DEATH IN THE LIFE OF CHILDREN

Death in the Life of Children

edited by
Kaoru Yamamoto

With the Assistance of

Judith M. Amsden	Holiday Park Elementary School, Phoenix, Arizona
M. Lynn Bessom	Moon Mountain Elementary School, Phoenix, Arizona
Paul W. Brewer	In private practice, Phoenix, Arizona
O. L. Davis, Jr.	University of Texas, Austin, Texas
Henry F. Dizney	University of Oregon, Eugene, Oregon
Joan G. Fassler	Yale University, New Haven, Connecticut
Rebecca M. Hawener	University of North Carolina, Greensboro, North Carolina
Alisa Davis Hazeltine	Sierra Christian School, Reno, Nevada
Carolyn E. Massad	Educational Testing Service, Princeton, New Jersey
Lorna Molinare	In private practice, Phoenix, Arizona
James D. North	Grimshaw Mortuaries, Phoenix, Arizona
Pamela K. Pillsbury	Mt. Whitney High School, Visalia, California
Sister Mary Ralph	St. Joseph's Hospital, Phoenix, Arizona

Original Contributions by

David H. Bauer   California State University,
                             Chico, California 95926

Maurine A. Fry   Arizona State University,
                             Tempe, Arizona 85281

Lynn Leonard   Foundation for Senior Adult
                             Living, Phoenix, Arizona 85021

Beverly H. Lewis   Avon Central School,
                             Avon, New York 14414

Rev. Paul W. Strickland American Baptist Churches,
                             Valley Forge, Pennsylvania 19406

Kaoru Yamamoto   Arizona State University,
                             Tempe, Arizona 85281

Contents

Preface

This book is geared primarily to our young colleagues in preparation. It is the final result of a cooperative venture, spanning a period of three years. The chapters were first prepared by a team of authors, consisting of a chaplain, a counselor for the aged, a school teacher, and three educational-developmental psychologists. They were then thoroughly examined in a retreat which was attended not only by the authors but also by a small group of select discussants. The latter included three teachers in preparation, a school teacher, three teacher educators, two educational psychologists, a clinical psychologist, a marriage-family counselor, a nurse, and a funeral director. The discussion at the meeting allowed the authors to improve and coordinate their contributions, and also provided the basis for the fifth chapter. I believe that the procedure is unique, and so is the product. Since the authors' goal was to open up a broad vista and share their thoughts on, and experiences with, this subject of common concern, the examination neither concentrated on any special subcategories of children nor elaborated upon numerous variations among different cultures and subcultures. These shall be for other books at other times. Our purpose here was to extend a general invitation for a joint exploration of *Death in the Life of Children*.

The retreat phase of the project was supported by the Grant Foundation, Inc., of New York, while Arizona State University offered continuous institutional assistance. I speak for all in expressing our gratitude to, in addition to the above two sources, our good teachers, faithful friends, and loved ones.

Kaoru Yamamoto

ix

When someone beloved has left,
it is **you** *who must let go.*

Prologue

Kaoru Yamamoto

Of all the tasks confronting young adults, the challenge of death is probably the hardest to face. For persons just beginning to assert their individuality, it is not easy to be reminded of the certainty of their obliteration. For persons now flowering into being, it is difficult to ponder the inevitability of nonbeing. In their exigent quest for significance in life, they are ill-disposed to reflect upon their imminent demise.[1] In a sense, however, that is the most critical time to place these matters in proper perspective, because meaningful life can hardly be defined against meaningless death and, in turn, meaningful death can seldom be related to meaningless life.

Bridges to Cross

For young people who are preparing themselves for a career in helping or ministering professions, including teaching, counseling, nursing, medicine, mortuary science, social work, and the ministry, the challenge is doubly daring. They must first resolve their own hang-ups ("complexes" in psychological parlance) concerning life, identity, and death, before they can hope to be of any assistance to their clients in the latter's efforts for growth. They must begin with themselves in learning to release, clarify, and accept their emotions and to integrate these with their thoughts, as well as with physiological givens. Only when they have tackled this personal task in earnest, they are capable of meeting others in need, particularly children, not merely as a dutiful professional, but as an understanding friend and compassionate human being.

In our highly mobile, nuclear family, where the number of supporting members has been reduced to minimum, it is difficult for a child to cope with loss of a dear person, especially when those few adults in his or her immediate circle tend to evade the issue. Indeed, "Death . . .

1

has become a taboo subject in American society and as such it is the object of much avoidance, denial, and disguise."[2] Nevertheless, death itself is certainly not dead. It is a fact of life which is as inexorable as ever, casting its long shadow across the allegedly carefree world of efficiency, comfort, and leisure. Accordingly, a serious examination of this subject is a requirement for those directly charged with nurturance of wholesome children[3] who love life but are not afraid of death.

When a student suddenly dies, what should a teacher do to bring the rest of the class face to face with the reality? How can a counselor help if a child reveals preoccupation with, and extreme fear of, death and dying? What is a nurse, a doctor, or an aide to do in working with a child who is slowly but certainly approaching his or her last moment on earth? What are some of the desirable parental actions for, and with, surviving siblings? How far should social workers or funeral directors go in their service to the mourning family? What attitudes are appropriate for ministers or friends in their supportive attempts for the bereaved? In every instance, the task is a shared one between the old and the young. Death unites, as well as sunders. Do the grown-ups, however, have what it takes to cope with the situation and lend a hand to those who are growing up? Remember, "A reservoir without water cannot take water to those who are thirsty. Neither can a starved person feed another out of full bounty."[4]

Unfortunately, budding professionals find little systematic help in their attempts to prepare themselves for encounters with death, not to speak of assisting children (and adults) in their experiences of dying, grieving, and reconstruction. It is peculiar not to find any extended discussion of this vital topic in influential treatises on mental health of Americans.[5] Similarly, the extent of analysis in representative textbooks in mental health, developmental psychology, and related fields is typically a fleeting comment or two on the Freudian concept of death wish, enumeration of some statistics on mortality, including suicide, or, at best, a mention of the presence of fear of death in children.[6]

However, there are probably some sixty books in print devoted to different facets of this overall topic. There are three recently initiated periodicals called, respectively, the *Omega, Journal of Thanatology,* and *Life-Threatening Behavior,*[7] as well as occasional articles in other journals in life and socio-behavioral sciences.[8] Because of their wide and varied foci, nevertheless, all these resource materials are not readily available to practitioners (in preparation). That is why we feel a volume of the present nature is useful. This book reviews man's relationships with death, particularly in the life space of the contemporary child, providing copious references as well as lists of suggested readings for those who wish to go beyond it.

To Weep a Little

"One runs the risk of weeping a little, if one lets himself be tamed," said the author of the charming book, *The Little Prince*.[9] Taming, in this context, means establishing ties with another being, coming to understand him, becoming responsible for him, and appreciating him as unique in the whole universe. To tame and be tamed—this is, in a sense, what our life is about. In so doing, and at the risk of crying a little, we nurture and cherish the precious beauty of love, faith, and hope.

That has been the case with a twenty-two year old young lady who provided us with the following candid recollection of her life prior to, and following, the death of her younger sister some ten years ago. With her explicit permission, and with our deep appreciation for her openness and willing cooperation, her account is reproduced here.[10] For obvious reasons, she remains unidentified, and all the names are fictitious.

* * * * * * *

I guess I just tell you what I remember. My sister June had leukemia. She was the third child in our family. I'm the oldest, and I have a brother who is about a year and a half younger than I am, and there was quite a bit of difference between my brother and myself and then the third child, June. We found out that she had leukemia when she was about, . . . I think she had just turned three years old. We had begun to suspect something; we had had her to the doctor's for having anemia and we thought that was all it was. I remember the day my parents had taken her to the hospital for tests and they came home and they called my brother and me into the bedroom and we all sat down on the bed and they, you know, began to tell us that they had found out that she had leukemia. There was no cure but they would try to keep her going as long as they could. My parents decided to be pretty honest with my brother and me, not to hide anything from us.

I think at the time I was about thirteen and my brother was around twelve. I remember, from then on, they never did tell June right out but she really sensed it; she was a bright little girl and she could feel it from the beginning. I remember towards the end when she started realizing. Things were pretty evident, you know, she was going in and out of the hospital quite frequently for blood transfusions. She could sense the feeling that I had, and one day she said to me, "Don't worry, Julie, things will be all right. I'll be all right." I was really close to her. I had always wanted a little sister and there was such a difference, I was about ten years old I guess when she was born. I really took up playing the mother role, you know, trying always to take care of her and stuff. It was really fun.

I think that it really hit us hard when she died. She was three years old when we found out that she had leukemia and she lasted, after that, for just about, . . . I think she died two days before her fourth birthday. So it was almost a complete year that we knew that she was going to die. When they told us that she had leukemia they said that she probably would last only another three or four months. They didn't expect her to last as long as she did. It was really a trial on our family. At the beginning it wasn't so hard because there wasn't much they could do at the hospital. But the last six months especially, she really began to bloat up, her body began to swell and she was uncomfortable a lot of the time and there were constant trips to the Children's Hospital in Oakmont. We were living down in that area when this happened. I remember days and days and days of sitting in the hall at the hospital with her looking at the little picture books that they have there and she was constantly having these blood transfusions.

I think the trouble was that the only medicine they had at the time for treating leukemia was cortisone and she would take that and then after a few treatments of it you become immune to it, you have to be off of it for awhile. So she would take it for awhile and her symptoms would go away and then she'd become immune to it and they'd have to take her off it until this immunity went away. That's when she really got bad. I think now they have quite a few different medicines that they can use for leukemia and they can keep switching them one after another. They develop immunities to the medicine, but they can keep rotating; by the time they get to the end of one, they can start the first one again. I think that they can keep leukemia patients living a lot longer now.

I remember we went through all different kinds of things. Of course, my parents were quite hysterical about it and we took her to just all kinds of specialists and doctors. And I remember at one time there was supposedly a place in Florida, a doctor in Florida who claimed that he could cure leukemia patients and, you know, it's pretty evident now, as it was evident then, that he was probably just a quack. But my parents were grasping for anything, and they even considered taking her to

Florida, until the doctors finally convinced them that there was nothing that could be done, and this guy was just, you know, an idiot, saying that he could perform these miracle cures and he really couldn't do anything. We went through all different things, she went to specialist after specialist trying to find out what could be done. We finally, I guess, reconciled ourselves to the fact that she was going to die, and there was just nothing that could be done.

There was a little boy whom we met at the hospital where we were taking her. He had leukemia also and was about her same age. He died about three months before June did, and this was kind of dramatic for my mother because she had spent all this time with the little boy and his mother and she kind of sensed, you know, what was going to happen. She had this preview of a little child dying.

As far as how it affected our family life, I think for awhile there we were really drawn closer together. We had this thing that we all had to fight together and we all had to keep our spirits up and we were trying to help each other. But towards the end things were really tough and we were under real pressure. I remember about the last two weeks when June really, really began to flare up and the doctor was pretty sure she only had a couple of weeks to live. Until that time my parents had· tried to keep her at home as much as possible and I shared a bedroom with her. The last thing they wanted at the time was for her to have to die in the middle of the night or something and have me wake up in the morning and find my sister dead in the bed next to me. So the last few weeks they moved her out to the hospital all the time. I never wanted to, you know, . . . I think about the last three days and she was so bad they, . . . I remember the last time I saw her at the hospital she was in an oxygen tent and I just couldn't handle it. I went there and I saw her in it, in that tent and it, you know, I more or less, you know, kept control while I was there, but she couldn't recognize us, she was almost in a coma. I remember, we left, and they sent us to some friends, my brother and me. My mom and dad spent all their time at the hospital the last few days, and I guess she didn't recognize them that much, but they wouldn't leave her.

And when she finally died, that's when the real pressure began in our family. I didn't go to the funeral. You know, I wanted to remember her as my little sister who was alive and playing, not as a little girl who was dead. I never went to the funeral. My brother wanted to see her, though, and he went down to the mortuary and he saw her before the funeral, even though he didn't go to the funeral. Even to this day my parents have this, kind of book of, you know, clippings and articles from her funeral and things. One of the worst things in the world, I wouldn't show this to anybody, but there was a picture of her taken in the coffin. My grandmother had this picture for quite awhile. She finally gave it back to Mom and this book, it's a book-type thing, it's in the bookshelf at home. I just, . . . so many times I've got right up to the point and almost touched it, touched the book and grasped it and was ready to look at that picture, but I, you know, never had any idea what she looked like after she died, but I just, I can't do it, I don't think I ever will now. I don't see any purpose in it. I think that picture should be destroyed. There's no need to keep anything like that. My grandmother came out for the funeral and stayed to help Mom and Dad for awhile.

I remember, you know, nothing was the same. It was just like I was living in a kind of a dream world. I tried to spend a lot of my time at my girl friend's house, you know, right during the funeral and things, because I didn't want to be around my parents. It was like I was more or less running away from the facts, but I couldn't stand it. There was just so much crying and they were fighting, fighting constantly. Every little thing would really flare up and they'd start a big fight. I guess about a week after the funeral my parents decided that we all needed to get away from the house that held those bad memories, and so they took us out of school for two weeks, my brother and me, and we went up to this cabin in the mountains and just stayed there. We talked quite a bit, and tried to, you know, come around to the fact that June was gone but we had to go on living. There, you know, there was nothing we could do, and there were still Joe and I, and Mom and Dad had to think about that. They couldn't keep thinking about June.

I remember the doctor, my mother's doctor, was always, . . . mother was still pretty young, and my mother's doctor always wanted her to have another baby after that, but she never would. My mom went back to work at the time. She thought that maybe if she were working she could keep her mind off it. I think it was a good thing. But I think that my parents almost came to the point of divorce and, you know, that because those few years after June died. . . . I do remember reading a magazine article that said in the death of children often times parents do divorce, and this is, . . . I just don't know how they avoided it. I'll never forget, they were just fighting and fighting and fighting, and I can remember I'd wake up in the middle of the night and hear them fighting, and it just gets to the point, you know, they never hit each other but lots and lots of screaming and I just felt like going and knocking on their door and telling them to please be quiet and I couldn't stand it any more. And finally I think it was about two or three years they just went through a really bad period and it was hard on my brother and me too, you know, seeing them the way they were.

But they finally came around and, you know, I think they realized that there was a struggle and they had gone through it together and they had survived. They had a lot more than they thought they had and there was no reason for them to fight like they did. They came really close to divorce, but they did finally make it, and they're really happy now. It's not too much any more. I remember we didn't even talk about June for a long, long time. We never mentioned her name in our house because it would just immediately bring up crying, you know, crying jags, and now we can talk about it, pretty openly. My mother, this morning, I was asking her some of the dates about how old June would have been, and she can even kinda smile a little. She can talk about it now more than she could.

I remember for about three or four months after June died I went through a really bad stage. I was having bad dreams about her. I was always dreaming that I was talking to her and that she was a little angel and stuff. These really wild dreams and, you know, at the time, I was really convinced that they were true and that I was really talking to her. Now, I look back on it and I see how much pressure I was under and why I was thinking those types of things. But, things are pretty open now.

The last time it really affected me was when I was a freshman in college. I had gone with a bunch of girl friends to see *Gone With the Wind* at a theater and the little girl in the movie looked identical to June. She just had the same face and the same hair and everything, and the little girl dies in the movie. I just really broke up in the theater and I think I went running out and I ran all the way home to the dorm by myself. I just went to bed and I was really crying. I couldn't explain to anybody what was wrong. I think that was the last time that it really affected me, and it has been about nine years now and we're, you know, we can talk about it pretty freely and pretty openly without any crying jags or anything anymore. The thing is that I think in a situation like this, . . . I'll never forget it, our family really went through a lot together and it just, it caused so much pressure that we either had to, you know, go one way or the other, and it almost was divorce and then they finally got together.

My mother even to this day is kind of overprotective of us kids. For, one of the symptoms of leukemia, June was always bruising really, really, really easy, and you could barely touch her and she would get a bruise. After June died, for years and years, my mother was just constantly taking us for physicals every six months right on the dot to make sure we were all right, and any time either one of us got a little bruise of any type, she was always rushing us to the doctor, to find out. I guess they're not too sure whether leukemia is hereditary or not, but she wasn't taking any chances. She was always, you know, kind of hesitant about letting us go camping with Girl Scouts or anything like that. She was always afraid something was going to happen and she couldn't stand to lose another one of her children.

I remember the time I was bitten by a dog after June had died, and we didn't find the dog and I had to start having the rabies treatments. The night before, I was very, very scared and, you know I was screaming, "Just let me take a chance, take a chance, and let me die, I don't want to have those horrible shots." And my mother just went completely crazy, you know, screaming at me, "I don't want to lose another child, you're going to have the shots no matter what." It ended up that I did go through the series of shots and then we did find the dog and it didn't have rabies. Kind of wasted effort. I'll never forget that, though.

*   *   *   *   *   *

Looking with the Heart

In the crucible of human tragedy, one often finds revealed the best qualities in a human being. The tenderest, bravest, and noblest deeds, thoughts, and sentiments are frequently seen under the worst conceivable circumstances to move us deeply. Death is no exception. Although we can never forget the reality that our loved ones died, we shall always remember that they lived to enrich us.[11] If we wept a little with Julie in reliving her experience, we have perhaps begun to comprehend the very simple secret which a fox shared with his friend, *The Little Prince*: "It is only with the heart that one can see rightly; what is essential is invisible to the eye."[12]

Paradoxically, it is not with our eyes we see, and it is not with the tangible we touch others. Life's mysteries are hard to unravel, but we can at least try to grow in wisdom, humility, and compassion through pleasure and pain, joy and sorrow. We can probably come to realize that understanding of death as a natural and significant experience is essential in giving life its meaning, and that caring, sharing, and daring are the indispensable characteristics for those who aspire to be of service to fellow human beings.

Do join us in our study, won't you?

Notes

1. Unless, of course, he is thrust into a holocaust of war, disaster, disease, or other intimate and sustained experience with death.

2. Robert Fulton, "On the Dying of Death," in *Explaining Death to Children*, ed. Earl A. Grollman (Boston: Beacon Press, 1967), pp. 31-47, quoted from p. 32.

3. For the purposes of our study, "children" include those from birth to about sixteen, with an emphasis on the elementary school age range. However, no hard and fast line of demarcation is indicated, because much of the discussion is relevant to the full life span of a person.

4. Dorothy W. Baruch, *One Little Boy* (New York: Dell Publishing Co., 1964), p. 24.

5. Examples are the publications of the Joint Commission of Mental Illness and Health, including its monograph series (Basic Books of New York) and *Action for Mental Health* (New York: John Wiley and Sons, 1961); James A. Davis, *Education for Positive Mental Health* (Chicago: Aldine Publishing Co., 1965); and S. B. Sells, ed., *The Definition and Measurement of Mental Health* (Washington, D.C.: U.S. Department of Health, Education and Welfare, Public Health Service, 1968). Even the generally excellent treatise on *What Is Fear?*, written for older children by Jean Rosenbaum and Lutie McAuliffe (Englewood Cliffs, N.J.: Prentice-Hall, 1972), avoids the subject of death!

6. My informal survey covered twelve titles in the area of mental health, eighteen in child development, eight in adolescence, and five in socialization. Minor deviations from the overall trend of complete neglect or silence were found in Louis S. Levine, *Personal and Social Development* (New York: Holt, Rinehart and Winston, 1963), Fritz Redl and William W. Wattenberg, *Mental Hygiene in Teaching* (New York: Harcourt, Brace and World, 1959), and L. Joseph Stone and Joseph Church, *Childhood and Adolescence* (New York: Random House, 1973), but most notably in Elton B. McNeil, *Human Socialization* (Belmont, Ca.: Brooks/Cole, 1969).

7. The *Omega: International Journal of Dying, Death, Suicide, Bereavement and Other Lethal Behavior* is edited by Robert Kastenbaum at the Department of Psychology, University of Massachusetts, Boston, Massachusetts 02116; the *Journal of Thanatology*, by Austin H. Kutscher at the Columbia Presbyterian Medical Center, 630 West 168th Street, New York, New York 10032; and the *Life-Threatening Behavior*, by Edwin S. Shneidman at the Neuropsychiatric Institute, University of California, Los Angeles, California 90024.

8. Some journals have published a special issue totally devoted to the topics of death and dying. A recent example is the Summer 1974 issue (Vol. 3, No. 2) of the *Journal of Clinical Child Psychology*, titled "Death and Children." Other periodicals regularly include articles on the subject—e.g., the *Hastings Center Report* (360 Broadway, Hastings-on-Hudson, New York 10706). For a recent, extensive bibliography, consult Robert Fulton, ed., *Death, Grief and Bereavement: A Bibliography, 1845-1975* (New York: Arno Press, 1977).

9. Antoine de Saint-Exupéry, *The Little Prince* (New York: Harcourt, Brace & World, 1943), p. 81.

10. At the retreat (see Preface), much lively discussion followed the rendering of this taped account. Some of the contents are presented in Chapter 5

beginning on page 115. For further examination of the dynamics surrounding this particular form of disease and death, see E. James Anthony and Cyrille Koupernik, eds., *The Child in His Family*, Vol. II, *The Impact of Disease and Death* (New York: John Wiley and Sons, 1973). In particular, contributions by Alby-Alby, Binger (two chapters), Futterman-Hoffman, Vernick, and Wolters.

11. This is the thought expressed by Earl A. Grollman in *Talking about Death: A Dialogue between Parent and Child* (Boston: Beacon Press, 1970); also see the following: Edgar N. Jackson, *Telling a Child about Death* (New York: Hawthorn Books, 1965).

12. Saint-Exupéry, *Little Prince,* p. 70.

Most of us are amazingly ignorant on the subject of death, an experience very prevalent and ostensibly intimate to us. It will indeed be a rare reader who does not find revealing the following discussion, presented by a sensitive counselor whose daily work with the aged raises many challenging questions about life, death, and dying.

1

Death in American Life

Lynn Leonard

The title of this chapter seems straightforward and simple. You and I are presumed to share a common understanding of the title's three key words. By "death" we mean the absence of life; by "American" we mean both the diversity and commonality of experience within the confines of our fifty states; by "life" we probably mean "awareness of experience."

If you do not agree with the meanings I have just presumed we share for these three words, you are in a position to appreciate the pitfalls of discussing death in American life. Even if we share meanings for these key words, our problem is still grave. For you and I cannot discuss death without examining life in our country. This task, in turn, necessitates an examination of all American ethnic, racial, geographic, socioeconomic and religious groups in our society. America is, and is not, a melting pot.

A time-honored resolution of such dilemmas is to talk in terms of the "average" American. The average American is a mythical person, sired by statistical analysis and nurtured by desires for definitional norms. You will never meet such an individual. He or she does not exist. I do not intend to compound my numerous descriptive dilemmas by attempting to provide prescriptions for your role in one of the helping professions. However, I have attempted to provide some information that will assist you in understanding the quantitative and qualitative changes in American mortality as well as some of the ways in which these changes affect American children.

The Demography of Death

Death was once both an expected and accepted part of American life. At the beginning of this century mortality rates were high, death during childbirth was frequent, and total life expectancy was brief when compared to life expectancy today. Death occurred at home and family members prepared the body for burial. Of necessity, children were exposed to the fact of death even as they were exposed to the fact of birth.

Since 1900 the picture of death in America has changed dramatically. The domain of death is now among the elderly who comprise almost 10 percent of our total population. Today nearly two-thirds of all deaths occur among those 65 and older while, in 1900, the majority (53 percent) of deaths occurred among those fifteen years of age and younger.[1] The overall death rate has decreased by almost 50 percent, from 17.2 deaths per thousand population in 1900[2] to 9.3 per thousand in 1971.[3] Correspondingly, life expectancy has increased from approximately 47 years for those born in 1900[4] to 71.1 years for those born in 1971.[5] Despite these remarkable gains, the United States still does not rank among the top ten countries of the world with respect to life expectancy. Among the countries outranking the United States in life expectancy are: Australia, Denmark, The Netherlands, New Zealand, Norway, Sweden, Belgium, France, East Germany, the Federal Republic of Germany, Switzerland, England, Wales and many others.[6]

These facts should indicate to you how infrequently the American child experiences the death of parent or sibling. In fact, a study of midwestern children (ages five through sixteen) revealed that 13 percent had never even known anyone who died.[7] Thus, today's children must cope not only with the pain of losing a parent or sibling through death, but they must also cope with the bewildering fact that their experience seems unique. Questions of "Why me? Why my family?" may be easily rephrased by the child to mean, "What did I do to cause this catastrophe?"

In 1900 children whose parent or sibling had died could not have felt so isolated in their bereavement. They could survey their world and discover that their experience was not unique. A fair number of their peers had lost a parent and many more had lost brothers or sisters through death. If children do attribute to themselves responsibility for their loved one's death, they had reason to conclude that their responsibility was no greater than many of their peers'. In addition, their parents' reaction to the loss of their sibling conveyed to them the message that "death is painful, but in no way unusual." Their peers provided additional models for coping with death.

Children today must frequently define for themselves the appropriate manner in which to respond to the death of parent or sibling. Their pain is compounded by confusion concerning the normality of their response to death.

Where and Why

Other aspects of death, causal ones, also have changed drastically since 1900. At that time influenza and pneumonia, tuberculosis and gastritis were the leading causes of death.[8] Today nearly 60 percent of total deaths can be attributed to two "killers," heart disease (38.6 percent) and cancer (17.3 percent).[9] Homicide accounts for an additional 8.5 percent of total death.[10] These causal factors of death, coupled with advances in medical technology, have altered the manner and setting in which death occurs. In 1900 the course of influenza, pneumonia, and gastritis was one of acute onset, followed by death in a matter of days or weeks. Lacking antibiotics and respirators, the patient usually was cared for at home. While these diseases provided some advanced warning of death, the terminal stage was usually not prolonged.

Death today is likely to occur either quite suddenly or after a prolonged terminal stage. In addition, the vast majority of deaths[11] occur in hospitals or nursing homes. What effect do these changes in the causes and locus of death have upon the child's experience of a loved one's death? (For a discussion of the dying child see Chapter 4.) The child must either come to terms with the abrupt death of a family member or friend, or he or she must adjust to the prolonged absence (due to hospitalization) and eventual loss of a loved one. Sudden death numbs the entire family, and frequently those to whom the child would turn for comfort and explanation are too stunned to help the child. Death has occurred "out there"—on the highway, on the job, or in the hospital emergency room. The funeral also occurs away from home, and frequently parents do not permit their child's attendance at the service.

When children are confronted with the protracted terminal illness of a family member, their situation is just as isolated as when death has occurred suddenly. You have read a transcript of a young woman's recollections of her sister's death from leukemia (see Prologue). The death was not a sudden one, nor was the young woman's loss confined to her sister. Her parents were also lost to her because they spent long hours at the hospital, a setting from which children under twelve years of age are usually barred. How different the child's experience of death must have been in the early part of this century when it occurred at home, within the purview of the child and within the bosom of the family.

There is another aspect of prolonged terminal illness that may contribute to the child's sense of isolation. Caretakers may be attempting to shield the dying family member as well as the child whose family member is the patient. The contemporary reality of institutionalized death has been studied by sociologists, nurses, psychologists, psychiatrists, and others. A recurring theme in their analysis has been the isolation of the dying person.[12] Glaser and Strauss have described the "closed awareness context" in which an attempt is made to prevent the patient from having knowledge of his or her impending death. Doctors, nurses, and family members were found to conspire to maintain a cloak of silence that prevented the dying patients from possessing knowledge of their true condition.[13] The effects of this cloak of silence upon the patient are readily apparent, but the effects upon a young member of a "conspiring" family could also be grave. One way to maintain the cloak of silence is by failing to inform a child that a brother, sister, parent, or grandparent is dying; or, having so informed the child, to prevent his or her access to the dying person. Either method leaves the child alone and bewildered.

Recently my judgment was questioned by a former Army nurse because I had given my eleven year old son a choice as to whether or not he wanted to visit his critically ill grandfather in the hospital. This woman informed me that (1) it would be traumatic for my son and (2) it would indicate to his grandfather the gravity of his condition. However, there were circumstances that made her objection invalid with respect to the conspiracy of silence. At the university medical center where my father was hospitalized, the medical staff followed a policy of honest communication with their patients. My father was fully aware of his condition, and this made it possible for him to speak openly with me about his anger and frustration over being deprived of health and future just as he was planning to retire. His doctors' honesty, which was candid but not cruel, also made it possible for him to ask for his grandson. An honest discussion with my son enabled him to choose to visit his grandfather, and I believe this visit gave the child a message that he had an important role to play within the family at a time of crisis. This personal experience has left me hopeful that no longer do the vast majority of doctors prefer not to tell their patients that the latter are dying, a trend that Oken documented in 1961.[14] Increasingly the morality of this maneuver is being questioned.

Modern Issues in Medical Ethics

The question of the physician's moral or ethical right to withhold from the dying person knowledge of his or her true condition is not the only ethical dilemma involved in American death today. While these areas of ethical murkiness have less immediate effect upon children than do the demographic factors previously discussed, they are crucial to a description of death in American life.

Earlier, I stated I presumed we agreed that "death is the absence of life," and that "life is awareness of experience." Actually, these definitions raise many questions and answer none. As you will soon discover, my definitional difficulties are shared by some of the best medical, legal, and ethical minds in America. Advances in medical technology have confused, not clarified, these issues.

Determining Death

For centuries the absence of heartbeat and respiration was generally accepted as the criterion for establishing the occurrence of death. The fallibility of these indicators was also recognized, and medical literature contains numerous citations of erroneously diagnosed death and premature burial.[15] Consequently, putrefaction came to be viewed as the only certain criterion for death, and varying time-spans between diagnosis of death and burial were recommended to insure that death was actual and not apparent. As a matter of fact, honors were accorded scientists for discoveries of "certain signs of death." The Prix Dusgate, a quinquennial prize of 2,500 francs, was awarded to Icard in the early 1900s for his discovery that when death had occurred, dye injected into the circulation did not result in coloration of the entire body.[16]

Avoidance of premature burial was the motivating concern for determining precise criteria for establishing the occurrence of death. While the widespread practice of embalming has eliminated the possibility of premature burial here in the United States, the importance of a precise definition of death has not diminished.

In 1967, Beecher stated that there were three competing definitions of death:

1. Irreversible destruction of brain matter with the resulting impossibility of regaining consciousness.
2. Heart death as determined by the moment at which spontaneous heartbeat could not be restored.

3. "Brain death" as established by electroencephalogram (E.E.G.).[17]

Beecher added that "any up-to-date determination of death would be a legal impossibility at this time, however theologically sound it might be."[18]

The occurrence of unpaired-organ transplants (i.e., a single heart as opposed to two lungs or kidneys), coupled with the possibility of "medical survival,"[19] has served to highlight the crucial issue of precise definitions of death. It has become an urgent matter to define death in a manner that

a. gives the dying patient every possible protection in terms of his rights;
b. protects the cardiac surgeon from allegations of violating moral, civic or criminal law; and
c. does not preclude a potentially life-saving operation for the patient desperately in need of a new heart.[20]

Glaser believes that this matter has been resolved by the recognition of the brain, rather than the heart, as "the seat of human life."[21] This resolution of the definitional issue of death was necessitated in part by cardiac surgeons' statements that "the donor's heart should be beating at the time it is removed.[22] In order to legally remove a beating heart it was necessary to locate the "seat of human life" in another organ.

The relationship between brain death and heart death is complex. Prior to the development of modern resuscitative techniques, the prolonged absence of heartbeat preceded and inevitably resulted in brain death. Conversely, severe trauma to the brain that affected those cells crucial to autonomic functions, e.g., heartbeat and respiration, resulted in heart death. The question of sequence (which came first) was of little importance because there were no known means for restoring or artificially maintaining heartbeat.[23]

Today medical technology makes it possible to restore and/or maintain heartbeat. Heartbeat can be restored and self-maintained because brain cells involved in autonomic functions are the last brain cells to be affected by oxygen deprivation. Cells in the neocortex, the part of the brain that developed most recently in evolution, control cognitive functioning. Such cells are the most sensitive to oxygen starvation.[24] Thus, it is possible for an individual to suffer injury to the brain that results in irreparable damage to the cognitive centers but does not result in heart death. Heart donors whose hearts are still beating at removal can thus meet the technical requirements for a pronouncement of death due to irreversible brain damage.[25]

While the thought of surgically removing a beating heart for purposes of transplantation is still unsettling to some people, it is, as Glaser stated, a question that has been resolved by accepting brain death as the criterion of death in such cases. However, Beecher appears to have been correct in pointing to the *legal* impossibility of defining death. Glaser made the same point when he cited a case in which an assault victim suffered irreversible brain damage. The family gave consent for use of his heart in a transplant operation, whereupon attorneys for the assailants claimed that their clients could not be charged with murder because the victim's (donor's) heart was removed while still beating![26] Thus, while we have better medical criteria for determining the occurrence of death, these criteria are of little assistance in providing legal determinations of death.

Defining Life

If physicians have provided more precise criteria for establishing the occurrence of death, it would seem plausible that a clearer definition of life would be implied. After all, life and death are relational concepts. One concept cannot be fully defined without reference to the other and, if one is fully defined, surely the other definition will follow. However, these two concepts are not parallel in the degree of meanings that they convey. Life connotes a wider range of meanings than does death. When we think of death, the state of being dead, we do not weigh qualitative/quantitative concerns. We do not think in terms of the length of one's death, nor do we think in terms of the quality of one's deadness.* We do, however, speak of both the length and quality of one's life. When we think of our own lives, it is possible for us to weigh the merit of a short, productive life versus a prolonged, less productive one.

Life and death concepts can be compared in other ways. Life can be defined as a process (a continuing development involving many changes) while death can be viewed as an event (a result, consequence, or outcome). Of course, dying is also a process and therefore can be experienced and discussed in the same qualitative/quantitative terms as life. Dying can be easy or hard, brief or prolonged. In addition, while

---

* Even when we do entertain thoughts about what "happens" after death, what we are questioning is the quality of *life* after death, not the quality of death.

the process of life encompasses the necessity of death, the event of death negates the possibility of life. However, death does assume the previous presence of life. That which was never alive cannot now be dead, but must be now as inanimate as before.

In summary we see that the processes of both living and dying can be described qualitatively and quantitatively while the event of death cannot be so described. Further, while the event of death cannot be prolonged, its occurrence can be postponed by prolonging either the process of living or the process of dying.

In our country, the ready access to the products of an advanced medical technology makes it imperative that physicians and laypeople realize that, "There is a difference between prolonging living and what can only be called prolonging dying."[27] The distinction of which is being prolonged—living or dying—perhaps can be made best on the basis of qualitative versus quantitative comparisons. But ours is a cultural climate in which quantity appears more highly valued than quality, a climate in which what is possible is presumed to be mandatory. As a result, the unquestioned use of radical medical intervention has become commonplace.

Schoenberg posed the problem of the possible versus the obligatory in question form: "Is it the physician's duty to preserve a patient's life simply because advances in sciences make it possible to accomplish?"[28] Fletcher has attempted a partial answer to the problem by making a distinction between *prolongation of life* (sustaining a life that otherwise might end) and *euthanasia* (merciful termination of a life that might otherwise continue).[29] Jones makes a plea for *agathanasia*, death with dignity, in which interventive measures are withheld if their application would mean only an artificial lengthening (greater quantity) of life that otherwise might end.[30] In the same vein, a Catholic theologian has argued that while an individual is obliged to take reasonable means to preserve life, he is not obliged to accept heroic means that involve excessive hardship for himself or others (diminished quality of life).[31] Roman Catholic dogma provides the most voluminous and cogent delineation, of which I am aware, of what *must be* or *need not be* done to preserve life. Church dogma distinguishes between *ordinary* and *extraordinary* means. The former are *obligatory*, the latter are not.[32] Dogma also employs the "law of double effect" in specifying which acts of intervention are moral for Catholic physicians and which are not. While it *is not* considered permissible to crush an infant's skull (primary effect) in order to carry through an otherwise impossible delivery and thus save the mother's life (secondary effect),[33] it *is* permissible to employ cobalt in treatment of a pregnant woman's uterus in order to arrest cancer (primary effect) even though the fetus will die due to the treatment (secondary effect).[34] The law of double effect is also the basis for the Church's position that morphine could be given to alleviate a person's intractable pain (primary effect) even though it is known to suppress respiration and could thus hasten his death (secondary effect).[35]

A third aspect of the Church's theology regarding interventive measures focuses on the doctor's role as an *active* or *passive* agent. It is acceptable for a physician to serve as a passive agent who permits death to occur by not employing extraordinary means to preserve life. The physician could not, however, function as an active agent in terminating life if such termination were intended as the primary effect. Nor could he morally serve as a passive agent by withholding ordinary means to preserve or sustain life.

Problems arise for the modern physician due to the fact that what was extraordinary only recently is so no longer. In addition, once heroic means for sustaining life are employed, the physician must assume the role of active agent when he instructs that they be discontinued. In assuming an active role, the ethical physician needs to be clear on the issue of primary effect. He may ethically intend to cease prolonging the process of dying and thereby afford the patient a death with dignity. This has been termed "negative euthanasia." While 87 percent of recently sampled physicians of all faiths stated that they favored negative euthanasia, only 80 percent stated that they practiced it.[36]

Distribution of Medical Care

Other ethical and moral questions arise regarding heroic acts for prolonging life. Who determines the recipients of heroic interventions and on what basis are such determinations made?

Sudnow found that perceived social status and moral character appeared to influence medical personnel's decision to employ heroic means. The aged, those attempting suicide, suspected criminals, prostitutes, "winos," and others assumed to possess little social worth were less often the recipients of heroic efforts to prolong life.[37] Yet Knutson has documented health professionals' expressed reluctance to answer such questions as, "In case of an epidemic in our society who should be taken care of first in the family, in the community, in society?"[38] Knutson feels that our cultural and ethical values induce guilt when one is asked to *say* that one individual is more valuable than another. Yet Sudnow's observations appear to indicate that medical personnel are less reluctant to *act* in a judgmental manner. Of course, in giving answers to Knutson's questions, health professionals were confronted with the necessity for formulating an answer on a rational, conscious level. Unfortunately, not all actions are preceded by these same qualities.

In 1968 the cost of the average heart transplant was placed at $20,000. The upper limit of potential recipients was 80,000 for the same year. The cost of transplants for 80,000 recipients would have required $1.6 billion, a sum approximately equal to the entire budget of the National Institutes of Health for 1968-69.[39] Knutson asks, "Is it better to spend a large portion of our financial resources for the benefit of relatively few persons or to put these same resources into services for a great many people?"[40] His answer is a summation of this current moral dilemma. "Decisions that are made on the basis of the greatest good for the greatest number inevitably bypass the needs of given individuals."[41]

While the ethics of modern medical practice have less immediate effect upon children than do the demographic changes that have so restricted their exposure to death, these ethical issues do bespeak the values of our society, values that children internalize unconsciously. From their exposure to television programs ("Marcus Welby, M.D.," "Medical Center," etc.) that frequently depict the utilization of medical heroics to preserve life, children internalize the commendable value that every human life is priceless. At the same time these romanticized programs encourage children to believe that socioeconomic status is not a factor in determining the recipients of preventive and corrective medical care. As both Sudnow and Knutson have demonstrated, perceived social worth and the ability to pay are prime determinants of the availability of quality health care. Lacking a realistic basis on which to reconcile these conflicting value messages, one wonders how children manage to do so.

Other values seem to underlie our current medico-ethical dilemmas. The quantity (duration) of life appears to be more highly valued than the quality of life. But, from my work with retired persons, I know that our senior citizens do not feel that society values them highly for having achieved an advanced age. Perhaps, then, the frequent use of medical heroics typifies, in a quite literal fashion, the old adage, "Never say die!" If this interpretation is valid, then, in our society, death may be experienced as the ultimate personal failure.

Death Attitudes in America

Toynbee has hypothesized that death is denied in the United States because it is considered un-American. Its occurrence contradicts the belief that the United States is an earthly paradise.[42] Howard and Scott believe that acceptance of death would negate the value that Americans place in their ability to obtain ultimate supremacy over nature. Other entrenched American values are also negated by death: the importance of companionship and the necessity of always being active.[43] Fulton[44] and Toynbee[45] conclude that the secularization of American society, specifically a weakened belief in an afterlife, also contributes to the death denial they feel prevails in the United States today.

These are interesting and perhaps valid beliefs about American death attitudes, although in many cases they are only inferences. Perhaps it would be helpful to examine both the behavioral basis for these inferences and the attitudes toward death that American laypeople profess.

Funerals in America

Because the funeral is a universal human event serving multiple functions, "its character, importance and frequency may be viewed as indicators of the place of mortality in a society."[46] Using the funeral as such an indicator, what is the place of mortality in America today? How have the demographic changes in death affected the traditional functions of the funeral as (a) a symbol of status transformation of the deceased, (b) an opportunity for public dramatization of grief, and (c) a means for disposing of the dead? Most important, what valid inferences with respect to death attitudes can be made on the basis of our current funeral practices?

On the basis of our current mortuary practices, it is difficult to view the funeral as symbolizing a dramatic status transformation of the deceased. The American public has accepted the practice of embalming as well as the presentation of a life-like corpse that "reposes" in a slumber room until time for the funeral service and burial. Funeral industry spokespeople state that the public both wants and needs to be presented with a life-like corpse.[47] While it is understandable that the bereaved might benefit from seeing that the signs of ravaging illness have been removed, the presentation of a life-like corpse need not be the only alternative. Much of the mortician's cosmetology is aimed at removing the pallor of death and replacing it with skin tones more reminiscent of a living person. I am unaware of any research that would definitively answer the question of whether it is the public or the funeral industry that wants and needs to see a life-like corpse in the coffin. If, in fact, it is the public that wishes the corpse to look as life-like as possible, then it would be valid to conclude that, to this extent, death is denied in our society today. Whatever the motivation for the practice of mortuary cosmetology, it is one that represents a fairly recent and radical departure from previous burial customs. This point was brought home recently when a colleague of mine, a woman in her fifties, stated that one of her clearest childhood recollections was sitting outside her neighbors' homes in New Mexico while waiting for her mother to finish bathing and wrapping a body for burial. Today it is a "rare phenomenon for the average individual to see an untreated dead person."[48] Preparing the body for burial is the exclusive responsibility of the mortician.

America is noted for its conspicuous consumption and funerals are no exception. In 1971 the average funeral cost $1,100.[49] However, contrary to the usual practice of maximizing opportunities for demonstrating the expense that has been incurred, Americans seem to be minimizing their opportunities to demonstrate publicly how costly a funeral they have provided their loved one. Murphy and Lester have found evidence that funerals have become less public and more private. Between 1929 and 1969 the hours set aside by families for condolence calls became restricted. By 1969 flowers were frequently omitted in the randomly sampled funeral notices that these authors studied. Murphy and Lester also noted a growing trend towards closed coffins and totally private funerals.[50]

While it is possible to interpret the privatization of funerals as indicative of death denial, other interpretations are possible. In a mobile society in which death occurs primarily among the elderly whose deaths are far less disruptive socially, it is possible that the privatization of the funeral is merely an accurate reflection of the diminished social status of the deceased. As Fulton has observed, "Retired from their work, freed from parental obligation, and often removed from the main current of social life, the death of the aged disturbs little the round of life today."[51] Perhaps some families prefer to restrict calling hours and request the omission of flowers because they anticipate that few people know the deceased or consider his or her funeral to be a significant social event.

On the basis of current funeral practices our only safe conclusion is that while funeral practices have changed (have become both more institutionalized and private), we can say nothing definitive about the motivational determinants of these changes. Our best available data regarding how Americans feel about death are derived from attitudinal surveys which provide partial answers to the following questions: Do Americans symbolize death? Is death ever an acceptable event? If so, under what circumstances? Do Americans plan for death? Do they discuss death with loved ones or friends? Do they think of death often? Do they state that they fear death?

Thoughts of Death

One of the most extensive recent surveys of individual attitudes and orientations toward death was conducted by Riley of the National Opinion Research Center, University of Chicago. The sample involved in this survey probably represents the population of the United States better than other studies that will be cited.[52]

Riley's study revealed that over two-thirds of the 1,482 sampled adults stated that they either often or occasionally thought of death. When death thoughts did occur, the vast majority agreed with the statement that, "Death is not tragic for the person who dies, but only for the survivor." There was also majority agreement with the statements that, "Death is like a long sleep," "Death always comes too soon," and "Death is sometimes a blessing." Only 14 percent of the respondents associated death with suffering.[53]

Responses to Shneidman's survey among the subscribers of *Psychology Today* magazine revealed that more than three-fourths thought of death either often, frequently, or occasionally. Only 15 percent of these respondents associated pain with dying.[54]

Shneidman's and Riley's findings appear to be consistent with each other despite the absence of quota sampling in the magazine survey. The majority of Americans do think about death, but only a small minority associates dying with pain and suffering.

Life after Death

Fulton's study of American attitudes towards death revealed that less than a majority (approximately 45 percent) of the 1,722 persons who responded to his questionnaire believed in a life after death. As might be expected, the majority of his respondents assigned secular rather than religious functions to the funeral.[55]

A similar percentage of the 30,000 *Psychology Today* respondents either strongly believed (23 percent) or tended to believe (20 percent) in a life after death. However, a majority of these respondents reported that they strongly wished there were a life after death.[56]

Planning for and Talking about Death

Riley found that the overwhelming majority of his respondents felt that it was better to make plans for death rather than ignore it. However, only one-fourth reported having made wills, funeral arrangements, or burial arrangements. Half of his sample had made a point of talking about death with someone dear to them, and a large majority reported having purchased life insurance.[57]

The voluminous response to the Shneidman survey is one indication of this group's willingness to discuss death—at least in writing. There were 30,000 respondents to the death survey, in contrast to 20,000 to the magazine's sex questionnaire.[58] Interestingly, only 30 percent of the death respondents reported that death was discussed openly during childhood in their homes. A slightly larger percentage could recall no death discussions in the home, and 15 percent recalled attempts to exclude children from death discussions in their childhood homes.[59]

Fear of Death

Americans do not frequently state that they fear death. Only 19 percent of Shneidman's respondents chose "fearful" as being most descriptive of their emotional response when thinking of their own prospective deaths. The majority stated that thoughts of their own mortality resulted in feelings of resignation in relation to life or pleasure in being alive. Thoughts of death were "discouraging," "depressing," or otherwise elicited feelings of purposelessness in 21 percent of the respondents. It is important to note that over three-fourths of these respondents were under thirty-five years of age, and over half were under twenty-five.[60]

In a study of elderly community volunteers (age sixty years or older), Jeffers, Nichols, and Eisdorfer found that only 10 percent of their group responded affirmatively when asked, "Are you afraid to die?"[61]

Distasteful Aspects of Death

Shneidman's 1971 study provided choices among the same responses that Diggory and Rothman designed in their attempt to understand the values destroyed by death.[62] The question was, "What aspect of your own death is the most distasteful to you?" The available choices were:[63]

		1961[64]	1971[65]
A.	I could no longer have any experiences.	4	1
B.	I am uncertain as to what might happen to me if there is a life after death.	6	3
C.	I am afraid what might happen to my body after death.	7	7
D.	I could no longer provide for my dependents.	5	6
E.	It would cause grief to my relatives and friends.	1	5
F.	All my plans and projects would come to an end.	2	4
G.	The process of dying might be painful.	3	2

The most distasteful aspect of personal death has shifted from an earlier concern for the effect on family and friends to one that focuses on the prospect of no longer being able to have experiences. This observation is striking because of the relative equivalence of the two groups studied. Both groups were predominantly youthful, unmarried, Protestant, and middle or upper-middle class.

It is also interesting to note that while only a small percentage of Americans associate pain or suffering with death, Item G was the second and third ranking distasteful aspect of death in 1971 and 1961, respectively.

Stability or Change in Death Attitudes?

While the most distasteful aspect in death contemplation seems to have changed during the past decade, there would appear to be a remarkable consistency among the death attitudes as revealed in the self-reports of some college students. In 1970 Lester[66] administered Middleton's 1936 death questionnaire[67] to students attending the same college where the questionnaire had been given thirty-five years earlier.

Lester found that there were no differences between the groups with respect to frequency of death thoughts and fear of death even though the 1970 group was less likely to believe in a life after death.[68]

Summary

At this point in our discussion it seems appropriate to recall Gertrude Stein's oft-quoted dying words, "But what is the answer?" After a moment of reflective silence, Miss Stein continued, "But then, what is the question?"[69] Perhaps a basic question to raise in summary is, "What does the foregoing description of death in American life tell us about the child's experiential basis for formulating a concept of death? Is the family likely to provide an open forum for a discussion of death-related questions, or are there fear-induced taboos that prohibit such discussions?"

Because of dramatic changes in the demography of death, few youngsters now encounter the death of peer or parent. Their most prevalent personal experience with death is the loss of grandparent or pet. All too often the pet is better known to the child than is the grandparent. Even when the grandparent shares the child's home, the youngster is unlikely to encounter death because, as we have seen, dying is done in institutions where children are rarely admitted. When death does occur, our modern funeral practices do not afford the child a realistic view of death. Either the coffin is closed or, if open, contains a life-like corpse.

Coupled with this paucity of death-related experiences is the likelihood that the majority of young Americans (as indicated by Shneidman's survey) are not afforded open home forums for discussions of death. However, it is unclear why this is so. The data marshalled in support of the "death denial hypothesis" are open to other interpretations.

Thus, while evidence of a death-denying American society is at best debatable, there is ample evidence that children are deprived of realistic death experiences as opposed to those presented by the various media, especially television. Consequently, in America today death is a void in a double sense. As always, we possess no knowledge of what happens after death; as never before, we possess little experiential knowledge of the events preceding death. It is as if the barrier that once divided the quick from the dead had now encroached upon the land of the living. If it is not possible to extend the bridge of understanding across the River Styx, perhaps it is not too late to buttress the pilings on this side of the shore.

Notes

1. Robert Fulton and Julie Fulton, "A Psychosocial Aspect of Terminal Care: Anticipatory Grief," *Omega* 2 (August 1971):91-100.
2. Ibid.
3. The United States Department of Health, Education and Welfare, The

National Center for Health Statistics, "Monthly Vital Statistics Report: Annual Summary for the United States, 1971," Rockville, Ma.: Author, August 1972.

4. Fulton, "Psychosocial Aspect," p. 91.

5. The United States Department of Health, Education and Welfare, "Vital Statistics," Table 3, p. 14.

6. Monroe Lerner, "When, Why and Where People Die," in *The Dying Patient*, ed. Orville G. Brim, Jr., Howard E. Freeman, Sol Levine, and Norman A. Scotch (New York: Russell Sage Foundation, 1970), pp. 5-29.

7. Matilda S. McIntire, Carol R. Angle, and Lorraine J. Struempler, "The Concept of Death in Midwestern Children and Youth," *American Journal of Diseases of Children* 123 (June 1972):527-32.

8. Lerner, "When, Why," Table 2, p. 14.

9. The United States Department of Health, Education and Welfare, "Vital Statistics," Table C, p. 3.

10. Ibid., p. 3.

11. Fulton and Fulton, "Psychosocial Aspect."

12. For discussions of the dying patient's isolation in hospitals, consult the following: Barney G. Glaser and Anselm L. Strauss, "Awareness Contexts and Social Interaction," *American Sociological Review* 29 (October 1964):669-79. David Sudnow, *Passing On: The Social Organization of Dying* (Englewood Cliffs, N.J.: Prentice Hall, 1967).

13. Glaser and Strauss, "Awareness Contexts."

14. Donald Oken, "What to Tell Cancer Patients," *Journal of the American Medical Association* 175 (April 1961):1120-28.

15. Keith A. Mant, "The Medical Definition of Death," in *Man's Concern with Death*, ed. Arnold Toynbee (London: Hodder and Stoughton, 1968), pp. 13-25.

16. Ibid., p. 20.

17. Ibid., p. 23.

18. Ibid., p. 23.

19. Howard E. Freeman, Orville G. Brim, Jr., and Greer Williams, "New Dimensions in Dying," in *The Dying Patient*, ed. Orville G. Brim, Jr., et al. (New York: Russell Sage Foundation, 1970), pp. xiii-xxvi, quoted from p. xiv.

20. Robert J. Glaser, "Innovations and Heroic Acts in Prolonging Life," in *The Dying Patient*, ed. Orville G. Brim, Jr., et al. (New York: Russell Sage Foundation, 1970), pp. 102-28, quoted from p. 108.

21. Ibid., p. 109.

22. Ibid., p. 108.

23. Mant, "Medical Definition," p. 23.

24. Ibid.

25. Glaser, "Innovations," pp. 108-10.

26. Ibid., p. 112.

27. Cicely Saunders, "The Moment of Truth: Care of a Dying Person," in *Death and Dying*, ed. Leonard Pearson (Cleveland: The Press of Case Western Reserve University, 1969), pp. 49-78.

28. Bernard Schoenberg, "Management of the Dying Patient," in *Loss and Grief: Psychological Management in Medical Practice*, ed. Bernard Schoenberg, Arthur C. Carr, David Peretz, and Austin H. Kutscher (New York: Columbia University Press, 1970), pp. 256-74, quoted from p. 256.

29. Ibid.

30. T. T. Jones, "Dignity in Death: The Application and Withholding of Interventive Measures," *Journal of the Louisiana Medical Society* 113 (May 1961):180-83.

31. "Catholic Theologian Defends Man's Right to Die," *Journal of the American Medical Association* 180 (April 28, 1962):23-24.

32. Gerald Kelly, *Medico-Moral Problems* (St. Louis: Catholic Hospital Association, 1958), p. 128.

33. Ibid., p. 65.

34. Ibid., p. 62.

35. Bernard Häring, *Medical Ethics* (Notre Dame, In.: Fides, 1972), p. 146.

36. Ibid., p. 147.

37. Sudnow, *Passing On*, pp. 98-100.

38. Andie L. Knutson, "Cultural Beliefs on Life and Death," in *The Dying Patient*, ed. Orville G. Brim, Jr., et al. (New York: Russell Sage Foundation, 1970), pp. 42-64, quoted from p. 51.

39. Glaser, "Innovations," pp. 119-20.

40. Ibid., p. 120.

41. Ibid.

42. Arnold Toynbee, "Changing Attitudes Towards Death in the Modern Western World," in *Man's Concern with Death*, ed. Arnold Toynbee (London: Hodder and Stoughton, 1968), pp. 13-25.

43. Alan Howard and Robert A. Scott, "Cultural Values and Attitudes Toward Death," in *Confrontations of Death*, ed. Frances G. Scott and Ruth M. Brewer (Corvallis, Or.: Continuing Educational Publications, 1971), pp. 16-25.

44. Robert Fulton, "On the Dying of Death," in *Explaining Death to Children*, ed. Earl A. Grollman (Boston: Beacon Press, 1967), pp. 31-47.

45. Toynbee, "Changing Attitudes."

46. Robert Blauner, "Death and Social Structure," *Psychiatry* 29 (November 1966):387.

47. Jessica Mitford, *The American Way of Death* (New York: Simon and Schuster, 1963), pp. 173-86.

48. Herman Feifel, "The Meaning of Dying in American Society," in *Dealing with Death*, ed. Richard H. Davis (Los Angeles: University of Southern California, 1973), pp. 1-8, quoted from p. 1.

49. Howard C. Rawther, "Comments on Ruth Mulvey Harmer's 'Funerals, Fantasy and Flight,'" *Omega* 2 (August 1971):155.

50. William J. Murphy and David Lester, "Changing Funeral Practices in America," *Psychological Reports* 27 (December 1970):886.

51. Fulton, "The Dying."

52. John W. Riley, Jr., "What People Think about Death," in *The Dying Patient*, ed. Orville G. Brim, Jr., et al. (New York: Russell Sage Foundation, 1970), pp. 31-41.

53. Ibid., pp. 36-37.

54. Edwin S. Shneidman, "You and Death," *Psychology Today* 5 (June 1971):43-45, 74-80.

55. Robert Fulton, "The Sacred and the Secular: Attitudes of the American Public Toward Death, Funerals, and Funeral Directors," in *Death and Identity*, ed. Robert Fulton (New York: John Wiley and Sons, 1965), pp. 89-104.

56. Shneidman, "You and Death," p. 74.

57. Riley, "What People Think," p. 38.

58. Shneidman, "You and Death," p. 43.

59. Ibid., p. 44.

60. Ibid., p. 77.

61. Frances C. Jeffers, Clauder R. Nichols, and Carl Eisdorfer, "Attitudes of Older Persons toward Death: A Preliminary Study," in *Death and Identity*, ed. Robert Fulton (New York: John Wiley and Sons, 1965), pp. 142-46.

62. James C. Diggory and Doreen Rothman, "Values Destroyed by Death," in *Death and Identity*, ed. Robert Fulton (New York: John Wiley and Sons, 1965), pp. 152-60.

63. Ibid., p. 154.

64. Ibid., Figure 2, p. 157.

65. Shneidman, "You and Death," p. 76.

66. David Lester, "Attitudes toward Death Today and Thirty-five Years Ago," *Omega* 2 (August 1971):168-73.

67. Ibid., p. 173.

68. Ibid., Table 1, p. 170.

69. Charles P. Curtis, Jr. and Ferris Greenslet, eds., *The Practical Cogitator* (Boston: Houghton Mifflin, 1945), p. 563.

Suggested Readings

Toynbee, Arnold, ed., *Man's Concern with Death* (London: Hodder and Stoughton, 1968).

A balanced presentation of original writings by historians, physicians, a journalist, and a theologian that provides a broad perspective on the topic of death. Of particular interest are Toynbee's chapter, "Perspectives from Time, Space and Nature," and his moving epilogue, "The Relation between Life and Death, Living and Dying."

Scott, Frances G., and Brewer, Ruth M., eds., *Confrontations of Death* (Corvallis, Or.: Continuing Educational Publications, 1971).

This book resulted from a seminar of the same title initiated at the University of Oregon in 1968. Chapters provide introductory comments describing how the materials are utilized in the seminar. Gwenn Nettler's chapter, "Review Essay: On Death and Dying," provides a needed corrective for the unchallenged assumption that death denial is totally maladaptive.

In working with children, it is important to recognize some of the qualitative differences in thinking between adults and children (i.e., the developmental trends), as well as the wide individual variations among children themselves. Here, an astute educational psychologist examines what we do and do not know about the concepts of death held by the young ones.

2

Images of Death in Children

Maurine A. Fry

"Now I lay me down to sleep
I pray the Lord my soul to keep
If I should die before I wake
I pray the Lord my soul to take."

The origins of this childhood prayer are apparently unknown, but for centuries large numbers of English-speaking children must thus have heard about death at an early age. Today, children also hear about death from fairy tales, books, television, and from conversations overheard directly or indirectly. What images of death have children formulated out of such experiences? How is this image of death changed and modified throughout childhood? Psychologists, as a group, have not shown much interest in these questions; but as always, there were pioneers.

Prior to the turn of the century, the psychological literature contained sporadic references to the child's image of death.[1] Anecdotal records of children's questions about death, reports of dreams and fragments of therapeutic interviews followed. These data were usually interpreted within a psychoanalytic framework,[2] where interpretations were generally speculative and lacked empirical support. Nevertheless, they have probably made an important contribution by pointing out the fact that the child *does*, indeed, think about death.[3]

In the following discussion,[4] the child's image of death is viewed from two perspectives. First, the child's thoughts on death were obtained from empirical, cross-sectional surveys whereby attention is focused upon the content of the child's thoughts or on *what* the child says he or she thinks concerning death. Second, the discussion examines *how* the child arrives at these conclusions regarding death. The child's thought processes are studied largely within the framework of the cognitive-moral developmental stage formulations of Jean Piaget and Lawrence Kohlberg.[5]

What Are the Child's Thoughts on Death?

Although chronological age is an admittedly crude indication of developmental level, it appears to be one of the primary covariates of the child's response to the question, "What is death?" Therefore, the data concerning the child's thoughts on death are reviewed within chronological age ranges. If readers will keep in mind that there are vast individual differences in the child's image of death within any given age group and if readers will accept limitations on generalizations that can be drawn, they will be aided in acquiring a picture of what is known of the child's concept of death. As with all aspects of physical and psychological growth, children are not very homogeneous and considerable variability likewise remains among adults.

Birth to Age Three

I have not found studies of thoughts on death among children younger than three years. The average child's limited experiential background and inadequate symbolic capability before age three probably account for the lack.

While death concepts in this age group have not often been studied, the child's response to separation from the mother has,[6] and death, of necessity, involves separation. One of the few investigators who has also considered the child's reaction to separation from the father is Ostrovsky.[7] The child's limited understanding of death, time, cancer, etc., does not insure emotional insulation, in fact the absence of such understanding may accentuate the emotional response to the loss of, or separation from, a parent or parent surrogate. Separation anxiety may be evoked, in part, because the difference between two hours, two days, two years, or forever, is not at all clear to the young child.[8] A more extensive discussion of the child's reaction to the loss of a family member is found in later chapters.

Ages Three to Five Years

The existing data for this age group are meager and the most thorough investigations were conducted prior to World War II with English and Hungarian children.[9]

Children from three to five years of age do have some first-hand experience with death in the form of wilted flowers, dead goldfish and other pets, and sometimes hearing of the death or funeral of a relative. Based upon these experiences most children in this age range will respond to questions about death. Many children conclude that death is "to go away" or "to go asleep."[10] For other three to five year olds death may be a gradual or temporary process. Dead people talk more quietly or run more slowly. "In the coffin, you can eat and drink."[11]

From these examples it is easy to see why some people have hypothesized that the child's anxiety or reluctance to go to bed at night or to have a parent take a trip may be associated with the child's concept of death. The death of a parent undoubtedly presents unique problems to the child of three to five whose concept of death is unrealistic. The child may assume that the dead parent could return if he or she wanted to, and sadness may be mingled with resentment at being abandoned.[12]

Synthesis of these data permits the interpretation that most children progress from no concept of death at age three to a vague, limited, or false concept of death (e.g., sleep) at age five. Young children do not yet distinguish completely between life and death. Fantasy still operates and is evidenced in a lack of awareness that everyone must die and in perceiving death as a temporary condition.

Ages Five to Ten

Empirical studies of the child's image of death are far more numerous among five to ten year olds than younger children. While controversy still surrounds the five to ten year old's image of death, two generalizations are fairly secure:

1. The child's concept of death becomes increasingly more realistic and complex between age five and age ten.[13] The increasing realism is best illustrated by examples from Anthony's study. Some of her five and six year olds still defined "dead" as "to go asleep." A modal response in this age group was, "When people get dead, they go in their grave." But some nine or ten year olds were defining "dead" in terms of logical or biological essentials, "When you have no pulse and no temperature and can't breathe."[14]

2. As the child advances from five to ten, death ceases to be something that only happens to some people. Awareness that everyone must die, that death is universal, is generally achieved by nine or ten.[15]

When one attempts to go beyond these broad generalizations

regarding the child's image of death from five to ten, the evidence is conflicting. For instance, controversy surrounds the following issues.

Anxiety. The authors of one of the largest studies of the concept of death among children and youth concluded that their subjects "showed almost no fright-laden or terrifying imagery."[16] This apparent lack of anxiety contrasts with the conclusion of another research team, perhaps because the children involved in the latter study were all psychiatric clinic patients.[17]

Much of the speculation and data prior to 1957 regarding the child's emotional response to the idea of death is reviewed by Alexander and Adlerstein in the introduction to their study in which they made use of more easily quantified measures of anxiety than had been typical in previous research.[18] Among male children from five to sixteen, Alexander and Adlerstein found that more emotion was aroused by words associated with death (e.g., buried, kill, dead) than by basal words (e.g., dress, happy, brave). Emotion was measured by the time required to respond with the first word suggested by a stimulus word and also by electrical conductivity of the skin, i.e., GSR. When the data were segmented by age group, the nine to twelve year olds revealed less emotional arousal than the younger (five to eight years) and older (thirteen to sixteen years) groups. The authors concluded that death has less emotional significance for the nine to twelve year olds because they are in a relatively tranquil period developmentally. In other words, during this period no great demand is introduced for a change in their overall response patterns.

A study by Safier is often cited in support of the notion that "death" is an anxiety-laden topic for five to ten year olds.[19] Safier examined the possibility of a positive relation between life concept and death concept formations among four to eleven year old boys. No measure of anxiety about death was involved and the author's only comment along these lines was that her seven and eight year old boys "expressed fear of the questions because they were afraid it was a 'test.'"[20] It seems unnecessary to belabor methodological and interpretive problems associated with these studies. Suffice it to say that findings on the degree of anxiety aroused by the topic of death or death words within this age group are confusing, and more careful research is needed before further substantive comment is possible.

Socioeconomic status. Socioeconomic status (SES) and its close correlate, general emotional health, seem to be related to what the child from five to ten years of age thinks of death, particularly its causes.

Exposure to death, violence, and physical aggression is more common in the life experiences of lower SES as opposed to middle SES children. McIntire, Angle, and Struempler found that their clinic children ($N = 50$) who were 85 percent white and lower to lower middle SES were four times as likely as the predominantly white suburban child to cite violence as the cause of death.[21] A relation between being seen at a psychiatric clinic and associating death with violence finds support in at least two other studies.[22]

Since many children seen by psychiatric clinics are from the lower SES levels, the variables of social status and emotional stability are often confounded with each other in studies involving clinic children. Emotional health may be a more potent factor than socioeconomic status in the violence-cause of death interplay, but we will not know this until samples of differing socioeconomic status but similar emotional health, and vice versa, are studied in relation to the child's concept of death.

Personification of death. Two-thirds of five to nine year old Hungarian children in Nagy's study imagined death as a distinct personality.[23] Either these children believed in the reality of the skeleton-man or they created their own idea of the death-man who catches people and carries them away. If you don't get caught, you don't die.

The conclusion that children of five to ten years tend to personify death in some form has probably been mentioned in far more discussions of the child's concept of death than it deserves to be. In addition to Nagy's data, this idea may have its origin in fantasy literature written for middle childhood which in no way reveals the real life interpretations children make. With the exception of Safier's study, investigations in England and the United States have rarely noted a tendency to personify death at any age.[24] Obviously, culture exerts an influence on the child's image of death.[25]

Irrevocability of death. Childers and Wimmer reported an increase with age in the child's understanding of death as irrevocable.[26] Nonetheless, nearly half of their ten year olds still thought death was revocable or were undecided. In contrast, McIntire et al. found among both Catholic and Protestant school children that the seven year old was more likely to accept death as total cessation than were younger or older children.[27] Beyond age eight, death as total cessation was less acceptable. A belief in spiritual immortality became increasingly common, a belief which accords with most Western religions.

Large scale cross-sectional studies or longitudinal studies (involving the same children being asked the same questions over this age span) will be needed to pinpoint the age, if it exists, at which most United

States citizens believe death to be irrevocable. As we will see, the question is far from settled even among older children of ages ten to sixteen.

Ages Ten to Sixteen

Following the lead of the McIntire et al.[28] comprehensive study of thoughts on death held by older children and adolescents, the following discussion is organized around five topics: (1) cause of death, (2) imagery associated with death, (3) after death?, (4) suicide, and (5) the significance of life.

Cause of death. After reading Chapter One, you know that most American children ten to sixteen years of age probably have little direct acquaintance with death. Only 3 percent of the McIntire et al. church school subjects ($N = 548$, ages 5-16) had lost a parent. Among clinic patients at the University of Nebraska ($N = 50$, ages 5-16), 14 percent had lost a parent. In spite of a lack of first-hand experience at home, children over ten years had some realistic acquaintance with the causes of death. A majority had known someone who died and had attended a funeral. This acquaintance apparently stops short of viewing the dead person, as 43 percent of those children from eleven to sixteen years had never seen a dead person.[29]

Death seemed to be attributed to different causes depending upon whether the child was asked, "Why do people die?," or "Why did someone that you knew die?" Deaths of known people were typically attributed to disease and old age, and a small minority to violence, accident, war, or suicide. The most common responses to why people in general die were old age, selected for death by God, disease, and violence, accident, war, or suicide.

Religious background seemed to influence the response to the general question, "Why do people die?" At age eleven, 22 percent of the Catholic children in this study cited selection by God as the reason people in general die. Only 2 percent of these same children cited selection by God as the reason someone they knew died.[30] Apparently, when considering the death of people in general, an informal conception of cause is induced via religious affiliation.

Imagery associated with death. Investigations have reached different conclusions on the degree to which children of ten to sixteen years are made anxious by death imagery. Unfortunately, anxiety has been measured more often by subjective impression than by some objective technique. It must be recognized, further, that objective measures of anxiety are not currently very satisfactory either.

McIntire et al. concluded that their subjects were not particularly anxious about death, but, interestingly, a significant minority of approximately 20 percent gave fantasy explanations of the state of the body in death which involved reincarnation.[31] Among these subjects, those who had lost a parent through death were far more likely to accept decomposition of the body after death than those children who had lost a parent through divorce or separation. Children from broken homes may be more anxious about many things, including death. Then again, a realistic perception of the body after death may or may not be an indication of anxiety about death.

Other investigators have inferred death anxiety to exist in adolescents. Kastenbaum's interpretation of his data was that the majority of his adolescent subjects were fearfully evading ideas and feelings concerning death.[32] The experimental evidence previously discussed of Alexander and Adlerstein also indicated that words associated with death aroused anxiety among preadolescents (ages thirteen to sixteen).[33] However, no firm conclusions may be drawn regarding the pervasiveness of anxiety aroused by the topic of death within this age group, or about the antecedent variables that may be associated with anxiety regarding death.

Anxiety about death in general is one thing, but anxiety about one's own death is another. Considering personal death undoubtedly arouses the adolescent's anxiety. Thomas Cottle has written a vivid description of thoughts of his own death during preadolescence.

Come to think of it, I do remember what I thought about death, or at least what I felt and did when I thought about it. First, the image that someday I just wouldn't be anymore always stung me in bed at night. Then a fright would envelope me, a physiological jolt that like an H-bomb hit every outpost in my entire body at once. Second, with knees folded up into my chest, I invariably sought to ward off the fright, employing the solution that when you're dead you cannot think about anything so it's not so bad, at least not as bad as what you're presently experiencing. Third, my warding off strategy never varied and never worked. Fourth, I spoke about this death thing with my friends and laughed as again and again I realized that millions of kids went through the same four steps. I wonder now whether anyone else still goes through them, not regularly of course, not often, but once in a while. One, two, three, four! explosion, and death has receded for the while, just as before.[34]

This description apparently strikes some adult readers as very unique. They don't remember having had such an experience. Others get a real feeling of "deja vu." It reminds them very much of their own adolescent encounter with thoughts of their own death, at least before they had essentially worked through thoughts and feelings surrounding "my death." Or was it that they just built better defenses surrounding such thoughts?

After death? In addition to asking traditional questions, McIntire et al. put some unique questions to children to reveal the child's view of consciousness after death.[35] These investigators asked children who had lost a pet, "Do you think the pet knows you miss it?" A "yes" response was interpreted as belief in cognizance after death. For the total group, "yes" responses decreased with age. However, at ages fifteen to sixteen, 33 percent of the clinic patients, 28 percent of the Protestants, and 12 percent of the entire group still attributed cognizance to the pet. "At all ages, the avowed belief in cognizance for self was much lower than for the pet."[36]

Among these primarily church school respondents, belief in spiritual continuation peaked at ages thirteen to fourteen.[37] The child's specific religious orientation was associated with belief in spiritual continuation after death. Nearly 90 percent of the Catholic and Protestant children in this age range believed in spiritual continuation, but only 60 percent of the Jewish children expressed such a belief. Within all three church school groups (Catholic, Protestant, Jewish), belief in spiritual continuation was unrelated to frequency of religious instruction; death or divorce in the family; death of a parent, sibling or peer; attendance at a funeral; total hours of television viewing per week; or type of favorite program.[38]

The divergent views of what happens after death found among ten to sixteen year olds seem merely to mirror the views of the adult population in America. As Gardner Murphy aptly noted, "I have also been impressed . . . with the cultural contradictions that lie even in the deepest scientific thinking about this whole matter. It seems to be assumed in our tradition that man is both terminated by death and capable of continuing in some other sense beyond death."[39]

Suicide. It seems to be characteristic of human beings that at some time during their lives they wish that they were dead. Hence, it is not so surprising that a fair proportion of children ages ten to sixteen say that they occasionally wish they would die. A much smaller number may have frequent death wishes. In the study by McIntire et al., 3 percent or eighteen children in their sample said that they "frequently" wished to die.[40] These children were all between ten and sixteen years of age, predominantly Protestant, members of intact families, and receiving religious instruction once a week. They seemed to view both life and death in a fashion more characteristic of children younger than their own age group, and they said their wish for death was precipitated by family arguments or fear of punishment.[41]

Some children in this age group do not simply wish to commit suicide or even merely make the attempt. Some succeed in killing themselves. Rate of death due to suicide is reported by the National Center for Health Statistics for age groups one to fourteen years and fifteen to twenty-four years. Among the younger group (ages one to fourteen), the estimated rate for 1971 was three-tenths of 1 percent, or 300 per 100,000 deaths in the population in this age range. Among the older group (those fifteen to twenty-four), the rate was 9.2 percent, or a little more than 9,000 per 100,000 deaths.[42] While the absolute incidence of suicide among one to fourteen year olds is certainly not high, one can decry the fact that any child in the United States should prefer to be dead rather than alive. The adolescent suicide rate, which has been increasing and continues to increase, is certainly cause for concern.

Significance of life. "What gives life its significance?" is not a question likely to be entertained by children less than ten years of age. It is even questionable whether many American adults would respond to this question with a logical, well-reasoned reply.

Evidence exists that the child's concepts surrounding moral judgment and his or her religion become increasingly abstract and complex from age ten to sixteen and so, too, do conceptions of the meaning of life.[43]

McIntire et al. asked all of their children (N = 598) the open question, "What does life mean to you?" The responses were categorized under one of five headings: (1) simple existence, including responses indicative of enjoying life's pleasures and interpersonal relationships, e.g., "grow up and get married," (2) theologic, (3) creativity or conduct of life—"be a good mother," "be of service to mankind," (4) biologic immortality—insure the genetic immortality of their parents, and (5) transcendental and other complex spiritual responses.

Among children with strong ties to organized religion, virtually no consideration was given to biologic immortality at any age. As a matter of fact, only one such response occurred among 598. Responses indicating that creativity or conduct of life gave life its meaning increased with age and attribution of theologic significance to life seemed to peak at ages eleven to thirteen and decline thereafter.[44] The dominant response in the oldest age group (fifteen to sixteen years) was that enjoyment of life's pleasures and interpersonal relations rendered life meaningful, i.e., the simple existence response type.

The reason children gave for life's significance varied with religious affiliation.[45] Catholic children gave the highest incidence of theologic responses and the Jewish children gave more significance to creativity and service than did non-Jews. However, discounting those who did not know what life meant to them or at least gave no response, simple existence responses made up the largest category of answers for all three religious groups (Catholic, Protestant, and Jewish), just as the pleasures of simple existence were cited by the largest number between ten and sixteen years of age.

When adolescents fail to express a meaning for life they may be suppressing thoughts of death.[46] This is one possible explanation among many, but there is some evidence that, among college students, an accepting attitude toward death is associated with seeing high purpose and meaning in life.[47]

Problems in Investigating the Child's Concept of Death

Before briefly summarizing what we know about the child's thoughts on death, it seems appropriate here to comment upon some of the difficulties that investigators have faced in attempting to study the child's concept of death.

One of the obvious problems is the availability of normal, healthy, ordinary children with whom to work. Death may or may not be a taboo topic, but death is not typically the subject of polite social conversation and many parents have undoubtedly refused or been reluctant to have their children questioned about it. A more severe social stigma probably attaches to sexual practices and attitudes, but in either case, it is especially difficult to gather a representative sample of the general population during childhood or adolescence.

Investigations of the child's concept of death share the basic problems associated with research into concept development in general. Many of these problems and issues have been discussed by Flavell in his recent review.[48] In relation to the work on death, one of the first things you note is that investigators seem to be trying to get at an entire conceptual system, rather than one concept. To a degree this is unavoidable,[49] but the attributes of a dead body do not have to include the concept of funeral, suicide, or reincarnation. Perhaps a less global approach, confined first to the simpler concepts that have a fairly well agreed upon "public" meaning, would be fruitful.

Since the concept is essentially within the child's head, a good deal of ingenuity is needed to develop stimuli (testing procedures) to tap dimensions of this concept and in refining reliable measures of the child's response to these stimuli. Although it doesn't eliminate all problems by any means, it would seem that greater use could be made of structured response formats. For instance, anxiety has often been studied in relation to thoughts about death, but apparently little attempt has been made to adapt such instruments as the *Children's Manifest Anxiety Scale* in some way to this purpose.

It is always easier to see what needs to be done than to do it. If the concept of death is viewed along some of the dimensions on which concepts differ (e.g., attributes, abstractness, generality), only the courageous experimenter need apply.

Summary of What the Child Thinks of Death

From birth until age sixteen, the child progresses from no image of death to, in some cases, a highly-structured, complex, and abstract image of death. The child from three to five may think of sleep or departure when he thinks of death. From five to ten, in most instances, the child progresses from a vague, unrealistic image of death to the general conclusion that death is the end of the life cycle or the opposite of "life," inescapable and universal. Beyond age ten, images of death become more variable, complex, and abstract, perhaps involving what comes after death and the value of life.

How the Child Thinks of Death

While reading the research presented in the preceding section, I, too, shared some of the investigators' dissatisfaction with *what* older children and adolescents thought about death. After pondering the source of this dissatisfaction, I concluded that it was important to identify the particulars of content in the child's image of death, and the dynamics as to *how* the child arrives at that content as two separate topics.

Obviously, if we are dissatisfied with the older children's thinking about death, we have examined their responses and they fell short of our expectations. In what way did they fall short? What was our expectation? Kastenbaum has considered this same question regarding the child's concept of death. He wrote, "We lack a truly convincing idea of the 'goal' or 'maturational outcome,' what the process of growth is moving toward."[50]

It seems to me that except for some publicly agreed upon aspects of death, e.g., what it means to be physically dead, we cannot specify a goal in terms of content or *what* the child should think.[51] In a society that allows considerable freedom of thought, it is difficult to invent an ideal image of life or death. But I still have expectations. I would like older children and adolescents to (1) respond, and (2) logically defend their response. It is sad that a large number of sixteen year olds say they "don't know" what life means to them. Does this mean they have never thought about it? Perhaps not, but they ought to think about it and they ought to be comfortable with their response, i.e., capable of defending it.

I am suggesting this capability, or this level of thinking, as a maturational goal. Further, I am suggesting this goal might be represented by Piaget's level of formal operational thought and Kohlberg's principled or postconventional morality. Whether or not we can all accept both of these representations is debatable and, if we can accept them, the route to them is relatively uncharted, but just thinking about it may be stimulating.

Piaget's Sequence of Cognitive Development

Piaget has outlined a theory of cognitive development and a sequence of developmental stages that are well supported empirically. The postulated sequence can be described in terms of four primary levels of cognitive development: (a) the sensorimotor, (b) the preoperational or intuitive, (c) the concrete operational level, and (d) the formal operational level of thought.[52]

The goal is the development of formal operational thought, but it is important to have some understanding of cognitive development that precedes and makes possible formal operational thought. As we review these stages we may gain some insight regarding "how" the child could have arrived at the answers that were reviewed in the first section of this chapter.

Sensorimotor period. In Piaget's view, thought evolves from the gradual internalization of action. The first two periods in his schema involve the development of cognitive substructures and functions that allow true thought or reasoning to emerge at around six or seven years of age.

The sensorimotor period extends from birth to approximately one and a half to two years. During this period, the child is learning to control and coordinate sensory and motor responses. No data on the child's thoughts on death during this period are available. The sensorimotor "infant lacks the symbolic function, that is, he does not have representations by which he can evoke persons or objects in their absence."[53]

Preoperational stage. The child's actions become increasingly more representative of the preoperational stage by one and a half or two and continue to be so until approximately six or seven years of age. During this period, tremendous representational ability develops, particularly in the use of symbolic language. This representational ability is basic to the development of later intelligence and provides "it with an unlimited field of application, in contrast to the restricted boundaries of sensorimotor action and perception."[54]

Piaget has attended to the complex subject of causality during this period. Parents can attest to the fact that the average child of three can drive you to distraction with "why?," "why?" Piaget has pointed out that these "whys" are a heterogeneous lot.[55] Some "whys" are questions of place or name, some reveal astonishment without expecting an answer, some reveal disappointment, some curiosity, but eventually the child searches for causes.

During this preoperational or intuitive period, the child is not interested in logical justification. He asserts without proving,[56] e.g., to be dead is to "be asleep" or "gone away." Lacking an understanding of chance events, the child looks for the why in fortuitous occurrences. He was naughty and grandma died that day. Was it his naughtiness that made grandma die?

The preoperational child endows inanimate objects with life and moving objects with activity of their own.[57] In Piaget's words,

> . . . life is a perfectly normal phenomenon, without any elements of surprise in it, up till the moment when the child takes cognizance of the difference between life and death. From this moment, the idea of death sets the child's curiosity in action, precisely because, if every cause is coupled with a motive, then death calls for a special explanation.[58]

In Piaget's view, it is precisely the phenomenon of death and questions revolving around it, "which will cause the child to leave behind him the stage of pure finalism, and to acquire the notion of statistical causality or chance."[59] With the advent of concrete operational thought he can reason that Grandma died, not because he was naughty that day, but because she happened to be involved in an accident on the freeway.

Piaget's description of prelogical processes is a way of looking at how, prior to nine or ten, the child might have arrived at his misconceptions regarding death.

Concrete operational thought. Almost all of those children over ten years of age whose thoughts on death were described previously seemed to be at least functioning within the level of concrete operations. This is not surprising since the ability to engage in concrete operational thought tends to develop around six or seven. However, the child in any period is considered to be gradually developing greater facility with the logical operations associated with that period, and it may be that logical reasoning in regard to death does not develop until the child has been using concrete operations for several years.[60]

Concrete operations make possible logical and more systematic thought, and only with the emergence of such a capacity can the child deal effectively with classes, relations, and the conservation of quantities.

Based on direct experience, however remote personally, the child capable of operational thought can reason logically about the facts of death. "Everyone just die." "The dead don't breathe."

In response to the question, "What do you expect to be doing sixty, seventy, eighty, or ninety years from now?," Farnham-Diggory found the child's awareness of his eventual death to be related to chronological age, whether he was a normal or a psychotic child (seven to sixteen years).[61] Among brain damaged children, the awareness was related to their IQ score. The children who realistically anticipated when their own death was likely to occur were on the average three years older than those who did not mention their own death. These data demonstrate that logical thinking in regard to death and time appear after some capability with concrete operational thought has developed.

Obviously, the achievement of logical concrete operations is a great advance over preoperational thought, but it has definite limitations. These limitations have been succinctly summarized by Elkind.

The [concrete operational] child can only reason about those things with which he has had direct personal experience. He has difficulty as soon as he has to deal with any hypothetical or contrary-to-fact proposition. In addition, while he can deal with two classes, relations, or quantitative dimensions at the same time, this is about the limit of his capabilities. As soon as more variables than two have to be taken into account in a systematic way, he flounders because he lacks an operational system appropriate to such situations. This is the fundamental deficiency of concrete operational thought.[62]

Formal operational thought. Obviously to reason very effectively about the value or significance of life and what happens after death, one has to be capable of considering hypothetical propositions and more than two variables at one time. Logical thinking in abstract terms is a difficult process to master, but it would seem to be a worthy aim to get as many of our adolescents and young adults as possible to this level.

The great breakthrough of the formal operational stage is that through "differentiation of form and content the subject becomes capable of reasoning correctly about propositions that he considers pure hypotheses."[63] This ability to draw the necessary conclusions from truths which are merely possible constitutes the beginning of hypothetico-deductive or formal thought.

Formal operations are often described as "operations upon operations," i.e., classifications and relations are liberated from their concrete or intuitive ties and logical inferences can be made on the basis of classifying classifications, combining combinations, and relating relationships. For example,

. . . you present the child with five jars A through E containing colorless liquids. The combination of A, C, and E produces a yellow color: B is a bleaching agent and D is pure water. The child has seen the color but not the method of obtaining it. The problem presented to him . . . is to discover the combination that will produce the color and to determine the roles of B and D. At age seven to eleven the child generally proceeds by combinations of two's and then jumps to a trial of all five together. After the age of twelve he proceeds methodically, testing all possible combinations of one, two, three, four, and five elements, and thus solves the problem.[64]

This ability to generate all possible combinations is a unique feature of formal operational thought and underlies many different types of accomplishment among which is a mode of thinking present in all scientific endeavor. The development of formal-operational thought also transforms the way in which adolescents think about moral questions. There is reason to believe that the development of formal operational thought is a necessary, but not sufficient condition for a child to attain Kohlberg's level of principled or postconventional morality.[65]

Kohlberg's Stages of Moral Development

Many of the important questions revolving around death and the value of human life obviously involve moral issues. Piaget's theory of cognitive development and original research on values and morality have served, in large measure, as the impetus for Lawrence Kohlberg's present cognitive-developmental theory and research on moral development.

Kohlberg and his colleagues have presented hypothetical moral dilemmas to varying age groups, both in cross-section and longitudinally. Based on the reasoning and responses of these children and young adults, Kohlberg has described three major levels of moral thought: the preconventional, conventional, and postconventional or principled level. Among middle-class children, the preconventional level is usually occupied by children from approximately four to ten years of age. The conventional level typically becomes dominant during preadolescence, and the postconventional level does not appear until adolescence, if it appears at all.

Each level has been subdivided into two stages. Kohlberg described these stages as "six definite and universal stages of development in moral thought."[66] One progresses through them one at a time and always in the same order without skipping any steps, i.e., one does not become capable of principled moral thought without first having mastered conventional moral thought.

A complete description of each stage would involve us in too much detail. The following capsule descriptions of each major level have been extracted from Kohlberg's more complete descriptions:[67]

> *Preconventional level.* At this level the child is responsive to cultural rules and labels of good and bad, right or wrong, but interprets these labels in terms of either the physical or the hedonistic consequences of action (punishment, reward, exchange of favors) or in terms of the physical power of those who enunciate the rules and labels.

Conventional level. At this level, maintaining the expectations of the individual's family, group, or nation is perceived as valuable in its own right, regardless of immediate and obvious consequences. The attitude is not only one of *conformity* to personal expectations and social order, but of loyalty to it, of actively *maintaining,* supporting, and justifying the order and of identifying with the persons or group involved in it.

Postconventional, autonomous, or principled level. At this level, there is a clear effort to define moral values and principles which have validity and application apart from the authority of the groups or persons holding these principles and apart from the individual's own identification with those groups.

The following responses to a moral dilemma involving mercy killing further clarify Kohlberg's view of the developmental pattern. A response illustrates each of the three major levels.[68]

Preconventional. Stage 2: Tommy, age thirteen (IV. Question— Should the doctor "mercy kill" a fatally ill woman requesting death because of her pain?): "Maybe it would be good to put her out of her pain, she'd be better off that way. But the husband wouldn't want it, it's not like an animal. If a pet dies you can get along without it—it isn't something you really need. Well, you can get a new wife, but it's not really the same."

Conventional. Stage 4: Jim, age sixteen (same question): "I don't know. In one way, it's murder, it's not a right or privilege of man to decide who shall live and who should die. God put life into everybody on earth and you're taking away something from that person that came directly from God, and you're destroying something that is very sacred, it's in a way part of God and it's almost destroying a part of God when you kill a person. There's something of God in everyone."

Postconventional. Stage 5: Jim, age twenty (same question): "Given the ethics of the doctor who has taken on responsibility to save human life—from that point of view he probably shouldn't but there is another side, there are more and more people in the medical profession who are thinking it is a hardship on everyone, the person, the family, when you know they are going to die. When a person is kept alive by an artificial lung or kidney it's more like being a vegetable than being a human who is alive. If it's her own choice I think there are certain rights and privileges that go along with being a human being. I am a human being and have certain desires for life and I think everybody else does, too. You have a world of which you are the center, and everybody else does, too, and in that sense we're all equal."

After seeing specific responses it is obvious that Kohlberg's moral hierarchy engenders controversy among psychologists and philosophers.[69] However, there is considerable agreement that Kohlberg's work is important. It is not essential (and is perhaps dangerous at this point) to believe Kohlberg has spelled out truth with a capital "T." But the real philosophic controversies center around whether or not Stage 6 represents a higher level of morality than Stage 5, or whether either represents a higher level than Stage 4. Getting adolescents and young adults to this level of debate would again seem to be a worthy objective.

Facilitating cognitive-moral development. Kohlberg rejects the thesis that morality and moral learning are fundamentally emotional and irrational processes. He also rejects the belief that morality is relative. Many psychologists part company with him on these two points but, beyond that, others will differ with his explanation of how moral values are learned. Kohlberg suggested that: (1) these broad moral principles are so natural and sensible that they don't have to be taught; their emergence needs merely to be stimulated; (2) growth in moral reasoning is a result of "cognitive conflict" at the stage in which the child is currently operating; (3) therefore, programs in moral education must include conflict and controversy if more mature stages of moral judgment are to be reached. Optimal conflict was judged by Kohlberg to be engendered when the children are exposed to arguments which are structurally one stage above their present level.

When the topic turns to the learning of principles, we do not know, as yet, how they are learned, nor how they might best be taught. Kohlberg's discussion raises more questions than it answers; it has tremendous heuristic potential: (a) Is cognitive conflict necessary for change? (b) What is the role of social reinforcement? (c) What is the influence of power and prestige attaching to those who think at a higher (?) level? (d) What part is played by the child's increasing role taking, as well as cognitive skill? (e) Can such learning be explained equally well by modeling (imitation/emulation) theory?

Kohlberg presents experimental evidence that his programs have been successful in changing *verbal* behavior. But although the judgment and reasoning behind behavior is indisputably important, in the final analysis, it is the behavior in many cases that must change. As yet, we have no idea what the effects of such a long-term program would be.

It is trite but true that, as with so many other areas of developmental psychology, we need answers that we don't have. The facilitation of cognitive development is certainly not a new concern and when we start talking about the learning of principles, moral or otherwise, there is much that we don't know. Our adolescents, and if recent surveys are accurate, any child of the seventies or eighties will be confronted with very real and personal issues revolving around death and the significance of life, e.g., population control, abortion, pollution, euthanasia, organ transplants, and the ever present possibility of nuclear warfare. For those of you who are interested in the helping professions, there is sufficient challenge here for a lifetime. Perhaps the first step is to be willing and able to debate the issues.

Notes

1. Anecdotes from J. Sully, *Studies of Childhood* (Longmans Green, 1895) are cited in Sylvia Anthony, *The Discovery of Death in Childhood and After* (New York: Basic Books, 1971); see, for instance, p. 51.

2. The following are only examples of work within the psychoanalytic framework: Phyllis Blanchard, "A Study of Subject Matter and Motivation of Children's Dreams," *Journal of Abnormal and Social Psychology* 21 (April 1926):24-37; H. Von Hug Hellmuth, "The Child's Concept of Death," *Psychoanalytic Quarterly* 34 (October 1965):499-516, (originally published in *Imago* 1 (1912):286-98. For a brief discussion of the interpretive debates among psychoanalysts regarding the child's concept of death, see the following: Bernard Steinzor, "Death and the Construction of Reality," in *Festschrift for Gardner Murphy,* ed. John G. Peatman and Eugene L. Hartley (New York: Harper & Brothers, 1960), pp. 358-75.

3. Paul Schilder and David Wechsler, "The Attitudes of Children Toward Death," *Journal of Genetic Psychology* 45 (December 1934):406-51.

4. In addition to the editor, the other chapter authors, and discussants, this chapter was certainly improved because Ann Cauble, Raymond Kulhavy, Loreen Shipley, and R. Keith Van Wagenen graciously consented to read and comment on it. The author is also indebted to Bonnie Janzen for help with the literature search.

5. Space prohibits presenting an adequate background on the work and thought of Lawrence Kohlberg and Jean Piaget. Interested readers are referred to recent texts in educational psychology or child development, such as: Robert M. W. Travers, *Educational Psychology* (New York: Macmillan, 1973), see pp. 80-88 and pp. 371-74; Robert E. Grinder, *Adolescence* (New York: John Wiley, 1973), pp. 186-210 and pp. 340-45. Other references are cited in the course of the chapter, but the reader may also be interested in the following original sources: Lawrence Kohlberg, "Moral Education in the School," *School*

Review 74 (Spring 1966):1-30; Jean Piaget and Bärbel Inhelder, *The Psychology of the Child* (New York: Basic Books, 1969).

6. John Bowlby, "Separation Anxiety," *International Journal of Psycho-Analysis* 41 (March-June 1960):89-113. Some of these studies are reviewed in the following chapter: Mary M. D. Ainsworth, "Attachment and Dependency: A Comparison," in *Attachment and Dependency*, ed. Jacob L. Gewirtz (Washington, D.C.: V. H. Winston, 1972), pp. 97-137.

7. Everett S. Ostrovsky, *Children Without Men* (New York: Collier Books, 1962); also see: Henry B. Biller, *Paternal Deprivation* (Lexington, Ma.: Lexington Books, 1974).

8. Robert R. Sears, "Attachment, Dependency, and Frustration," in *Attachment and Dependency*, ed. Jacob L. Gewirtz (Washington, D.C.: V. H. Winston, 1972), pp. 1-27.

9. Anthony, *Discovery of Death*; and Maria Nagy, "The Child's Theories Concerning Death," *Journal of Genetic Psychology* 73 (September 1948):3-27.

10. Anthony, *Discovery of Death*, p. 52; and Nagy, "Child's Theories," p. 12.

11. Nagy, "Child's Theories," p. 9.

12. This reaction in the case of Tom (age 5) is discussed in Ostrovsky, *Children*, p. 117.

13. Anthony, *Discovery of Death*; Perry Childers and Mary Wimmer, "The Concept of Death in Early Childhood," *Child Development* (October 1971): 1299-1301; Wayne Gartley and Marion Bernasconi, "The Concept of Death in Children," *Journal of Genetic Psychology* 110 (March 1967):71-85; Matilda S. McIntire, Carol R. Angle, and Lorraine J. Struempler, "The Concept of Death in Midwestern Children and Youth," *American Journal of Diseases of Children* 123 (June 1972):527-32; and Nagy, "Child's Theories."

14. Anthony, *Discovery of Death*, pp. 50-54.

15. Anthony, *Discovery of Death*; Childers and Wimmer, "Concept of Death"; and McIntire, Angle, and Struempler, "Midwestern Children."

16. McIntire, Angle, and Struempler, "Midwestern Children," p. 531.

17. Schilder and Wechsler, "Attitudes of Children."

18. Irving E. Alexander and Arthur M. Adlerstein, "Affective Responses to the Concept of Death in a Population of·Children and Early Adolescents," *Journal of Genetic Psychology* 93 (December 1958):167-77.

19. Gwen Safier, "A Study in Relationships Between the Life and Death Concepts in Children," *Journal of Genetic Psychology* 105 (December 1964):283-94.

20. Ibid., p. 292.

21. McIntire, Angle, and Struempler, "Midwestern Children," p. 531.

22. Schilder and Wechsler, "Attitudes of Children"; and Martha Wolfenstein and Gilbert Kliman, eds., *Children and the Death of a President* (Garden City, N.Y.: Doubleday, 1965).

23. Nagy, "Child's Theories," p. 25.

24. Anthony, *Discovery of Death*, p. 75; Gerald P. Koocher, "Childhood, Death, and Cognitive Development," *Developmental Psychology* 9 (November 1973):369-75; McIntire, Angle, and Struempler, "Midwestern Children," p. 531; and Safier, "Study in Relationships," pp. 292-93.

25. Personification of death seems to be reflected in the Mexican custom of taking entire meals and especially bakery goods to the cemetery on the Day of the Dead and leaving them for the dead to eat.

26. Childers and Wimmer, "Concept of Death."

27. McIntire, Angle, and Struempler, "Midwestern Children."

28. Ibid.

29. Ibid., pp. 528-29.

30. Ibid., p. 529.

31. Ibid., p. 529.

32. Robert Kastenbaum, "Time and Death in Adolescence," in *The Meaning of Death*, ed. Herman Feifel (New York: McGraw-Hill, 1959), pp. 99-113.

33. Alexander and Adlerstein, "Affective Responses."

34. Thomas J. Cottle, "The Connections of Adolescence," *Daedalus* 100 (Fall 1971):1177-1219; quoted from p. 1196.

35. McIntire, Angle, and Struempler, "Midwestern Children," p. 529.

36. Ibid., p. 529.

37. Ibid., p. 530.

38. Although there is no specific mention of a belief in spiritual continuation in the abstract, Bolduc found a relation between a cognitive measure of the child's (ages nine to fourteen) concept of death and having experienced the death of a parent or sibling. See: Jeannette Bolduc, "A Developmental Study of the Relationship Between Experiences of Death and Age and Development of the Concept of Death," *Dissertation Abstracts* 33 (December 1972):2758-A.

39. Gardner Murphy, "Discussion," in *The Meaning of Death*, ed. Herman Feifel (New York: McGraw-Hill, 1959), pp. 317-40, quoted from p. 333.

40. McIntire, Angle, and Struempler, "Midwestern Children," p. 530.

41. These associations are not necessarily in agreement with those found in other studies of adolescent suicide. Adolescent suicide is a complex topic in its own right. Many references to the topic of suicide are included in Chapter 5, but the reader who is particularly interested in adolescent suicide might begin with the following source: Jerry Jacobs, *Adolescent Suicide* (New York: Wiley-Interscience, 1971).

42. U.S. Department of Health, Education and Welfare, National Center for Health Statistics, "Monthly Vital Statistics Report: Annual Summary for the United States, 1971," Rockville, Md.: Author, August 1972.

43. See, for example: David Elkind, "The Child's Conception of His Religious Denomination: III. The Protestant Child," *Journal of Genetic Psychology* 103 (December 1963):291-304; and Sol Kugelmass and Shlomo Breznitz, "Intentionality in Moral Judgment: Adolescent Development," *Child Development* 39 (March 1968):249-56.

44. McIntire, Angle, and Struempler, "Midwestern Children," p. 531.

45. Ibid., p. 531.

46. Ibid., p. 532.

47. Joseph A. Durlak, "A Relationship Between Individual Attitudes Toward Life and Death," *Journal of Consulting and Clinical Psychology* 38 (June 1972):463.

48. John H. Flavell, "Concept Development," in *Carmichael's Manual of Child Psychology*, ed. Paul H. Mussen, 3rd ed. (New York: John Wiley, 1970), pp. 983-1059.

49. Ibid., p. 986.

50. Robert Kastenbaum, "The Child's Understanding of Death," in *Explaining Death to Children*, ed. Earl A. Grollman (Boston: Beacon Press, 1967), pp. 89-108, quoted from p. 91.

51. As mentioned in Chapter 1, the medical profession has not achieved a totally acceptable definition of biological death, but there is public consensus regarding the basic physiological condition of a corpse.

52. Piaget does not use the term stage or period to imply that children move from discrete stage to discrete stage in development. Rather, he views cognitive development as a continuous and cumulative process. In various publications, the precise breakdown of stages that Piaget uses may vary from three to eight. Four are used here because it is perhaps more traditional and it facilitates relating to Kohlberg's work.

53. Piaget and Inhelder, *Psychology*, p. 3.

54. Ibid., p. 91.

55. Jean Piaget, *The Language and Thought of the Child* (Cleveland: Meridian Books, 1955), see Chapter V.

56. Ibid., p. 178.

57. Piaget uses the term "animism" to describe the child's assignment of life and life-like qualities to inanimate objects. Readers interested in this concept might begin with the following: Göte Klingberg, "The Distinction Between Living and Not Living Among 7-10-Year-Old Children, With Some Remarks Concerning the So-Called Animism Controversy," *Journal of Genetic Psychology* 90 (September 1957):227-38; and Safier, "Study in Relationships."

58. Piaget, *Language and Thought*, p. 210.

59. Ibid., p. 185.

60. The following investigation supports the view that the longer a child has been conserving (the hallmark of entering the concrete operational period), the more adept he is at classification and seriation tasks: Ronald Zellner, "An Empirical Investigation of the Relation Between Conservation and the Concrete Operations of Classification and Seriation," Ph.D. diss., Arizona State University, 1973. Koocher, "Childhood, Death," found among seventy-five Midwestern children of ages six to fifteen a clear relation between responses regarding the causes of death and a measure of Piaget's levels of cognitive development.

61. Sylvia Farnham-Diggory, "Self, Future, and Time: A Developmental Study of the Concepts of Psychotic, Brain-Damaged, and Normal Children," *Monographs of Society for Research in Child Development* 31 (No. 1, Whole No. 103), 1966, pp. 1-63.

62. David Elkind, "Cognitive Development in Adolescence," in *Understanding Adolescence: Current Developments in Adolescent Psychology*, ed. James F. Adams (Boston: Allyn and Bacon, 1968), pp. 128-58, quoted from p. 141.

63. Piaget and Inhelder, *Psychology*, p. 132.

64. Ibid., p. 134.

65. Lawrence Kohlberg and Carol Gilligan, "The Adolescent as a Philosopher," *Daedalus* 100 (Fall 1971):1051-86, see p. 1071.

66. Ibid., p. 1066.

67. Lawrence Kohlberg, "Implications of Developmental Psychology for Education: Examples from Moral Development," *Educational Psychologist* 10 (Winter 1973):2-14.

68. Lawrence Kohlberg, "From Is to Ought," in *Cognitive Development and Epistemology*, ed. Theodore Mischel (New York: Academic Press, 1971), pp. 151-235, quoted from pp. 168-69.

69. For an introduction to this debate, see the following: R. S. Peters, "Moral Development: A Plea for Pluralism," in *Cognitive Development and Epistemology*, ed. Theodore Mischel (New York: Academic Press, 1971), pp. 237-67; and William P. Alston, "Comments on Kohlberg's 'From Is to Ought,'" in *Cognitive Development and Epistemology*, ed. Theodore Mischel (New York: Academic Press, 1971), pp. 269-84.

Suggested Readings

Anthony, Sylvia, *The Discovery of Death in Childhood and After*, 1st Am. ed. (New York: Basic Books, 1972).

The author's broad scholarship makes this book well worth reading, even if you aren't particularly interested in the child's concept of death.

Grollman, Earl A., ed., *Explaining Death to Children* (Boston: Beacon Press, 1967).

A variety of viewpoints are represented by the various authors. In total, this volume contains some of the best practical, though tentative, suggestions on dealing with children. The final chapter on the use of literature may be particularly helpful to those in daily contact with children.

As is the case everywhere in this book, the unique qualities of the author shine through in the following chapter. He is a minister who has long served fellow humans in suffering as a compassionate chaplain. His dynamic interpretations of faith and living-learning add much to our understanding of death and life.

3

Grief, Mourning, and Reconstruction

Paul W. Strickland

Death and Living—Learning

One of the goals of education is to teach people to think for themselves. They can! Another goal of education is to awaken in persons an awareness of their emotions, to be able to cry when they are sad. It is possible to help children learn how to meet the hard places of life in such a way as to grow stronger by having lived through them. It is a premise of mine that we can do something more or different than we have done in the past, and hopefully it will be more effective.

There is no prior preparation for living, that we know about for sure, that is! But we can set up some simulated situations from which we can learn. We can be sensitive enough to the hurts of one another to learn from one another, and pool our resources to cope better with the stress of life. We can be open to the living-learning opportunities as they happen to us to learn something rather than let them happen without experiencing anything. After all we are human, and one of the qualities of human beings is the capacity to experience compassion and caring, if not love. And the root meaning of compassion is "to suffer with." Children can learn the meaning of the proverb, "Share a sorrow and you cut it in half; share a joy and you multiply it by two."

Lamers suggests the following guidelines when talking with a child about death:

1. Attitude more important than words.
2. Talk before the need arises.
3. Begin at child's level.
4. Let the child talk.
5. Try to answer all questions.
6. Make yourself available to the child.[1]

If you are relaxed and calm and dignified, yet approachable, children will be able to feel they can trust you, even if they do not want to talk

57

with you at the time. We cannot deceive children for very long. They easily see through our falseness, whether it is verbalized or not. They seem to read our muscles if not our minds! Some have called it a visceral level of communication. But their own efforts to find meaning in a time of acute stress are often damaging to themselves. It is better to supply them with the simple facts than to leave them on their own to figure it out for themselves.

A sixteen year old girl was in the hospital with acute pain from a terminal illness. A visitor observed, "She should be out dating and finding out what life is all about."[2] But life isn't all about how to have a good time. There are disappointments in life also. There is sickness and pain. Therefore, this girl was also finding out what life is about. Certainly not what life is *all* about, but surely about a part of all life, namely death itself.

A father said to his son, "Your problems are as big to you as a boy as mine are to me as a man." That's a relationship of respect. We can permit children to be children, while teaching them what's involved in being human. When we shield children from significant family events they may feel we are saying, "I don't respect you enough to allow you to become involved. You are too weak. You may get upset." It may also say, "You upset me and I don't want that." Children need to know that we are willing to struggle with them, not leave them to figure it out for themselves alone. That's what *living* together involves. I know no pat solutions or simple answers to such situations, since to be truly alive in the *now* requires some degree of alertness, discipline, and patience. The rewards of being awake like that can be exciting for all of us. Who knows, adults might start growing again if they (we!) adopted such a life style!

Quickly replacing a pet that has died can rob a child of the refining benefits of grief. Living through grief must start somewhere. A Chinese proverb illustrates this principle: "I hear and I forget, I see and I remember, I do and I understand." A child said it like this: "My mama has shown me so many times I haven't learned it for myself." Effective teaching and learning permits participation, not just imparting what has been learned. There was a teacher who always kneeled when he talked with children. He did not want to look down on them. He was equally dramatic in teaching adults. He left an indelible impression on many. His attitude was that of a great teacher—looking at life from the perspective of the student. I know, I was one of his students.

A father had been quiet and thoughtful. It was Saturday afternoon. He was lying on the floor sprawled out on his back. His young daughter asked, "How are you today, Dad?" "Very well, why do you ask?" "I had some things I wanted to talk with you about, but not when you have too many things on your mind." Parents have problems of their own, but children need and respond to undivided attention. The teachable moment occurs infrequently. All who are teachers need to be sensitive to these opportunities of living-learning. It is likely to occur in the context of some emotion, perhaps caring if not love.

This principle is described in the children's classic by Margery Williams, *The Velveteen Rabbit*.[3] The following dialogue is between two of the toys: " 'Real isn't how you are made,' said the Skin Horse. 'It is a thing that happens to you. When a child loves you for a long, long time, not just to play with, but really loves you, then you become real.' 'Does it hurt?,' asked the Rabbit. 'Sometimes,' said the Skin Horse, for he was always truthful. 'When you are real, you don't mind being hurt.' " The classic is a parable about life for adults too. It is about how it is okay to be angry or sad and to cry real tears. It also illustrates warmth, caring, and love. A teen-age psychiatric patient in my experience found this parable expressed the meaning she found for her life through a therapeutic relationship. It helped her clarify what she had experienced and put her experience in concepts she could begin to live with.

It is not possible to shield someone from all pain and sadness. In fact, to avoid the pains connected with grief and the expression of the emotion necessary may be the prelude for morbid grief or hostile delinquent behavior. For example, if a student has shown marked change in irritability, it might be good to explore what losses the student has experienced recently and how he or she has learned to cope with them. To deny release of one emotion may block the flow of other emotions, including those that are pleasurable. It is to die a little inwardly. It is to pour the child into a mold rather than to permit individuality. It is to impose on him or her some of our death-defying concepts.

Antoine de Saint-Exupéry describes the process of separation in *The Little Prince*.[4] The story is an allegory about a little prince who encounters the author while he works on his disabled plane in the Sahara Desert. Following a series of conversations about life on another planet as well as the mystery of the desert and simple things like flowers and stars, the little Prince is about to die from a snake bite. He says to the author, "It is a good thing to have a friend, even if one is about to die. One runs the risk of weeping a little, if one lets himself be tamed . . . you will suffer, I shall look as if I were dead, and that will not be true

. . . you understand . . . it is too far, I cannot carry this body with me. It is too heavy. But it will be like an old abandoned shell. There is nothing sad about old shells." At the heart of this fantasy, there is a comment from the fox who was standing nearby that describes a kernel of truth. "It is only with the heart that one can see rightly; what is essential is invisible to the eye." In another part of the process of separation there is the following conversation: " 'What are you trying to say?' 'In one of the stars I shall be living. In one of them I shall be laughing. And so it will be as if all of the stars were laughing, when you look at the sky at night. . . . You—only you—will have stars that can laugh!' And he laughed again. 'And when your sorrow is comforted (time soothes all sorrows) you will be content that you have known me. You will always be my friend. You will want to laugh with me.' " Learning how to cope with loss can be as simple and profound as learning how to say "Hello" and "Goodbye."

Preparation for Loss and Separation

The person who is most alive can cope best with death. That person will not feel the loss less. The person may feel the loss more, since his or her capacity to experience feeling is likely to be more keenly developed. However, one way to help children develop resources for coping with death is to help them come alive.

Leonard applies this principle to education and ecstasy.[5] On entering his classroom a boy exclaimed, "This room says yes." His teacher had succeeded in providing an environment for wonder and creative perceptual learning. "The small child's sensory experiences start long before nursery school. Ideas and concepts may be formed later, but these early sensory experiences have a vital impact on his emotional and intellectual development."

Some children do not learn to stand alone because they have not learned to be with others. For separation to be successfully worked through, togetherness must be accomplished someplace. Otto Rank focused on "the trauma of birth." He felt the later crises in life are a variation on this theme. The painful experience of birth for the child leaves him or her with a measure of primal anxiety. Other experiences of separation or "rebirth" provide opportunity for "growth-dilemma."[6]

Children who have experienced separation of any kind need to experience the opposite, that is, to keep in contact with someone. That contact for some may be literally through tactile contact.[7] A twelve year old girl spent fourteen months in the hospital with a terminal illness. Her home life was one of noncommunication. She did not talk to anyone in the hospital. This was quite frustrating to some of the staff who attempted to establish contact with her. The chaplain visited her daily through her last nine months of living. He did not require verbal response from her. She sensed his acceptance. She reached for his hand one day. They maintained this touch contact for brief intervals daily, rarely saying a word. One day when he realized that she was in a comatose condition, he spoke to her. He was holding her hand at the time. She squeezed his in response. She died later that day.[8] This human relationship has had a profound influence on the life of that chaplain.

Reassurance cannot be dispensed in a cheap manner. Something significant may be happening, even when there is no verbal communication. People experience feelings of detachment as a part of the bereavement process. Many have said, "My arms feel numb," or "My arms don't seem to belong to me." Charles Mayo, the younger of the famed Mayo brothers, is reported to have said, "When I die, I hope someone I love will hold my hand." The most valuable resource to be offered a grieving person is human contact. That contact may be blundering. It is rarely provided with perfection. But a blundering contact is more meaningful than being abandoned through indifference or embarrassment.

Touch helps people cope with feelings of detachment. People learn through their fingers and ears and all other senses. Neale tells of an ancient legend: "Once all creatures were required to pass through a narrow gate to the corpse of a goddess on the other side. Those who went through the gate and touched her dead body became human beings. Those who refused to touch death became animals and vegetables."[9] The person who has experienced an honest confrontation with death can relax and get on with the business of living. Indeed, everybody needs a day off, including a day off from the truth, whatever that is. But the best way to cope with preoccupation about death is to have an honest confrontation with it in order to move on to something else.

The Meaning of Rituals and Grief Work

Children and ceremonies have a natural affinity. If there were no funeral rituals, children would invent their own. Therefore, children should be free to attend funerals and to participate with other family members in rituals associated with death and the separation process.

However, no child should be forced to attend a funeral, to participate in the funeral, or to touch a dead body. No other person should be forced either. People need and respond to a measure of freedom.

However, changes in family life, especially involving childrearing practices, will alter funeral practices. Increasing depersonalization in urban life and loss of small meaningful group involvement will also have its effect. But a child should not have to wait until the death of a loved one to be hurriedly and frantically informed by a weeping mother that people are buried in special gardens or that stones or plaques are placed on each grave to indicate who is resting there.

The origin of funeral customs is in antiquity. Some of these practices developed for scientific or chemical reasons. Scientific knowledge changes. Customs resist change. They may have taken on religious significance and sanction. Some of these habits outlive their usefulness, leaving cultures in transition. A funeral that represents relationships, ideas, or values individuals no longer believe in or hold true may serve to thwart and anger them rather than achieve its intended purpose.

One group attempting to obtain simplicity, dignity, and economy in funeral arrangements suggests the following: "With children, as with adults, an understanding and acceptance of death can best begin in the absence of family sorrow. Parents should help their children become familiar with the world of nature, of which we are a part. Through exploring the woods and fields and by keeping pets, children can have firsthand contact with birth and death and with parental encouragement, learn to accept and have reverence for the whole process of life."[10] The goal of such groups is to establish a framework in which a sensitive and meaningful funeral or memorial service can be provided. It is no easy task.

A funeral serves as the rite of separation. The bad dream is real. The presence of a casket gives visual evidence of this reality. It changes the process of denial to acceptance of reality. All the emotional reactions a child is likely to experience associated with a loss by death (sorrow and loneliness, anger and rejection, guilt and anxiety about the future, and nameless fears) can be lessened when children feel that they know what is going on, and that adults are not trying to hide things from them. The funeral provides the time for community expression of grief. It is also a time when love is freely given. The sorrow of one becomes the sorrow of all. Grieving children must be given more than comfort. They must be given assurance that they will be loved and looked after. Children look to parents, teachers, and other significant adults for clues as to how they are expected to respond at a funeral. And when adults respond appropriately, chances are that children will also, and that they will grow emotionally as a result.

General customs are needed that permit personal sharing as a reminder of group resources.[11] Customs are also needed in which there is an attempt to give meaning to the events, permitting sufficient time for personal reflection. The events may be too deep for words.

Jackson quotes Eric Lindemann as saying, "The funeral service is psychologically necessary in order to give the opportunity for 'grief work.' The bereaved must be given the capacity to work through his grief if he is to come out of that situation emotionally sound."[12] He quotes another psychiatrist, Knight, as stating that parents and teachers "need to understand thoroughly the steps seen in the normal grief reaction, in which the work of mourning must be done, the bondage to the deceased broken, and new relationships formed. The rituals and customs associated with death and dying should be understood and evaluated from the standpoint of how well they help people do the necessary work of mourning and how well they succeed in preventing pathological grief reactions which now or later lead to illness."[13]

And Kübler-Ross also writes, "The most meaningful help that we can give any relative, child or adult, is to share his feelings before the event of death and to allow him to work through his feelings, whether they are rational or irrational."[14] It may be desirable but not necessary to introduce a course on death in secondary or elementary education to accomplish this. The topic can be introduced as a natural part of the regular learning process with occasional reference to authors who are dead, or in response to an acknowledged need like the death of a plant or a pet. There is also an increasing supply of useful picture books, parables, and folk stories available.[15] Stories of death and abandonment serve the function of learning on the level of fantasy to cope with one's fears and to reassure oneself of the unreality of fantasied terrors. The frequent reporting through mass media of death by violent means as a result of war, murder, or accident gives an inadequate model for death and dying.

Search for Models*

Stated simply, role theory indicates that children learn by imitating. They first playfully copy and subsequently acquire the behavior of

---

* I am indebted to Paul W. Brewer, Ph.D., for these notes on the search for models. Dr. Brewer is a clinical psychologist in private practice in Phoenix, Arizona.

key people in their lives, particularly that of their parents and of other significant persons. Almost equally important models are children's stories, fairy tales, the theatre, and the ubiquitous television screen. The dearth of death and mourning models in real life situations due to our culture's conspiracy of avoidance leads to a heavy reliance on pre-manufactured material.

To rephrase the main thesis: one of our major difficulties in encountering death is the almost total lack of suitable models. Even worse, whatever models exist are of a theatrical, overly dramatized, or overly sensationalized nature. They are grossly misleading. They almost resemble a hall of mirrors, where one mirror reflects the picture of another mirror, and so on, ad infinitum; while the original may have been perceived quite accurately, the constant redoubling of the reflection becomes confusing and misleading.

As most authors have indicated, the process of dying in our culture is typically physically isolated, an almost hidden event, frequently occurring in a well-guarded institution. It is seldom witnessed and portrayed accurately. Some exceptions to this are the very sensational killings, such as that of the alleged presidential assassin Oswald by Ruby—which was also theatrical, "unreal," and on-camera.

Nevertheless, death is quite frequently shown in the literature, in the movies, and on television. It would be safe to say that death is one of the favorite roles of actors: tragic death, heroic death, violent death, patriotic death, cowardly death, painful death, and many other death patterns and models. This was dramatically portrayed by the Actor, one of the main protagonists in the play *Rosencrantz and Guildenstern* by Tom Stoppard. He freely places death in the realm of acting. The Actor gives an example, where he attempted to provide the pinnacle of realism—and also thrills—by having an actual death occur on the stage. Since the play takes place in medieval Denmark where death penalty for minor infractions was common, he persuaded a judge to have a young boy (whose crime had involved a minor theft) hanged on the stage. Much to everybody's disappointment, the little boy just cried copiously; his death was an audience flop—it wasn't "well acted" at all.

When we see violent death, as for instance portrayed in the film *The Godfather*, it is typically dramatic, gory, but mercifully brief. The media have not been either capable or willing to portray long lingering death, the ups and downs of a long terminal illness: the loneliness, isolation, fears of the patient, the terror of the relatives, and the contrived professionalism of the caretaker establishment; the time element of prolonged suffering, the false hopes, or the setbacks apparently cannot be adequately portrayed in the telescoped time available on the stage or on the screen—between commercials.

One notable exception is the recent Bergman movie *Cries and Whispers* showing the final days of a dying person and the reactions of her sisters and of her servant girl. The servant girl at least provides a model of humanness and a capacity for empathy and coping. Judging by the public response, this type of presentation is too difficult to tolerate. Few parents would consider it to be suitable for children.

Considerable dissonance, then, exists between death as portrayed by the public media, and death as actually experienced. Dissonance has to be resolved in fairly predictable ways. The individual feels that he or she is not living up to expectations, feels unique, different, unworthy, unable to live up to standards which have been set for him or her.

(Dr. Brewer has described the need for models well with some suggested alternatives. Perhaps some more adequate models will come from the use of this book as an educational tool.)

Rituals in Various Cultures

Rituals of all kinds seem to have more meaning for those who feel themselves to be members of minorities. These rituals, whether related to death or not, may well provide evidence of group solidarity for which members of the majority may feel less intense need. The need for some sense of belonging is still there. It may be satisfied in a different manner, though there is some evidence that persons need both small and large group involvement. Something is lost for those who know only fringe participation in large groups without any of the intimacy of a small group.

Prescribed and accepted rites grow out of small, close-knit cultures. Something is lost by too much mobility and mixture of cultures. But there is enough that is basic to being human that we can develop new customs in our culture to meet changing circumstances rather than discard all that has been used as if it is only superstitious or without meaning.

Most recorded human societies developed rituals for mourning, some more formal than others. Generally the bereaved have changed their physical appearance through such things as special clothing, a black arm band, or change in their hair care. Others therefore could see that they were in mourning and could respond in a prescribed manner. The mourner was permitted to go through a *rite de passage*—a formal withdrawal from society, a period of seclusion, and a formal reentry into society.

Few cultures have retained an accepted social ritual for the initial recognition of loss, or for the first contact between a mourner and his neighbors. This makes it even more necessary that persons in mixed cultures develop greater sensitivity to the nonverbal clues people give to great loss expressed daily and often without any recognition or response. (This is not a problem for Orthodox Jews, however. The mourner is greeted in their culture with a salutation, "I wish you long life," which requires no reply. Then the conversation proceeds normally.)

Funerals tend to reflect the basic philosophy of the culture in which they are performed. The Amish bury their dead in plain wooden coffins in an atmosphere of great cleanliness and quiet solemnity. Everything is very plain and simple. No flowers are used. Most relatives live nearby and are expected to be present, including babies. Before the funeral begins, food that is simple but plentiful is served. The meal is a time for quiet reflection, even on the part of small children. Then the funeral ritual itself is generally quite long. Prayers and scriptures are read in German. Hymns are sung slowly in unison almost like a chant. Men of the Amish faith always dig and close an Amish grave. After the burial many of the mourners stand around and chat, then gradually return to their homes. The Amish also lead lives of peace, serenity, and contentment. Their lives are characterized by hard work and simplicity.[16]

Some cultures provide a fixed period of time for mourning, thus encouraging the expression of grief with expectation to move on to other adjustments at the end of the stated time. Orthodox Jews encourage the dead to live on in memory through prescribed visitation of the grave on the anniversary (counted by the Jewish calendar) of the death.

Burial implies the acceptance of a style of mourning of a different nature from that implicit in cremation, involving some form of perpetual care and continued expense to keep green the memory of the dead. These later practices inhibit time-limited mourning for some. Some may return so frequently to the site of the burial they have difficulty getting on with the business of living. Typically, for the mourning process to be successful, there is a period of intense grief characterized by weeping, some loss of appetite and weight, some sleep disturbance, withdrawal from some social activities followed by return to physical and social homeostasis. Roman Catholics were permitted for the first time by papal decree in 1963 to arrange cremations.[17] At the turn of the century less than 1 percent of the United State's dead were cremated. By 1950 the figure had risen to about 3.8 percent. However, the proportion has declined slightly since then. On the other hand, 60 percent or more of all disposals in England were by cremation, and 50 percent for western Australia by 1950.

Mourning parties may be a means of group expression to the value of life in the presence of death. An overnight vigil the night after death may be a reminder that the dead will not be abandoned. For example, in Hungary after the body has been placed in the casket, "A three-course feast is held in its presence. This is called the 'Last Supper,' because it is actually the last meal eaten in the presence of the dead. The death vigil is kept by relatives and neighbors, and the body is not left unattended, even for a moment. Such attendance is called, 'keeping the vigil,' or 'mourning.' "[18]

Such customs also become a means of regrouping resources through marathon fashion to cope with the stress of readjustment. It is interesting that such events are referred to as a wake through such phrases as, "The mourners eat and drink while the dead is being waked."[19] Could it be that food and drink are used without rational statement as an aid to socialization and as relief from the pain of loss?

Some cultures provide opportunity for the overt expression of anger in their mourning rituals. For example, the dead person's property was destroyed by various Indian tribes in the southwestern United States. Or more indirectly, mourners were encouraged to inflict various mutilations on themselves as a sign of the pain caused by the dead. These rituals may have been extreme, but according to some psychoanalysts anger is inherent in all mourning. Therefore, one of the main functions of the mourning process is to work through and dissipate this anger in a symbolic, or some socially acceptable, manner. Teachers can at least permit, if not encourage, the recognition of this process as normal before it becomes repressed and therefore pathological.

Practice seems to indicate there is greater rivalry among the poor for an elaborate funeral than among the rich. This may be caused by exploitation on the part of some funeral directors of the anger that most mourners feel. When the anger is self-directed it becomes guilt. And the guilty can be prompted to pay off his guilty conscience by buying a more expensive funeral than he can afford. Elaborate funerals may also occur without this stimulus. Some choose to "make it" in death who did not achieve financial success in life.

For all people everywhere, funerals and funeral ceremonies satisfy basic needs, relieve suffering, and help to rescue death from meaninglessness. In fact, another definition of man might be, "He is a being that buries his dead with ceremony."[20]

Normal Grief

It is not necessary to have a concept of death to experience grief. It is necessary only to experience a sense of loss. Children can grieve. People can grieve without understanding why. Children can feel without having a rationale for the feeling.

Rogness has written, "Grief is as universal as death. Sometimes it may cripple, occasionally it ennobles. Grief is not the occasion for heroism. If we have loved, we suffer. It is as simple and as human as that. To grieve is to be human, and to be human is good."[21]

Grief has been too easily identified with pathology as if something that is sad is necessarily bad. At least we tend to look for glib solutions and simplistic answers. Some have been deeply damaged through grief. Others have completed the work of mourning in such a manner as to become more sensitive to the needs of others, with greater inner strengths to live meaningfully in the face of great stress.

Gorer quotes Melanie Klein in support of this proposition as follows:[22]

If the mourner has people whom he loves and who share his grief, and if he can accept their sympathy, the restoration of the harmony in his inner world is promoted, and his fears and distresses are more quickly reduced.

. . . people who fail to experience mourning. Feeling incapable of saving and securely reinstating their loved objects inside themselves, they must turn away from them more than hitherto and therefore deny their love for them. This may mean that their emotions in general become more inhibited; in other cases it is mainly feelings of love which have been stifled and hatred is increased.

Klein feels it is necessary for human infants to pass through a crisis in development she calls the "depressive position." The ego of the child is forced in this process to develop methods of defense that are "fundamental to the whole ego-organization."[23]

Lindemann described the course of normal grief as follows:

The duration of a grief reaction seems to depend upon the success with which a person does the grief work, namely, "emancipation from the bondage to the deceased, readjustment to the environment in which the deceased is missing, and the formation of new relationships." One of the big obstacles to this work seems to be the fact that many patients try to avoid the intense distress connected with the grief experience and to avoid the expression of emotion necessary for it.[24]

Oates has outlined how normal grief moves through six stages:

1. The shocking blow of the loss in itself.
2. The numbing effect of the loss.
3. The struggle between fantasy and reality.
4. The break-through of a flood of grief.
5. Selective memory and stabbing pain.
6. The acceptance of loss and affirmation of life itself.[25]

Bowlby believes the behavior sequence of mourning for human beings begins with anxiety and anger, proceeds through pain and despair, and if fortune smiles ends with hope.[26] This is based on his assumption that "once a child has formed a tie to a mother-figure, which has ordinarily occurred by the middle of the first year, its rupture leads to separation anxiety and grief and sets in train processes of mourning."[27] He believes a child of six months has the emotional capacity to experience a significant relationship and the meaning of loss sufficient to cause grief.

This illustrates the importance of dependence in human development from which human beings are never fully weaned. Nothing that lives is more dependent than, or dependent over as long a period of time as, a human infant.[28] The measure of independence we achieve in adulthood is on a continuum. Some persons function like a clinging vine, holding onto others closely. Some persons withdraw from other people, or do not permit them to get close emotionally. They hold them at an emotional arm's length. Some persons alternate between apparent warm relationships and cold aloofness. For most of us, our dependent-independent needs are not likely to remain static, but fluctuate to some degree depending on a variety of factors and circumstances.

While our culture may encourage a patient resignation in the face of grievous loss, angry violent feelings nonetheless well up and must be recognized as an "essential ingredient of grief. Grief is a peculiar amalgam of anxiety, anger, and despair following the experience of what is feared to be irretrievable loss."[29] This is more than separation anxiety. And how important it is that adults, and all who have a teaching role, recognize and permit this phase of the mourning process to occur. For if there is no protest, there is no grief. If persons do not permit themselves to experience protest (grief), they have given up without a fight. Later this may be repeated so frequently that it becomes a life style, one of giving up. Those who give up so easily have already experienced a measure of inward death.

As a part of the process of protest, love for the lost object is replaced by hatred of it, according to Bowlby. All this is difficult for the grieving person to accept, since it requires internal reorganization. Bowlby reminds us that all human beings are reluctant to face disorganization.[30] It is interesting that in the discipline of economics the term "depression" connotes a reduction in economic activity accompanied by some degree of disorganization and then of reorganization. Therefore, this describes another necessary part of the mourning process. Some disorganization is necessary before reconstruction can be successful. "Looked at in this way the behavioral processes going with depression can be seen to have an adaptive function."[31] Human life is more intertwined and complex than the world of economics. The process of coping with real or apparent loss in either is not easy. But the patterns of behavior which have grown up in interaction with the lost object are no longer appropriate. And if they linger and persist then they would be maladaptive. Only by breaking them down is it possible for new ones to be developed in relationship with new objects. Such disorganization is painful and involves some risk, but it seems indispensable for reconstruction, a necessary part of being alive.

Bowlby summarizes his position by suggesting that at all ages (infants and young children over six months, and adults) "the first phase of mourning is one of protest, the second one is of despair, and the third one of detachment."[32] Having successfully achieved these, it is possible to move on through reconstruction to live again.

Anticipatory grief. It is possible for persons to approach death with a growth-orientation. One of the most influential psychologists of our day, who died in 1970, Abraham Maslow, wrote the following statement after a massive heart attack:

> My attitude toward life changed. The word I use for it now is the post-mortem life. One very important aspect of the post-mortem life is that everything gets doubly precious, gets piercingly

important. You get stabbed by things, by flowers and by babies and by beautiful things—just the very act of living, of walking and breathing and eating and having friends and chatting. Everything seems to look more beautiful rather than less, and one gets the much-intensified sense of miracles. I guess you could say that post-mortem life permits the kind of spontaneity that's greater than anything else could make possible. If you are reconciled with death or even if you are pretty well assured that you will have a good death, a dignified one, then every single moment of every single day is transformed because of the pervasive undercurrent—the fear of death is removed.[33]

Blevins, working with a group of persons in a hospital setting experiencing life-threatening illnesses has written, "Growth is the result of internalizing hope and finding some meaning to life. Growth is never complete and is in a continual state of becoming."[34] He states there are no ready answers as to how persons facing death can continue to experience growth by giving hope to one another, and by helping professional people understand the human experience more effectively. But he has underscored the following concepts:

1. Death is a natural event in human experience!
2. Dying is a social process. Persons need the resources of a group, rather than attempt to cope with the experience alone. People feel comfortable in exposing their fears or apprehensions regarding death when others in the group setting are neither repelled, frightened, nor give the appearance of deserting them. The group helps to take the focus off the subject matter and to develop a sense of sensitivity for others who are also human.
3. People can learn and grow. Didactic methods can assist in the learning process, including how to cope with loss, even that associated with one's own death.

We experience grief regarding the death of others. We also experience grief regarding our own death, or perhaps anticipatory grief. Such grief is normal as we each seek to live our own life and die our own death. A child with cancer expressed her fear in arithmetical form:

2 Nice
2 Be
―――――
4 Gotten

Play can be therapy for grief. Adults can learn a great deal by ob-
serving the play of children. Kastenbaum describes the origin of the
delightful game "Ring-Around-the-Rosy." Medieval society was almost
totally helpless against the bubonic plague. Adults could not ward off
the Black Death. But children joined hands in a circle of life. They
chanted a ritual, "Ring-Around-the-Rosy, . . . all fall down" moving in
a reassuring rhythm of unity. This may have been playing-at-death
because after having fallen down they could rise to play again. But their
play was also an "artful response to harsh and overwhelming reality."[35]

Games of make-believe violence using realistic toys for weapons
allow children to explore their real feelings related to other situations
from life. Adults may fail to understand the meaning of children's play
when they have not seen the stimulus. For example, the behavior in
play may not seem to be death-related, but this should not rule out the
possibility that it might be understood at least partially in those terms.

Furthermore the game of peek-a-boo may have greater implication
than alternating states of terror and delight. It involves concepts of
disappearance and return, of taking risks, of experiencing minimal
frustration and disappointment. To be sure it involves concrete
thinking for the very young. But abstract concepts grow from what is
experienced as safe. Kastenbaum believes, "The very young child must
be aware of changes, losses, and disappearances if he is eventually to
comprehend what 'stays,' what 'goes,' and what 'comes and goes.' Even
very young children encounter losses, ends, and limits. Without an
ability to fathom these experiences, they could not form protoconcepts
of constancies, beginnings, and possibilities."[36]

Even in the midst of play the problem of death might very well be the
prime challenge that sets in motion children's curiosity and mental
questing. Death may provide much of the motivation for their intellectual development. There is evidence that children are experiencing
maturation earlier than at the turn of the century in physical respects
and from the knowledge explosion. Could it be that adults are stunting
the growth of children as persons when they prevent their participation
in matters related to death? Children need to express through talk,
play, or somehow the strong emotions associated with death rather
than let these accumulate inside to erupt in some more harmful form
later.

Developmental trends. Children understand death in a variety of
ways depending on their stage of development. An infant of six months
experiences death as separation. The toddler recognizes the death of a
bird or a pet as a change of state, though not as a final process. School-
age children begin to recognize the significance of death as their concept

of time, space, and self develops. But not until about the age of nine do children recognize death as an inevitable experience that may happen to them (see Chapter 2 for the details of the developmental trends).

On the other hand, persons find purpose through meaningful relationships. The qualities that contribute to rich human relationships include warmth, honesty, tact, strength, openness, directness, empathy, and sensitivity. Those who practice these qualities can help children cope with loss and disappointment without spoiling or coddling them and robbing them of their personhood. Children enjoy responsibility scaled down to their size. All persons do not possess these qualities in equal proportion. All teachers should not attempt to relate to children in grief in the same manner. After all, teachers are persons too, not puppets. Some will be more effective than others. And we can rely on the strengths of one another rather than attempt to do all things equally well. Other help is also available through student personnel services, counselors, psychological services, clergy, parents, and other students.

Normal grief restated. All researchers seem to agree that there are three phases in normal mourning: a short period of shock, a period of intense grief, and a period of recovery and the resumption of normal social life. If for any reason the third stage is not reached, it is as if grief itself has been buried inside the person to erupt in some other form later.

The second stage can be short-circuited by treating all mourning as morbid, by a general conspiracy to pretend that death has not occurred and that no one is grieving, by persons hovering too closely and not permitting reasonable privacy for the mourner, and by delaying the expression of grief through too much busy-ness. In this latter instance, it is important to note that having something to do after a personal loss is often a healing blessing. Even the routine of providing for physical necessities may serve to carry people past dead center on their way to living again. In fact, drudgery can be a blessing. Therefore, ceremonies and the participation in them have always been recognized as an effective method of channeling energy and releasing tension in the period of crisis. These rituals provide an effective way of saying to each participant, "I can do something. I am not paralyzed." Some may discover, "I can find some meaning from these events, perhaps not the same meaning they have for others, but meaning for me."

Delayed Grief

The teacher and principal had known that Nicky had no father, but they were not aware of the devastating effect a divorce of eight years could have on a child. At nine he had become belligerent at home, a severe stutterer, frequently involved in fights at school, destructive with neighbors, and below average in his school work.[37] The school situation frequently becomes the main focus of the displacement when grief has not been worked through successfully otherwise.

Martin, while working as a staff member in a psychiatric center, stated that about 60 percent of his psychiatric patients had problems related in some way to loss. He said, "Again and again we are asked to see kids with 'school-phobia.' This is a misnomer. It is really a 'loss-phobia.' They are afraid to leave home for some reason. Perhaps they have suffered a loss or perhaps they feel guilty. When a loss occurs, respond to it."[38]

When the work of grief is thwarted, then it is displaced in withdrawal or aggressive behavior. Shoor describes the interrelationship of unwisely managed grief and juvenile delinquency. In speaking of numerous boys and girls whose lives had exploded in violence, promiscuity, and theft, he stated, "These are not children who hated. These are children who mourned. Delinquent behavior by children and adolescents is sometimes a substitute for grief reaction."[39]

The child who angrily wishes his mother to drop dead for not having gratified his needs will be traumatized greatly by the actual death of his mother, even if this event is not linked closely in time with his destructive wish. Children more than adults experience the effects of magical thinking.[40]

The distress of dogs and other animals who have lost a master to whom they are strongly attached illustrates the effects of bottled up or delayed grief. This occurred with Stasi, a female mongrel of Chow and Alsatian ancestry which the Austrian ethologist Konrad Lorenz had bred. "At seven months he [Lorenz] began to train her, but a couple of months later he had to be away and left her at home. Her behavior during this separation (four months duration) is not recorded, but on reunion she was in a 'frenzy of joy.' When after a few weeks, however, he began to prepare for a second departure, 'the dog became noticeably depressed and refused to leave my side for an instant. With nervous haste, she sprang up and followed every time I left the room, even accompanying me to the bathroom.' At departing she became desperate; and in the weeks following the second separation she became an unruly delinquent dog. She roamed restlessly about the district, was no longer house-trained, and refused to obey anybody. She also became increasingly ferocious."[41]

Some children have not experienced the quality of caring to provide the kind of togetherness referred to in the first part of this chapter. They have existed in emotional emptiness. They may not yet have discovered the meaning of being human. Schrut describes how Donald at seven and a half years of age had learned a self-destructive way of life. He had been unable to reach his adoptive mother by good behavior. Instead, she rewarded him with attention when he participated in self-destructive behavior. Therefore, he discovered or was clued into a type of behavior that led to numerous suicide attempts. He also seemed prepared to meet other interpersonal crises in life with a similar reaction of self-destructiveness. Schrut's description follows:[42]

It was only his difficulty in school that brought him to therapy, when the teacher complained of both the learning activity and his "deliberately falling out of chairs and throwing himself onto the ground." Once, following a minor quarrel with his mother, Donald tearfully told her he would kill himself. He disappeared for ten minutes. When she became uneasy and went to look for him, she found he had tied a rope around his neck and had thrown it over a rafter in the garage, securing it with a slip knot as he had learned from TV and play with the neighborhood boys. She caught him before he could jump off the box, which he had prepared after careful testing. Both his parents agreed he could well have hanged himself fatally had he carried out his threat. Despite all her admonitions and punishments, he continued to misbehave frequently in front of her as she stated angrily that sometimes right after, "I whack him, he would run right into the street again laughing at me while he does so, although he knows I will just whack him again."

Somehow this expression of "concern" was more satisfying to Donald than the emotional emptiness of his life. He seemed programmed for further self-destructiveness until he could learn from other interpersonal relationships a more creative way of life. In psychotherapy at the urging of the child's therapist, this mother told about her hidden bitterness in failing to conceive and having to adopt a child. She had attempted to prove that she was a valid woman through childbirth. She had struggled also with strong ambivalence about becoming a mother at all. This was intensified in turn by her hostility to the child who now became the symbol of her failure.

I wonder if a sensitive teacher could have detected something about this child's life style at an earlier age or before the pattern had developed to such an extreme degree. Certainly it would have taken sensitiveness to clues without reacting to them personally or without attempting to fix blame. This school did serve as the place of referral for a deeply troubled child. I hope others in similar need will experience equal help.

The more we make death as a process unmentionable in polite society and therefore referred to only in morbid terms, the more we guarantee the continuation of horror literature. When society prevents persons to come to terms with basic issues like birth and death in an open and dignified manner, then it will be done surreptitiously.

Gorer has written:

> The problem of dealing with sex in secular terms has been discussed with increasing clarity for the better part of a century. Although there is still no complete consensus on the most appropriate social ways of dealing with sexual urges, there is now a very general recognition that human beings do have sexual urges and that, if these are denied outlet, the result will be suffering, either psychological or physical or both. But there is no analogous secular recognition of the fact that human beings mourn in response to grief, and that, if mourning is denied outlet, the result will be suffering, either psychological or physical or both. At present death and mourning are treated with much the same prudery as sexual impulses were a century ago.[43]

Perhaps we need a crusade with a slogan like "Let's not abolish sorrow!" or with Charlie Brown, "Good Grief!" All mourning is not an indication of weakness or selfishness. If one can deny one's own grief, how much more easily can one deny the grief of others; and one possible outcome of the public denial of mourning is a great increase in public callousness.

Coming Alive

I was surprised when a friend said enthusiastically that he enjoyed a thunderstorm. I was amazed when a woman said with equal enthusiasm that she got a thrill out of watching a blizzard—from inside a strong cabin!

Some people seem to court danger, flirt with disaster, and even dare death occasionally. One friend during World War II drove his jeep through no-man's land crossing a narrow bridge, fully conscious of the risks he was taking. He returned with no injury fortunately!

Were they seeking some form of neurotic pleasure or punishment? I think not. The rest of their life style was not that of dare-devils. Perhaps they were living in the consciousness that some risk is necessary to be alive, really alive.

One contemporary black preacher, Gardner Taylor, has said:[44]

It is natural for us to want to avoid pain and discomfiture. Only the morbidly diseased person courts hurt and enjoys being wounded. So many of us are obsessive on the other side. We intend to avoid pain and trouble at any price. "I don't want to get hurt," is the theme of so many of us. We go through life studiously avoiding all situations that might involve damaged emotions and bruised feelings. So we go sliding through the days. But this is not living. True living consists of believing greatly, not narrowly, parochially, coyly. True living consists of risking grandly, not pettily and miserly. True living consists of loving deeply, not cautiously, carefully. True living consists of daring nobly, not hedging every action.

Could it be that's why Kübler-Ross found black people culturally better prepared to help others die? Could it be that's the way to learn empathy, rather than just sympathy? Could it be that only those who are willing to risk facing death will know what it means to be truly alive?

One way of finding *life* is to be in tune with another person, being so much together that each inwardly says "yes" to what has happened between them, whether the relationship is sustained or fleeting: "You heard me with understanding." "Like wow! That's what I was trying to say!" I have been there.

Another way of discovering *life* is by an attitude of such inward quietness that time itself seems to stand still. Such times may be so full of meaning that you will want to breathe deeply. It may happen in the quietness of a great forest, or simply watching a bird fly or a child laugh. I have been there.

Or a third way of encountering *life* may occur, though perhaps more deliberately than either of the other methods. The first two occur almost by accident, certainly not by strain. The latter comes out of courage to confront stress, rather than turning away as if we could escape disappointment forever. It comes to those who have discovered the truth in "Strength is made complete through weakness" (II Corinthians 12:9, paraphrased). I have been there.

These are the three methods in which I have encountered LIFE so full and meaningful that something within me named it "God." Such is the nature of ultimate reality for me. Perhaps courage for the latter method of finding life came from the former. But not until a person has found meaning through the rough experiences of life has he or she truly lived.

Notes

1. William Lamers, Jr., *Death, Grief, Mourning, The Funeral and the Child* (Chicago: National Funeral Directors Association, 1965).
2. "Shoulditis" characterizes an unrealistic approach to life in this instance. The attitude of "shoulditis" may undermine effective communication, especially where there is limitation to freedom of choice. And the attitude of our approach to one another is as important as the words we express in our verbal communication, as Lamers observes above.
3. Margery Williams, *The Velveteen Rabbit* (Garden City, N.Y.: Doubleday, 1922), p. 14.
4. Antoine de Saint Exupéry, *The Little Prince* (New York: Harcourt, 1943), pp. 87, 91, 99, 104.
5. George B. Leonard, *Education and Ecstasy* (New York: Delacorte, 1968).
6. Otto Rank, *The Trauma of Birth and its Importance for Psychoanalytic Therapy* (New York: Harcourt, 1924).
7. This concept is described by: Ashley Montagu, *Touching* (New York: Harper and Row, 1972).
8. C. Rabon Stephens, "The Chaplain's Ministry to the Dying Child," unpublished paper, Chaplain, Walter Reed Army Medical Center, Washington, D.C., 1973.
9. Robert E. Neale, *Living with Dying* (Phoenix: Grimshaw Mortuaries, 1971).
10. Ernest Morgan, *A Manual of Simple Burial* (Burnsville, N.C.: Colo Press, 1971), p. 12.
11. This point is made by many others, particularly: S. I. Hayakawa, *Language in Thought and Action*, 2nd ed. (New York: Harcourt, Brace & World, 1964).
12. Edgar N. Jackson, *For the Living* (Des Moines, Ia.: Channel Press, 1963), p. 91.
13. Ibid., p. 91.
14. Elisabeth Kübler-Ross, *On Death and Dying* (New York: Macmillan, 1969), p. 180.
15. Some examples include: James Agee, *A Death in the Family* (New York: Grosset & Dunlap, 1967); Ambrose Bierce, "An Occurrence at Owl Creek Bridge," *In the Midst of Life and Other Stories* (New York: New American Library, 1976; on film from Contemporary Films, McGraw-Hill, 330 W. 42nd St., New York, N.Y. 10036); Margaret W. Brown, *The Dead Bird* (Reading, Ma.: Addison Wesley, 1958); Anne Frank, *The Diary of a Young Girl* (New

York: Simon & Schuster, 1952); John Gunther, *Death Be Not Proud* (New York: Harper, 1949); Oscar Lewis, *A Death in the Sanchez Family* (New York: Random House, 1969); Martha Wolfenstein and Gilbert Kliman, eds., *Children and the Death of a President* (New York: Doubleday, 1966).

16. Robert W. Habenstein and William M. Lamers, *Funeral Customs the World Over* (Milwaukee: Bulfin Printers, Inc., 1963), pp. 709-17.

17. Ibid., pp. 370-74.

18. Ibid., p. 459.

19. Ibid., p. 629.

20. Ibid., p. 757.

21. Alvin N. Rogness, *Appointment with Death* (New York: Thomas Nelson, Inc., 1972), p. x.

22. Geoffrey Gorer, *Death, Grief, and Mourning* (Garden City, N.Y.: Doubleday, 1965), p. 140.

23. Ibid., p. 139.

24. Eric Lindemann, "Symptomatology and Management of Acute Grief," *American Journal of Psychiatry* 101 (July 1944): 141-148, quoted from p. 143.

25. Wayne E. Oates, *Anxiety in Christian Experience* (Philadelphia: Westminster Press, 1955), pp. 52-54.

26. John Bowlby, "Process of Mourning," *International Journal of Psychoanalysis* 42 (July-October 1961): 317-340, quoted from p. 331.

27. Ibid., p. 317.

28. This point is made also by: Ashley Montagu, *On Being Human* (New York: Hawthorn Books, 1967).

29. Bowlby, "Mourning," p. 331.

30. Ibid., p. 336.

31. Ibid., p. 335.

32. Ibid., p. 338.

33. "Editorial," *Psychology Today* 3 (August 1970):16.

34. Donald J. Blevins, "Living with Imminent Death," Master's thesis, Seattle Pacific College, Seattle, Washington, 1972.

35. Robert Kastenbaum, "The Kingdom Where Nobody Dies," *Saturday Review—Science* 55 (December 1972):33-38, quoted from p. 34.

36. Ibid., p. 37.

37. Hella Moller, "Death: Handling the Subject and Affected Students in the Schools," in *Explaining Death to Children*, ed. Earl A. Grollman (Boston: Beacon Press, 1967), pp. 157-60.

38. Edward A. Martin, *Children—and the Truth about Death* (Phoenix: Grimshaw Mortuaries, 1971).

39. Quoted by Jackson, *Living*, p. 27.

40. For clarification of this concept, see: Everett S. Ostrovsky, *Children Without Men* (New York: Collier Books, 1962).

41. Bowlby, "Mourning," p. 329.

42. Albert Schrut, "Suicidal Adolescents and Children," *Journal of American Medical Association* 188 (June 1964):1103-1107, quoted from p. 1106.

43. Gorer, *Death*, p. 128.

44. Gardner Taylor, "Only Scarred Hands Heal," unpublished sermon, Pastor, Concord Baptist Church, Brooklyn, New York, 1973.

Suggested Readings

Feifel, Herman, ed., *The Meaning of Death* (New York: McGraw-Hill, 1959).

Feifel traces in basic style how the concept of death has undergone a number of fundamental changes through the centuries, using illustrations from man's social and intellectual history.

Grollman, Earl, *Talking About Death* (Boston: Beacon Press, 1970).

This book is written in a thoroughly readable manner by one comfortable with the value of human relationships and is a follow-up on the theme developed in *Explaining Death to Children* edited by the author in 1967.

Jackson, Edgar N., *Understanding Grief* (New York: Abingdon Press, 1957).

This pioneer in death education has had considerable influence on American funeral customs. He describes grief here in readable and elementary terms.

Neale, Robert E., "Death and Education," *Pastoral Psychology* 22 (November 1971):33-74.

Neale has outlined five sessions in death education, using the following themes: denial, fear, grief, belief, and martyrdom. He gives practical suggestions for content and procedure of a nontechnical nature based on sound research. This syllabus in death education is compiled by a clergyman whose interest includes play as reflected by his basic book *In Praise of Play* published by Harper and Row in 1969.

Switzer, David K., *The Dynamics of Grief* (New York: Abingdon Press, 1970).

Switzer traces the personal dynamics of grief through its source, its pain, and its healing as a psychologist and a pastoral counselor. This is primary source reading.

Some observers have called the United States child-centered. When death strikes a child, however, many contradictory faces of this culture surface to challenge the easy generalization. In the following chapter, the full range of related issues is discussed by a concerned educational psychologist who urges us on to better appreciation of what life is about.

4

What of the Dying Child?

David H. Bauer*

Individually and collectively man stands alone as "life being aware of itself."[1] Throughout human history this awareness of finite being in the face of infinite nonbeing has led human beings to their noblest accomplishments in courage and love, as well as to the depth of despair in guilt and anxiety.[2] Paradoxically, their awareness of ultimate separation (death) from their own being and the rest of humanity causes them to question the very meaning of life itself.

The poignancy of death, however, reaches a peak when a child has specified for him or her a time for dying. It seems that the prospect of the death of a child threatens the essential order in nature and the purpose of life. In a sense, it represents a violation of the trust: "To everything there is a season, and a time to every purpose under the heaven" (Ecclesiastes 3:1). Naked, human beings stand helpless in a universe out of which they attempt to structure meaning. The death of a child raises doubt, and man faces despair. On the death of her cherished eight year old nephew, Emily Dickinson revealed her feelings of forlorn hope:[3]

> "Open the Door, open the Door, they are waiting for me," was Gilbert's sweet command in delirium. Who were waiting for him, all we possess we would give to know—Anguish at last opened it, and he ran to the little Grave at his Grandparents' feet—All this and more, though *is* there more? More than Love and Death? Then tell me its name.

How children face death depends on their developmental capacity to understand its meaning (see Chapter 2) along with the characteristics of the environment created by those who care for them. Through interactions with parents, physicians, nurses, hospital staff, and others, dying children may experience either a meaningful life pervaded by a sense of hope or a meaningless one dominated by feelings of despair.

Even though nearly overwhelmed by their feelings of loneliness, sadness, and powerlessness, those who surround dying children need to express courage and love as they care for them and share in their remaining life.

In this chapter some specific problems generated by the ending of life in childhood along with some ideas for dealing with them are discussed. For instance, of what significance is the past and brief remaining life of terminally ill children? How should they be handled, and their loneliness, fear, pain, and anguish be treated? How may siblings, parents, and classmates be prepared for the child's approaching departure? What role should religious, medical, and educational personnel be playing in the process and its aftermath?

Children in Crisis

Loneliness

To be is to be alone, and we experience aloneness both as the inspiration of solitude and the pain of loneliness. In quiet solitude while listening to music, reading poetry, skiing down a mountainside, or walking along a beach at sunset, we may feel alone, but we are not lonely. Loneliness always returns to us, nevertheless, for there are times of boredom, illness, rejection, separation, and death in each of our lives. Loneliness is an intrinsic quality of human existence which gives rise to one of humanity's deepest needs: "The question of how to overcome separateness, how to achieve union, how to transcend one's being and find atonement."[4]

During infancy and early childhood this need for contact may temporarily remain unresolved, while during preadolescence and in time of serious illness feelings of loneliness reach full significance.[5] Yet, beyond the existential loneliness which all children feel, separation from parents only adds to the dying child's feelings of isolation. Statistics indicate that in 1967, for instance, seven out of ten deaths took place in institutions, the vast majority of which were general hospitals.[6] For the dying child, these statistics may mean separation from family and feelings of abandonment at a time when he needs most the feeling of security engendered by attachment.

Attachment and loss. Attachment to a mothering person provides a basis through which children develop a sense of trust in the world, of unity with the human family, of personal invulnerability and omnipotence of self. The protection and love offered by mother allow children to feel as the psalmist David did, promising, "A thousand shall fall at thy right hand and ten thousand at thy left, but it shall not come nigh thee," while loss of mother through separation may result in mistrust of self as well as the rest of the human community.

Bowlby has observed that separation resulting from hospitalization after a child has developed a reasonably secure relationship with his mother results in a predictable sequence of behaviors which may undermine his basic trust in people.[7] The initial phase in the sequence is characterized by protest and it may last only several hours or as long as a week or more. The second phase is one of despair in which the child appears to be in deep mourning, and he or she may cry intermittently or monotonously. The final phase is distinguished by detachment in which the child becomes increasingly self-centered and preoccupied with such things as sweets, toys, and food. The child neither cares when nurses come and go, nor shows interest in parents as special people. He or she may seem happy and cheerful, but no longer concerned about anyone.

Unfortunately, it seems that children adapt to separation from parents by keeping their relationships with people on a superficial level in order to protect themselves from further hurt. In their desperate attempt to defend themselves, children who are separated from parents may unwisely give up their attachment to people in favor of attachment to things. Furthermore, children's inclination to adjust by detachment may be encouraged by the way they are treated by hospital staff. Instead of a loving mother to reassure a frightened child at night, for instance, a hospitalized child may be attended by several staff members who, because of the number of children to be treated may not have the time or necessary patience for fondling. Furthermore, since mothers communicate genuine affection for their children in many subtle ways including the manner of changing diapers, handling feedings, and responding to cries of distress,[8] messages conveyed by busy hospital staff as they carry out their assigned duties may not have mother's reassuring qualities. Moreover, hospital staff who must change shifts at regular intervals, whose primary concern may be the physiological well-being of children, and whose ward assignments change regularly, may have limited time to devote to frightened children.

Dehumanization. Despite the humanitarian motivations of most hospital staff members, the dying child's feeling of abandonment generated by separation from family may be compounded by the quality of the child's interpersonal interactions with staff. In a comprehensive study of the life of terminal patients and their families in hospital settings, Glaser and Strauss made the following observation concerning the dynamics of nurse-patient interaction:[9]

> . . . when it comes to the duties of medical care, nurses cannot literally avoid the patient. They can, however, employ "expressive avoidance"; that is, they avoid him as a person while they are fulfilling the medical duties. They ignore him, treat him as a body (that is, socially dead), wear bland professional facial expressions, exude dignity and efficiency, and refuse or evade conversation, or else do their chores quickly and "get out" before the patient can say anything.

The tendency on the part of hospital staff to interact with the dying in a way which tends to dehumanize them is documented further by Quint who notes that,[10]

> . . . both physicians and nurses limit their contacts with those who are dying unless medical treatment or hospital routine require their presence. The general practice of not talking to the dying patient about his dying serves to isolate him from meaningful interactions with the significant persons in his life and prevents him from preparing for his own death. If he is surrounded by a conspiracy of silence, then all relationships become superficial. Under these conditions he is also likely to be given physical care in a routinized and impersonal manner.

Avoiding contact with patients may reach an extreme with terminally ill children. Due to their possession of attributes such as youth and beauty which are highly valued in society (referred to as social loss value), personal contact with children and their parents is held to a minimum, and nurses may attempt to protect themselves from being hurt by "personally focusing their attention on the disease or treatment process."[11] No general policy exists in most hospitals regarding the degree of personal or parental involvement in caring for children. Consequently, in general hospitals "psychological and social aspects of terminal care may be good, but are carried out on the basis of private initiative and judgment rather than as part of accountable decision-making."[12] As a result, there is danger that children already suffering from separation and detachment will become progressively more isolated.[13]

Anxiety. Among the consequences of dehumanization in, and socialization into, the hospital's institutional structure generally is the development of anxiety. More specifically, progressive isolation from parents and friends as well as hospital staff may exacerbate already existing feelings of loneliness resulting from the terminal illness itself. Moreover, when isolation is compounded by feelings of confusion, monotony, and powerlessness the conditions are set for experiencing intense anxiety.[14] An eleven year old boy revealed his feelings of confusion and loss of control in the following account of life in a large metropolitan hospital:[15]

> I didn't know what they were going to do. I didn't know what they were going to feed us, or what they were going to let us do—stand up or sit, or let us see our mothers, or something like that. I didn't know what they were going to do.

A study conducted at the City of Hope, Duarte, California, revealed a number of clearly definable sources of fear in children suffering from cancer, leukemia, or blood disease despite an ongoing Parent Participation Program.[16] Ages of the children in the study ranged from one to thirteen, and all the children have ultimately died. Three distinct sources of fear were identified for different age groups of children. Children in the age range birth to five suffered most from separation from their parents; those in the age range five to ten experienced most fear in reaction to medical procedures; children over ten suffered most from the fear of death itself. Although these young patients may have experienced all three fears on a conscious or unconscious level regardless of age, the sources of fear reported by children of various ages correspond to the major developmental changes observed in children's conceptions of death.[17] It is interesting to note that only in older children did the fear of the concept of death itself become their paramount concern. At younger ages, fundamental anxiety about death was expressed through more specific fears involving separation and medical routine.

General feelings of confusion, loss of control over even simple life functions, and anxiety are commonly associated with life in total institutions such as prisons, mental hospitals, and orphanages where there are barriers to social intercourse with, and departure to, the outside world,[18] and they contribute greatly to the anguish which terminally ill children experience. Despite the fact that "hospitalization may do a child more harm than good—not only in contributing to his sense of abandonment, but in the development of terrifying fears, anxiety, and traumas which survive long after the physical defect has been rectified,"[19] children are still separated from their parents, subjected to depersonalizing and monotonous institutional routine, and denied opportunity for determining their own fates even to a modest degree.

Frustration and Anger

Very early in life children realize that they have desires of their own which need to be gratified, and failure to achieve a reasonable amount of wish-fulfillment results in frustration and feelings of anger. Terminal illnesses, however, impose countless and varied limits on children's ability to obtain gratification so that anger and frustration inevitably arise.

Frustration. Seriously ill children, for instance, may become frustrated as they valiantly attempt to "stand on their own two feet," while their anger is displaced to people and events which surround them such as hospital routine, attending personnel, parents, and other patients.

Well-intentioned adults may only aggravate the condition by imposing rigid restrictions on activities in the hope of avoiding unnecessary injury to their children. Personal exploration and gratification of desires within some reasonable limit are nevertheless essential under any circumstances. Too stringent controls on even seriously ill children's behavior may result in situations where they turn things around and consider as evil only the fact that there are limits to their behavior. Too much shaming of their actions may lead to a secret determination to try to get away with things when adults are not present to enforce controls.[20]

In hospital settings especially, children are subjected to a variety of restrictions which become obstacles to gratifying personal wishes and feeling a sense of control over their lives. In most hospitals, staff members see to it that the goals of the institution are met first, and the young child is forced to conform to them.[21] Even for adults, but especially for children, hospital staff enforce a strict code for socializing them into the culture of the "sick" and making them into "cooperative" patients.[22] The objective of compliance with routine at the expense of fulfillment of personal wishes is carried out on many fronts including restricting parental visits to one or two a week and by the assumption by part-time personnel of many parental functions.[23]

The following list of rules, which was *drawn up by children* on a hospital ward, reveals a number of sources of frustration for terminally ill children who may actually need more than an ordinary amount of protection:[24]

Table 1

Hillside Hospital Club
Good Chart

1. Do not talk at nap
2. Do not talk at dinner
3. Do not talk at night
4. Do not be bad
5. Do not talk in school
6. Be a good sport
7. Do not shoot sticks
8. Do your homework when the teacher tells you to
9. Do not say bad words
10. Do not swear
11. Do not talk so loud
12. No toys on bed pan
13. Obey the nurses
14. Listen to the doctors
15. Little folks should be seen and not heard
16. Do not fight or throw things
17. Kiss the girls all you want
18. Do not trade toys
19. Don't throw toys
20. Be good at the workshop

Repression of anger. Hospitalized children face countless daily frustrations as a consequence of limitations imposed by separation and by threats to autonomy (control of their own fate) stemming from both omnipotent adult authorities and overpowering physiological forces. To make the situation all the more impossible, hospital staff have little tolerance for young patients' aggressive behavior and provide few opportunities for their expression of anger. Indeed, Quint points out that some forms of patient behavior are more acceptable than others, and "staff endorsement is unlikely when the dying patient makes many demands for time and attention, or when he overtly expresses anger or criticizes their actions."[25] Paradoxically, socialization into the hospital environment seems to encourage the development of hostile thoughts and emotions in children but demands that they repress their feelings.

Nevertheless, even healthy children express their feelings of anger through their actions. Studies conducted in American nursery schools indicate that some sort of conflict occurs in free play situations about every five minutes for boys and every seven or eight for girls.[26]

Although there are sex differences in the mode of expression, anger itself seems to be universal at least at younger age levels. Unfortunately, the tendency in general American culture, and particularly in hospitals, is to suppress the expression of anger (some form of aggressive acts), rather than to route it into more socially acceptable and constructive channels through informal discussions, story construction, play, art, fantasy, or other creative outlets.

Guilt, Anxiety, and Fear

Anger not expressed constructively or directed outwardly is frequently turned inward against the self in the form of guilt and anxiety,[27] and as noted previously, these vague feelings set the stage for more specific fears. Since children are not able to identify clearly a source for their feelings of guilt and anxiety, they use instead a symbolic representation, through which they can express their feelings.[28] Seriously ill children, for instance, may believe that their pain and suffering are punishment for some transgression against the wishes of parents or other adults. In other instances, in a desperate attempt to defend against self-blame, children may project their anger onto other people or things in their environment.

On the other hand, children may anthropomorphize their feelings in the form of monsters, ghosts, animals, or even animated machinery, and these constructions may in turn frighten them even more. Bettelheim reports an incident in which a girl who deeply repressed her anger represented her anxiety in the form of a ghost which she was afraid would eat her up.[29] It seems almost contradictory that, in her valiant attempt to deal with her own repressed feelings, this child constructed an image which threatened her even more.

Unfortunately, surrounding adults have little sympathy for, or understanding of, children's fears as expressed through their symbolic representations, and they may frustrate a child further by their lack of insight. When, however, an eight year old describes death as, "A dead person who doesn't have any flesh any more, only bones,"[30] it is easy to see how such an image might threaten a child who projected anger onto it. Furthermore, entry into the hospital environment with its foreign sights, sounds, and smells provides countless opportunities for anxious children to express their feelings of anxiety as more specific fears. Even mature adults become disoriented and fearful when deprived of information concerning, and control over, their own fate.[31]

It may be expected that children develop fears when they are separated from familiar places, people, and things; subjected to sundry treatment regimens; socialized to repress their feelings; and isolated from parents and family.

Helping Children in Crisis

Down through generations and over the course of the life cycle, human beings meet crises, overcome despair, and construct an acceptable reality by means of their symbols. Language, play, dreams, and fantasy not only provide mechanisms for expressing feelings, but they also act as vehicles for communication between isolated people and means of structuring life in the quest for inner peace. With the help of these various forms of symbolic representation, children organize the sequence of momentary experiences spatially as well as temporally to make their life what it is and what it might become.

Constructing Life-Space

Language is an important mode of symbolization throughout the life cycle. Even children under six years of age utilize language for expressing their feelings and thoughts and for structuring reality.[32] Prior to six, however, children's language and thought tends to be egocentric, meaning they may not attempt to place themselves in the point of view of the listener.[33] Children may not wish to tell a listener anything by what they are saying. Often, they simply use the listener as a model for their own constructions and verbalize most of what they are thinking.

Language and thought. This egocentric orientation in children's thought and language manifests itself in a number of important ways. For example, it seems that children under six would rather have factual descriptions of events than cause-effect explanations in response to their questions, and they repeat these descriptions to adopt them as their own. In other words, explanations which children give for events reflect not necessarily their own constructions, but adults' thinking which has been adopted without conscious intent. Up to about age seven, children "invariably imagine that they have discovered by themselves what in reality they are only repeating from a model."[34]

The preference for descriptive rather than cause-effect explanations, the tendency toward imitating a model, and the egocentric character of children's language and thought have profound implications for those who wish to help dying children. For instance, in the following incident reported by Kübler-Ross,[35] a young child suffering from acute leukemia reveals how her egocentric orientation helped her resolve a crisis situation.

> In our hospital we saw a small child with acute leukemia. She made the rounds and asked the adults, "What is it going to be like when I die?" The grownups responded in a variety of ways, most of them unhelpful or even harmful for this little girl who was searching for an answer. The only message she really received through the grown-ups' response was that they had a lot of fear when it came to talking about dying.

> When the child confronted the hospital chaplain with the same question, he turned to her and asked, "What do you think it's going to be like?" She looked at him and said, "One of these days I'm going to fall asleep and when I wake up I'm going to be with Jesus and my little sister." He then said something like "That should be very beautiful." The child nodded and happily returned to play. Perhaps this is an exaggerated example, but I think it conveys how children face the reality even of their own death if the adults in their environment don't make it a frightening, horrible experience to be avoided at all costs.

For this child a simple description of what might take place following death was sufficient explanation for her question. Moreover, even though in the past the child probably had someone explain death to her from this Christian perspective, she now accepts the answer and adopts it as her own. For children under six or seven, organic life is a sort of story regulated according to the wishes and intentions of the one who brought it into existence,[36] and whether that creator is perceived as God, a parent, or some other personified power is irrelevant. What is important is that events are not perceived by young children as resulting from pure chance or physical cause-effect. Rather, events are invariably under the control of a creator. Consequently, to help young children confront unknown and uncertain events in their lives, parents and others need to provide a system of symbols such as religion, a philosophy of life, or some other scheme through which children may come to conceptualize, with the help of language, the power which controls events.

Empathic listening. Although the age of transition from egocentric to more socialized language and thought is somewhat variable, by age ten or eleven the majority of children have made the change and recognize physical cause-effect relationships as well as the universality of death.[37] Among the more frightening consequences of children's loss of their egocentric orientation is that, despite the social quality of language, children recognize their separation from the rest of humanity. Since during early childhood, children's thinking was not clearly differentiated from the language and thought of models, they easily identified with others and felt related to the group. On the other hand, older children who have lost their egocentrism realize their independent existence, feel the loneliness of life, and recognize the permanent separation from loved ones implied by death.

To help children express their fear, anger, and frustration, and feel less separated from the group, concerned adults need to provide ample opportunities for them to communicate with others. For example, private conversations with a sympathetic person who listens empathically may help children overcome their feelings of separation. Persons who take the role of active listener need not feel that they must have all the answers to children's questions. Rather, accurate recognition of children's feelings without agreeing or disagreeing with them seems important.

"Real communication occurs . . . ," says Carl Rogers, "when we listen with understanding."[38] When we see the expressed idea from the other person's point of view; when we see how it feels to him; when we achieve his frame of reference. These are the times we truly communicate. Attainment of such a perspective requires that we become mature persons ourselves so that our responses to those in anguish may reflect not our own egocentric point of view but that of the speaker. When this type of active listening is achieved, those who cry out may feel that they have been more deeply heard and so feel less alone. However, those who dare to listen actively need the courage to hear deeply and to share in human suffering.

Individual and group discussions. In addition to being deeply heard by a sympathetic listener, the opportunity for children to communicate with others is important. For instance, informal discussions among fellow patients on a hospital ward encourage the development of a sense of camaraderie which is extremely helpful in overcoming loneliness and in strengthening hope.[39] Also, informal contacts with physicians, nurses, aides, and volunteers may help children develop trust in those people who tend to assume parental responsibilities. These are the ones who must meet children's emotional needs, and to do this successfully demands personal involvement with young patients. Those who keep their relationships with dying children on a strictly professional basis to protect themselves from being hurt are not likely to be helpful human beings.

Play and drawings. "A child's play," says Vygotsky, "must always be interpreted as the imaginary, illusory realization of unrealizable desires."[40] Through their play, and in their paintings and drawings children express themselves and master reality.[41] Children's play provides the means by which they redeem failure, strengthen hope, and construct reality, and we need to recognize that, "To 'play it out' is the most self-healing measure childhood affords."[42]

A poignant illustration of how the drawing process helps children communicate feelings and resolve fears is provided by Kübler-Ross who described a sequence of drawings completed by an eight year old boy suffering from an inoperable brain tumor. In an early picture, the child represented death as a huge military tank confronting a small, helpless child who futilely waved a stop sign in a desperate attempt to halt the tank's advance. In the last picture he drew before dying, the child outlined a peace dove soaring in flight. The tip of the wing was colored bright yellow, as if reaching into the sunlight. "And this boy, through a telling lapse in speech, confirmed his self-identification with the peaceful, free-flying bird. He pointed out the splash of color as 'a little bit of sunshine on *my* wing.' "[43]

In another case not involving a terminal illness, four year old Sylvia was referred to a play therapist to attempt to resolve some fears and anxieties which resulted from a traumatic experience when, with no explanation or preparation by her parents, she had been taken to the hospital for minor surgery. The following passage is an excerpt taken from a session in which Sylvia was sweeping thick globs of blue and green finger paint around on some paper with both hands.[44]

Sylvia: The water, The water, These are big waves.

Therapist: You've made the waves and the water.

Sylvia: Swish, Swish, Woooo.

Therapist: The waves make funny noises.

Sylvia: Give me black. Give me black. (Therapist gives her some black finger paint.)

Sylvia (changing her voice dramatically): Here comes the ghost!

Therapist: The ghost is coming.

Sylvia (forming a black shape in the middle of the paper): Wooooooo.

Therapist: The ghost goes "Wooooooo." The ghost is right in the middle of the water.

Sylvia (grinning up at the therapist): I like this.

Therapist: You like to do this. You like to mess with the finger paints.

Sylvia: Look. Look. I am the ghost that lives under the water. See?

Therapist: That is the ghost that lives under the water.

Sylvia: I am the ghost that flies in the open window at night.

Therapist: You are the ghost that flies in the open window at night.

Sylvia: It scares me.

Therapist: Your ghost scares you.

Sylvia: Yeah. (She swoops her hands through the blue-green water.) Go away. Go away!

Therapist: You are sending the ghost away.

Sylvia: Wooooooo. Wooooooo. (Grins up at therapist.)

Therapist: The ghost is saying "Wooooooo."

Sylvia: The ghost is all gone.

Therapist: The ghost is gone now.

Sylvia: Find him.

Therapist (examining the paper): The ghost is not there.

Sylvia (shaking her head emphatically): The ghost is not there. (Once more she smears the finger paints around in free, circular swoops and then she moves away from the table.) Now I'll play in the sand.

Through her play Sylvia was able to overcome most of her fears which were represented as the ghost in her story and which remained nameless. In her play Sylvia had control over her ghost and could bring it forth or destroy it at will. Finger paints, which were her own choice, constituted a perfect medium with which to express a ghostly visitor.

Despite the recognition given to play as a means through which to help emotionally disturbed children develop healthy personalities, little recognition has been given to the role of play in helping children without these disturbances meet the exigencies of their lives. In the decision to provide opportunity for play therapy, it must be remembered that therapists assume that disturbed children most likely have been deprived of normal opportunity for expressing their secret feelings in play with the sanction of an understanding adult. In most families, an understanding grandmother or favorite aunt may play the necessary role for a child during crisis.

For terminally ill children who experience deep feelings of loneliness, anxiety, fear, and anger, just such *normal* opportunities may be lacking. On wards where hospital staff are limited and many children are kept, opportunities for having an adult to themselves are limited.[45] Tragically, in most hospital settings, little chance exists for play away from other children in a time and place that is theirs alone with an adult.[46] Moreover, few hospital staff members have been made aware of the significance to children of having an adult who not only sets limits on their behavior but also actively listens to and reflects with empathy what the child is communicating. Perhaps, what is needed to help children as well as adults confront a life crisis are helpers who recognize the "importance to take off one's professional white coat and just be a human being."[47]

Dreams and fantasy. Dreams are the least understood form of symbolism, but they provide an important mechanism through which children's deepest feelings reach conscious expression, most primordial desires are fulfilled, and terrifying fears are expressed.[48] For children threatened at the basic levels of existence, dreams become a potentially powerful means of constructive expression on the one hand, but are also potentially dangerous. For instance, in some cases dreams may enable children to construct a more acceptable reality. In other instances, because children have little control over their dreams, terrifying nightmares may serve to frighten children already in anguish. In both cases, dreams communicate deep feelings and needs to those who listen closely.

Up to age seven or eight, play dominates children's thoughts to such an extent that it is very hard to tell deliberate invention from fantasy that children believe to be the truth.[49] Moreover, during childhood, dreams, play, and imitation are not clearly differentiated from one another.[50] Consequently, children can resolve some of the fear, anger, loneliness, and frustration expressed in dreams by gaining control over them in their play. Play may allow children to work through fears under much more controlled circumstances than exists in night dreams.

On the other hand, daydreams and other more controlled forms of fantasy need to be encouraged in children. For adults as well as children a rich inner life provides an essential means of fulfilling wishes and meeting crisis. Take, for example, the experience of Viktor Frankl who reports that in times of extreme stress such as were found in Nazi concentration camps, a deep inner life provided a "refuge from the emptiness, desolation, and spiritual poverty of his existence, by letting him escape into the past."[51] Just as expressed so eloquently by the words, "The angels are lost in perpetual contemplation of an infinite glory," dreams, fantasy, and reflection enable children to commune with a power neither they nor we truly understand.

In dying children and adults, helpers might inspire self-fulfillment through various forms of fantasy. Reading poetry, taking time for prayers, telling stories with a spiritual meaning, and allowing children to construct their own stories or supply endings to those related by adults, all encourage the development of a rich inner life.[52] Most important is probably allowing time for serious reflection and quiet conversation with adults who have a deep spiritual dimension in his or her own life. Through genuine caring, active listening, and encouraging discussions among those who share a common fate, individuals surrounding the dying may help them feel a sense of unity and atoneness with the human family, may draw them closer to God, and encourage them to fear less the time after death.

Constructing Life-Time

Children develop their conceptions of time by the purposeful satisfaction of desires through language, play, fantasy, and dreams.[53] Obviously, for children who are terminally ill as well as for those who care for them, the character of this conception has profound significance, for it invariably affects the quality of life till death. The perspective on future-time constructed by children depends, however, largely on the goals they set, and the goals children strive toward are influenced heavily by interactions with significant people in their social environment such as parents, teachers, and, in the case of hospitalized children, nurses and physicians. What type of perspective on future-time, then, does the American cultural environment encourage in children? Of what significance is this perspective in the life of dying children?

Thing among things. Sociologists have observed that the rapid growth of industry and technology over the last century has encouraged Americans to establish as their overriding objective the production and consumption of "bigger and bigger," "better and better," and "more and more," goods and services.[54] As a result, the people themselves have become an element in the process of manipulated production and consumption. They have become a thing among things. Unfortunately, children's daily lives reflect this basic technological orientation, and we need not look beyond their everyday experience to find examples of the predicament. Children's lives are well-ordered with each moment filled with some activity, something which must be done, seen, said, or planned. Seldom do children exist in a moment in which they do not care what comes next and their only concern is with the meaning of an experience as it occurs. Rarely do they have an opportunity to experience and learn to appreciate the world within themselves that may become a part of life.

It is generally agreed, for example, that the prevailing pattern of socialization in the so-called middle class setting encourages impulse-renunciation rather than impulse-gratification,[55] and that the schools embrace this middle class value system.[56] Schools encourage delay of gratification in children in many ways. Among the more important of these encouragements is through the system of rewards and punishments in which children are graded at prescribed intervals, given lock-step homework assignments, and promoted on a regular basis.

Unfortunately, once such a perspective is inculcated in children, it is difficult to alter. Thus, well-socialized children who suddenly find themselves with serious illnesses which limit the range of their activities and have uncertain outcomes have difficulty adjusting to the new demands. Children who become hospitalized, for instance, carry the expectation that their caretakers will establish for them a well-formed, sequentially patterned set of goals into an institutional environment in which the goals for recovery are less well defined and much more uncertain. As a result, children may make valiant but unsuccessful and disappointing attempts at setting new goals for themselves—goals which reflect their organized and patterned life style, but which fail to meet the demands imposed by their illness and hospitalization. Davis, in his study of the impact of serious illness on children and their families, reports the following incident in the life of a child suffering from spinal paralytic poliomyelitis (polio).[57]

More typically, children explored such questions as "When will I be able to sit up?" "How will I know if I am going to wear a brace?" "When do you get a wheelchair?" "How will I know when I'm due to go home?" They attempted to delineate the telling clues and interdependent sequences. The neophyte on the ward was told by the veteran of three or four months what to look for and what kinds of ambulatory advancement and privilege followed certain events and conditions. These predictions came to serve as provisional signposts for the child, who tried to assess their validity by comparing them with what others had told him and what he himself was able to observe. For example, after his second month of convalescence Johnny Lawson announced to the interviewer that he would be going home soon. (Actually, he was not discharged until five months later.) Johnny explained that another boy who, according to Johnny, had been "sicker," was then being fitted for a brace. Being fitted for a brace, Johnny had learned from the other children, meant that the boy would be going home soon, and so, therefore, would he.

The children in Davis's study were mostly from middle socioeconomic families, and not surprisingly, they typically experienced great difficulty in adapting to the time schedule for recovery imposed by the uncertainties of their illness. Little information is available concerning the impact of comparable situations on children being reared in cultural settings having different time-perspectives. However, one might expect differential reactions to such uncertainties since studies showed that some children in America are socialized in environments in which, "the future is vague, unstructured, ambiguous and without consensual markers."[58]

Obviously, a mode of socialization that encourages delay of gratification may result in a time-perspective which favors success in economic aspects of life. When children are confronted with life crisis situations which have uncertain and unpredictable outcomes, however, such an orientation may be less advantageous.

In addition to having difficulty in adjusting their time-perspective to accommodate an uncertain future, the deferred gratification pattern may lead to other difficulties for terminally ill children. For instance, because of their tendency toward impulse-renunciation, children may experience difficulty in expressing their feelings. As a result there may be a tendency for them not to share their fear, pain, and anguish with others, but rather suffer in solitude. Moreover, socialization that encourages impulse-renunciation is a precondition for children coming to believe that their feelings are bad or that their actions are inappropriate. Need we look further for a major contributor of unnecessary anxiety in terminally ill children?

Life without life within. A distressing consequence of socialization into a culture preoccupied with technology and veneration of materialism is the generation of an anxiety of meaninglessness. "This anxiety is aroused by the loss of a spiritual center, of an answer, however symbolic or indirect, to the question of the meaning of existence."[59] More specifically, consider for a moment that in American culture young children are encouraged to defer their immediate desires so that they might obtain material rewards later in their lifetime. As a result, rather than engaging in activities which might have personal significance, very early in their lives children are required to pursue goals which are set for them by significant persons such as parents and teachers but which they may perceive as of little concern. Instead of being encouraged to construct a life which has personal significance, children develop a perspective in which meaning is perceived only in reference to some external material objective. Consequently, life loses essential qualities of spontaneity and creativity, while the value of human life itself tends to be judged on the basis of the person's potential contribution to the productive sphere.

This anxiety of meaninglessness seems to be reflected in the way the dying child is handled. Glaser and Strauss, in an investigation of the experiences of terminally ill patients and their families in hospitals, noted that, "In our society, certain values are highly esteemed—among them youth, beauty, integrity, and parental and marital responsibility—and when the terminal patient strikingly embodies such values, staff members tend to react to the potential or actual loss to his family or society."[60] These reactions by adults, which reflect their own preoccupation with potential or actual contributions by isolated individuals to the material world, are not necessarily the concerns of dying children, nor are they especially helpful to them.

In general, it seems that medicine is preoccupied with crisis-oriented, individual medical treatment at the expense of the welfare of the group. As a result, "Often no costs are spared to prevent the death of *one person* (in part this occurs because our financial mechanisms for subsidizing such treatment are biased in this direction). Conversely, few funds are available for attacking the problem of how best to prevent diseases from becoming too far advanced."[61]

A more constructive perspective to have might include an appreciation of life at the moment, set within the context of the collective evolutionary history of humanity. The current perspective, which encourages self-fulfillment through isolated accomplishments by the person in the secular world, forfeits an appreciation of the commonality of human fate. Consequently, for adults at least, the death of an isolated individual, for example, a politician of some stature, may take on such significance that grief is "shared throughout the nation and the world,"[62] while not even passing note is made of the fact that American Indians, as a group, have the highest infant mortality rate in the nation, that their life expectancy on reservations is one-third shorter than the national average, or that on reservations the incidence of rare diseases such as otitis media (an ear infection which is the leading cause of hearing loss in children), which responds readily to treatment, is not rare at all.[63]

The sting of individual death might be tempered if death were viewed more as "the regular, indispensable condition of the replacement of one individual by another along a phyletic stem. Death—the essential lever in the mechanism and upsurge of life."[64] If death were regarded less as an event to be avoided at all cost to human suffering and dignity, then individual life might take on a deeper meaning. Furthermore, if surrounding adults feared death less they might have greater courage to become emotionally involved with the dying and so dehumanize them less.

"Healthy children," Erikson points out, "will come not to fear life if their elders have integrity enough not to fear death."[65] A sense of integrity in the face of death, however, is derived from the strength of spiritual commitment.[66] Adults who are wise enough to realize the commonality of human fate as evidenced in the cycle of generations, "the cycle of one generation concluding itself in the next, and the cycle of an individual life coming to a conclusion,"[67] may help children perceive their own unique contribution to the spectrum of life regardless of its length. Through appreciation of the cycle of life and through identification with the human family of all ages, individual life acquires new meaning. Just as in fantasy an eight year old may identify with a free-flying bird, so may children find comfort in the realization of the ultimate relatedness and universality of life. In addition, adults may come to evaluate the significance of life according to its depth, not its length, and according to its intrinsic quality as an expression of the grander scheme of evolutionary history rather than exclusively as a function of its actual or potential social loss value.

Constructing life within. Regrettably, the present cultural matrix does not encourage development of this type of perspective. Furthermore, the current tendency on the part of adults to deal with death by disguising and avoiding it serves to direct children's attention further away from a spiritual confrontation with the problem of death. Moreover, the modern trend toward adoration of medical technology not only reflects the basic materialistic structure of the society but again focuses attention on a physical resolution of the problem of dying rather than a spiritual one. For example, in hospitals, children are socialized into believing that listening to physicians, taking their medication, and the like will make them into whole persons again, whether or not this is in fact the case. Davis reports that, "a recurrent theme running through their stories on the Children's Apperception Test was that of a sick animal hero who, because he obeyed the doctors and his parents, recovered and was then able to join all other animals in play."[68] The *Children's Apperception Test,* a psychological projective technique involving the construction of stories to fit a series of vague animal pictures, revealed these children's needs and their beliefs regarding forces that might facilitate or interfere with satisfaction of those needs.

What seems to be reflected in hospitals and the children they allegedly help is the tendency in society to develop the power necessary to face existence not from sources within themselves, but rather from external ones such as the family, medical technology, physicians, or some other extrinsic power source. Since each individual faces death essentially alone, however, it seems important that children be encouraged to develop early in their lives some internal source of strength in addition to the support provided by external accoutrements. Indeed "if there is any responsibility in the cycle of life it must be that one generation owes to the next that strength by which it came to face ultimate concerns its own way."[69]

Since children rely on adult explanations for their construction of reality, parents, teachers, hospital staff, and others may have profound influence on the development of an inner source of power for living. For instance, when adult explanations for events focus exclusively on mechanical operations in the physical world, then power is perceived in these external sources; when explanations concentrate on the actions of people such as parents, physicians, hospital staff, etc., the child invests power in them; and when explanations and interpretations include some reference to a spiritual force in the individual's life, children may be inspired to perceive power in it.[70] Encouraging children to search within themselves through dreams, play, fantasy, and prayer in order to construct answers to their questions of life and death may help them develop a spiritual source of power in their lives. By allowing time for fantasy, adults may become teachers in the truest sense of the word as they help the young regain a dimension of life lost in their own culture.

What of the Dying Child's Loved Ones?

Loneliness, frustration, anger, fear, and guilt are all emotional crises which dying children face. But what of their family and friends? How are they handling the child's approaching departure and the aftermath of this tragedy? What possible meaning may be made of the death of a child by those left behind?

Family in Crisis

The parents. Parents as well as their dying children experience the loneliness that is inevitably a part of separation and the solitude of suffering. Parents may feel the anguish of loneliness, for instance, when they are asked to make decisions which affect their children's lives or when they wait in helpless anticipation of the outcome of diagnostic tests, surgery, and the like. One anxious father gave the following account of his feeling of loneliness:[71]

> It was a terrible responsibility, being required to make a decision, a life and death decision for someone else. This awful feeling, this overwhelming sense of responsibility, I could not share with anyone. I felt utterly alone, entirely lost, and frightened; my existence was absorbed in this crisis. No one fully understood my terror or how this terror gives impetus to deep feelings of loneliness and isolation which had lain dormant within me. There at the center of my being, loneliness aroused me to a self-awareness I had never known before.

Any parent who has comforted a sick child through even a minor illness may bear witness to the loneliness of which this father speaks. On one occasion I recall, our son underwent some diagnostic blood tests, and the physicians provided little information other than that the results of the test would be available in several days. Unfortunately, the ambiguity and uncertainty of the situation set the conditions for a nightmare of terror with flights of fantasy in which we imagined the worst possible outcome. No one could have known, including the attending physician, the total isolation and disorientation felt at that time as we waited for the test results. Utterly shaken to the core of existence, I could do little more than helplessly wait.

Among the more obvious preconditions for the feeling of loneliness described above were helplessness and uncertainty. Not knowing what to do, or what the outcome might be, was the critical feature which made these situations terrifying and totally disorienting. Whether or not families should be made aware of a diagnosis involving a terminal illness is an unresolved problem, however. For instance, in dealing with parents of children with leukemia some medical authorities advise facing the fact immediately, recognizing its fatal consequences, and involving families in an active program of open and honest communication among themselves and with attending personnel. Others advocate a more optimistic approach emphasizing aggressive treatment and the possibility of long term remission of symptoms. In this case, confrontation with a diagnosis which implies impending doom is unnecessary. On the other hand, some physicians and hospital staff advise a course of action lying somewhere between these two extremes so that parents, children, and staff may communicate openly without the risk of giving up hope.[72]

Unfortunately, the psychosocial dynamics of life in hospitals do not always provide an open awareness context for patients or their families. In some cases terminal patients and their families may be kept totally unaware that the patient's condition is even serious ("closed awareness" described in Chapter 1). In other less closed contexts, family and staff may know of the terminality, but the information is withheld from the patient. Under these circumstances, patients may become suspicious and embark on a plan for finding out more about themselves ("suspicion awareness"). Discovery of terminality under these conditions may lead to yet another, and perhaps least desirable, situation. In this case, family, staff, and the dying patient know of the terminality, but each party pretends not to know (mutual pretense). This pretense context does not lend itself to effective interpersonal communication within the family and frequently results in very brief and shallow interactions with the dying patient. Furthermore, the mutual pretense situation "eliminates any possibility that staff members might 'work with' patients psychologically, on a self-conscious professional basis."[73]

Although sweeping generalizations about disclosure of terminality to patients and their families are not warranted at this time, in many cases the situation is made more traumatizing for them both by the uncertainty, suspicion, and depersonalization which result from well-intentioned attempts to protect parents and siblings from knowing the seriousness of an illness. Even though dying children themselves may need to be allowed to set the pace as far as their own recognition and acceptance of their condition are concerned, the possible consequences for the family circle of secrecy, deception, and uncertainty may be more devastating than confronting a diagnosis of terminality.

Studies indicate that in more than half the families who have a terminally ill child, more than one member is undergoing psychiatric care a year after the child's death, and that two out of three couples end up divorced after the child dies.[74] As a result of divorce, children lose a parent as well as a sibling, while parents add to their already overloaded burden of guilt. For a family that experienced one crisis, divorce compounds a tragic episode in their lives.

Even before their children die, however, families need to begin to make many adjustments in their life styles to accommodate demands made by various physical handicaps which dying children may develop. For instance, adverse changes in children's physical appearance due to extreme loss or gain in weight, orthopedic disabilities, and other disfigurements, which are negatively valued in our society, as well as limitations on their social activities such as play and school attendance, impose new conditions for the family. Moreover, changes in dying children's personalities resulting from their hospital experiences and adjustment to their disabilities necessarily modify the dynamics of family life. As a result, families with dying children along with the children themselves need to begin to discover new meanings and purposes in their lives as their life circumstances are altered.

Despite the major adjustments that are apparently necessary during time of crisis, families typically do not recognize the need for change on their own. Moreover, closed, suspicion, and mutual pretense awareness contexts do not encourage such recognition. Davis, for instance, found that parents of orthopedically handicapped children tended to defend against the possible negative meanings associated with the visible defect by maintaining that nothing had changed and that the handicapped child was the same as he or she had always been.[75] Tragically, a deliberate effort was made on the part of families, and parents especially, to develop a sense of sameness and continuity with the past in the face of monumental changes in their real life situations. Although some continuity with the past is important in maintaining family stability, confrontation with the necessity for change seems vital if the destructive forces surrounding family crisis situations are to be dealt with effectively and somewhat controlled.

Another problem often confronting parents with dying children is guilt. For instance, parents may feel some responsibility for their child's condition, or they may spend an inordinate amount of time with the dying child and so neglect their other children. Furthermore, because of the extreme demands seriously ill children may make on parents' time and energy, they may become frustrated and angry with the dying children themselves. Since anger is regarded as an inappropriate emotion to feel for seriously ill children, parents may feel guilty.

Perhaps the most tragic consequence of parental guilt is that in attempting to deal with it, individual parents may defend against their own self-blame by projecting blame onto their spouse and others. As a result, a vicious cycle of anger, blame, and guilt may destroy precious family unity at a time when it is needed most. Moreover, parental guilt may be projected beyond the family circle as parents blame hospital staff or even other children who share in the lives of their dying child such as classmates, fellow patients on the ward, and the like.

The siblings. Despite the range and severity of reactions children manifest to the death of a sibling, the most neglected members of the family are the siblings. Emphasis is placed on dealing with dying children and their parents, while siblings, if not totally ignored, are at least pushed into the background. A common practice is for pediatric wards to restrict visitors to persons over twelve years of age, while lengthening the time allowed for parental visits. As a consequence, children who already have difficulty differentiating fantasy from reality are deprived of opportunity to satisfy some of their curiosity concerning their sibling, while their parents spend increasing amounts of time away from home as they care for the dying child. Furthermore, siblings may feel angry with parents or the dying child, and they may actually confuse desires for a child's death arising from their anger with the eventual reality of the child's death. Children then may experience feelings of profound guilt either before the sibling's death when he or she is forced to undergo repeated hospitalization and treatments or afterward.

Siblings of dying children show many immediate reactions to the death including loss of appetite, dazed status, incessant talk about death as well as more enduring symptoms such as nightmares, speech disturbances, enuresis, antisocial acting out, and severe anxiety states.[76] Moreover, in a study of children's disturbed reactions to the death of a sibling, Cain, Fast, and Erickson[77] found that 50 percent of the cases studied showed guilt as an initial and persistent reaction which was still very much noticeable five or more years after the sibling's death. Guilt was handled differently by the children depending on their personality structure. Reactions such as depressive withdrawal, accident-prone behavior, punishment-seeking, constant provocative testing, and exhibitionistic use of guilt and grief as well as many forms of acting-out were among the adjustments made. Obviously, the resulting deterioration in their behavior affected their performance in school giving them further grounds for guilt and feeling that they were no good.

Other serious reactions to death of a sibling uncovered by Cain, Fast, and Erickson included distorted concepts of illness and death, heightened fear of death, and disturbances in cognitive functioning especially with respect to their concepts of time and causality. More specifically, though it must be remembered that all the children studied were already in therapy, 40 percent of cases they examined showed either immediate, prolonged, or "anniversary" hysterical identification with the dead child's symptoms. Others believed that they would die at the same age as the sibling, that they had the same disease as their sib, or that coughs, colds, "high temperatures," and bruises led to death. Also, the majority of cases studied showed heightened fear of doctors and general confusion about the benevolence of God. In addition, looming large as a response to death of a sibling was an intense fear of death which was exacerbated by the fact that notions of parental omnipotence, all-powerfulness, and effectiveness as protectors went crashing.

Furthermore, since many parents felt some guilt over the death of their children they did little to encourage independence in the surviving siblings, but, rather their normal parental concerns were intensified to extremes of overprotection, restrictiveness, and infantilization. As a result, children became generally immature, passive-dependent, and fearful, feeling small and ineffective in an increasingly dangerous world. (Many, but certainly not all, of the responses described in this section may be seen in Julie's account introduced in the Prologue. Hers was a "family in crisis," but a family that succeeded in coping with it in spite of everything.)

Family Participation

A number of hospitals have begun parent participation programs which seem to lessen the anxiety experienced by terminally ill children as well as provide a means for dying children to deal with the anxiety which they already have.[78] Furthermore, parent participation provides an opportunity for alleviating parental guilt by actively involving them in the care of their children. Despite the benefits which accrue to parents and their terminally ill children, a rigorous program of parent participation at the expense of the siblings may have adverse effects on them.[79] Some pediatric wards have extended visiting hours, while others allow mothers to move right into the hospital. Although circumstances vary, and children differ in their capacity for dealing with separation, a program of total family participation may be of more help, especially for young children, than strictly parent-oriented efforts.

Such a program of total family participation may be particularly important to siblings' future emotional and social development. Since overprotective parents may easily encourage the development of dependent personalities, attending medical personnel along with the clergy may help parents develop the courage to allow children to become independent, while they help siblings through a very difficult period in their lives. Furthermore, in young children who experience difficulty differentiating wishes from reality, a comprehensive program of participation involving parents, clergy, and medical personnel seems essential if siblings are to avoid feeling unnecessary guilt.

Another important function of family participation programs would seem to be the provision of an opportunity for families to interact with people outside their immediate circle who could make suggestions regarding necessary adjustments in their life style. Perhaps some of the conditions within the family that result in divorce and disturbed reactions in siblings might be recognized and treated well before the children die. Moreover, opportunity for families, hospital staff, and clergy to interact might help to initiate some creative alternatives in the purposes and meanings of their lives, after the death of their child.

The Widening Circle

Despite the observation that during the elementary school years the neighborhood is as important a part of children's lives as is their immediate families,[80] the social relationships of dying children which extend beyond their families have not been recognized. For instance, there is a paucity of information concerning the playmate's reactions to the dying child's absence from their group and about how they treat the child when he or she returns home for visits and attendance at school. Although some meager data are available concerning peer responses to the return of polio victims after long periods of hospitalization, little is known about the reactions classmates have to the news of death of one of their members.

Children afflicted with polio who returned after lengthy hospital stays typically experienced placement in a marginal position with respect to playmates, while their identification as handicapped altered their pattern of friendships.[81] Following their initial exclusion, handicapped children tended to give up old friendships in favor of new patterns with other marginal members of their group. Unfortunately, it is not known, "Whether such marginal friendships function as a temporary way station in a life-career passage to a new, handicapped-oriented identity or endures as a kind of socially marginal sequestered place, neither wholly within nor wholly without the world of normal peers."[82] Tragically, in American culture, social stigma accompanies many types of disabilities including deafness, blindness, as well as speech defects and emotional disturbances, and the stigma may be so isolating and difficult to confront that families may resort to moving out of a community to avoid contact with old acquaintances.

But, need families of seriously ill children face social stigma in addition to their primary crisis? Can residents of an increasingly urban, technological, and individualistic society regain some sense of community so that they might help their neighbors and grow in character as a result of their misfortune? Teachers, for instance, might help dying children as well as their siblings by fostering the development of a sense of community in classmates. By providing opportunities for children to interact with and help in caring for those who are different due to a physical disability, teachers might not only contribute significantly to the handicapped child's welfare but also to the emotional and social development of their more fortunate peers.

Perhaps the "milk of human kindness" does not flow whenever there is tragedy but needs to be cultivated and nurtured in children's lives. It may be that from misfortune children may learn of the need for relatedness and fulfillment through the unity of humanity as well as fulfillment in isolation. Maybe from the suffering and seemingly meaningless suffocation of a life in childhood may grow a victory.

Sound strange? Let me explain. Through sharing in the remaining life and the death of a classmate, children may come to understand more deeply the value of human life and the meaning of suffering. In a world in which the mass media have depersonalized and routinized dying, children might regain an appreciation of their own life as well as their neighbor's. Furthermore, by confronting the reality of death early in life, children might develop the courage to face their own life whatever the future holds. By facing death a new spiritual dimension may unfold in children's lives which can help them live through crisis.

In conclusion, the death of a child may give meaning to life for those who try to understand. By sharing in the death of a loved one, those who survive might find depth and meaning in their own lives as well as in others. Out of the loneliness of shared tragedy our children may draw the bounds of human kinship wider and closer than we have ever dreamed. From the utter feelings of helplessness surrounding the death of a child, our children may appreciate the loneliness in life and generate for humanity a "spirit of the earth."[83]

Notes

* I wish to thank Dr. Sara Allen Spear of California State University, Chico, California, and Miss Julia I. Lynch, Glenn County Schools, Willows, California, for their suggestions regarding an earlier version of this chapter.

1. Erich Fromm, *The Art of Loving* (New York: Harper & Row, 1956).
2. Paul Tillich, *The Courage to Be* (New Haven, Ct.: Yale University Press, 1952).
3. Thomas H. Johnson, *Final Harvest: Emily Dickinson's Poems* (Boston: Little, Brown and Co., 1961), p. xii.
4. Fromm, *Loving*, p. 9.
5. Clark E. Moustakas, *Loneliness* (Englewood Cliffs, N.J.: Prentice-Hall, 1961), p. 35.
6. Monroe Lerner, "When, Why, and Where People Die," in *The Dying Patient*, ed. Orville G. Brim Jr., et al. (New York: Russell Sage Foundation, 1970), pp. 5-29.
7. John Bowlby, *Attachment and Loss*, Vol. I: *Attachment* (New York: Basic Books, 1969).
8. Ray L. Birdwhistell, *Kinesics and Context: Essays on Body Motion Communication* (Philadelphia: University of Pennsylvania Press, 1970).
9. Barney G. Glaser and Anselm L. Strauss, *Awareness of Dying* (Chicago: Aldine Publishing Co., 1965), p. 237.
10. Jeanne Quint, *The Nurse and the Dying Patient* (New York: Macmillan, 1967), p. 224.
11. Ibid., p. 106.
12. Anselm L. Strauss and Barney G. Glaser, "Patterns of Dying," in *The Dying Patient*, ed. Orville G. Brim Jr., et al. (New York: Russell Sage Foundation, 1970), pp. 129-55, quoted from p. 130.
13. Glaser and Strauss, *Awareness*.
14. E. Paul Torrance, *Constructive Behavior: Stress, Personality, and Mental Health* (Belmont, Ca.: Wadsworth, 1965).
15. Fred Davis, *Passage Through Crisis* (Indianapolis: Bobbs-Merrill, 1963), p. 52.
16. Joseph M. Natterson and Alfred G. Knudson, "Observations Concerning Fear of Death in Fatally Ill Children and Their Mothers," *Psychosomatic Medicine* 22 (November/December 1960):456-66.
17. Marjorie E. Mitchell, *The Child's Attitude to Death* (New York: Schocken Books, 1967).
18. Erving Goffman, *Asylums: Essays on the Social Situation of Mental Patients and Other Inmates* (Garden City, N.Y.: Doubleday, 1961).
19. Moustakas, *Loneliness*, p. 36.
20. Erik H. Erikson, *Childhood and Society*, 2nd ed. (New York: W. W. Norton, 1963), p. 253.
21. Davis, *Passage*.
22. Ibid.
23. Ibid.
24. Ibid., p. 122.
25. Quint, *The Nurse*, p. 118.
26. Boyd R. McCandless, *Children: Behavior and Development*, 2nd ed. (New York: Holt, Rinehart and Winston, 1967).

27. Torrance, *Constructive Behavior;* see also: Karl Menninger, *Man Against Himself* (New York: Harcourt, Brace and World, 1938).

28. Torrance, *Constructive Behavior.*

29. Bruno Bettelheim, *Love Is Not Enough* (New York: The Free Press, 1950).

30. Robert Kastenbaum, "The Child's Understanding of Death: How Does It Develop?" in *Explaining Death to Children,* ed. Earl A. Grollman (Boston: Beacon Press, 1967), pp. 89-108.

31. Glaser and Strauss, *Awareness.*

32. Jean Piaget, *The Construction of Reality in the Child* (New York: Basic Books, 1954).

33. Jean Piaget, *The Language and Thought of the Child* (New York: Meridian Books, 1955).

34. Ibid., p. 35.

35. Elisabeth Kübler-Ross, "Facing Up to Death," *Today's Education* 6 (January 1972):30-32, quoted from p. 31.

36. Piaget, *Language and Thought,* p. 185.

37. Ibid.

38. Carl R. Rogers, *On Becoming a Person* (Boston: Houghton Mifflin, 1961), p. 331.

39. Renee C. Fox, *Experiment Perilous* (New York: The Free Press, 1959).

40. Lev S. Vygotsky, "Play and Its Role in the Mental Development of the Child," *Soviet Psychology* 5 (Spring 1967):6-18.

41. Piaget, *Construction of Reality.*

42. Erikson, *Childhood,* p. 222.

43. "Dealing with Death: Thanatology Looks at the Doctor and the Dying Patient," *Medical World News* 12 (May 1971):30-36, quoted from p. 35.

44. Virginia Axline, *Play Therapy,* rev. ed. (New York: Ballantine Books, 1969), pp. 187-88.

45. Glaser and Strauss, *Awareness;* see, also: Quint, *The Nurse.*

46. Davis, *Passage.*

47. Elisabeth Kübler-Ross, "The Dying Patient's Point of View," in *The Dying Patient,* ed. Orville G. Brim, Jr., et al. (New York: Russell Sage Foundation, 1970), pp. 156-70, quoted from p. 167.

48. Jean Piaget, *Play, Dreams and Imitation in Childhood* (New York: W. W. Norton, 1962).

49. Lev S. Vygotsky, *Thought and Language* (Cambridge, Ma.: The M.I.T. Press, 1962).

50. Piaget, *Play.*

51. Viktor E. Frankl, *Man's Search for Meaning* (New York: Simon and Schuster, 1962), p. 38.

52. For an overview of available children's books to help in discussing death with children see: Eulalie Steinmetz Ross, "Children's Books Relating to Death: A Discussion," in *Explaining Death to Children,* ed. Earl A. Grollman (Boston: Beacon Press, 1967), pp. 249-71.

53. Piaget, *Construction of Reality.*

54. Warren G. Bennis, "Beyond Bureaucracy," in *Current Perspectives in Social Psychology,* ed. Edwin P. Hollander and Raymond G. Hund (New York: Oxford University Press, 1967), pp. 565-72.

112   DEATH IN THE LIFE OF CHILDREN

55. Louis Schneider and Sverre Lysgaard, "The Deferred Gratification Pattern: A Preliminary Study," *American Sociological Review* 18 (April 1953):142-49, quoted from p. 142.

56. McCandless, *Children*.

57. Davis, *Passage*, p. 75.

58. Theodore S. Sarbin, "The Culture of Poverty," in *Psychological Factors in Poverty*, ed. Vernon L. Allen (Chicago: Markham Publishing Co., 1970), pp. 29-46, quoted from p. 33.

59. Tillich, *Courage*, p. 17.

60. Glaser and Strauss, *Awareness*, p. 38.

61. Richard M. Bailey, "Economic and Social Cost of Death," in *The Dying Patient*, ed. Orville G. Brim, et al. (New York: Russell Sage Foundation, 1970), pp. 275-302, quoted from p. 285.

62. Martha Wolfenstein and Gilbert Kliman, eds., *Children and the Death of a President* (Garden City, N.Y.: Doubleday, 1966), p. 217.

63. Edgar S. Cahn, ed., *Our Brother's Keeper: The Indian in White America* (Washington, D.C.: New Community Press, 1969).

64. Pierre Teilhard de Chardin, *The Phenomenon of Man* (New York: Harper & Row, 1959), p. 312.

65. Erikson, *Childhood*, p. 269.

66. Tillich, *Courage*.

67. Erik H. Erikson, *Insight and Responsibility* (New York: W. W. Norton, 1964), p. 133.

68. Davis, *Passage*, p. 70.

69. Erikson, *Insight*, p. 133.

70. Ernest Becker, *The Birth and Death of Meaning*, 2nd ed. (New York: The Free Press, 1971).

71. Moustakas, *Loneliness*, p. 2.

72. See, for example: John Peterson, "Life With a Dying Child," *The National Observer*, December 16, 1972. For more comprehensive discussions of problems associated with, and suggestions for, management of dying patients and their families, see the following works: Elisabeth Kübler-Ross, *On Death and Dying* (New York: Macmillan, 1969); David Sudnow, *Passing On* (Englewood Cliffs, N.J.: Prentice-Hall, 1967); and Avery D. Weisman, *On Dying and Denying: A Psychiatric Study of Terminality* (New York: Behavioral Publications, 1972).

73. Glaser and Strauss, *Awareness*, p. 78.

74. Peterson, "Dying Child."

75. Davis, *Passage*.

76. Beatrix Cobb, "Psychological Impact of Long Illness and Death of a Child on the Family Circle," *Journal of Pediatrics* 49 (December 1956):746-51.

77. Albert C. Cain, Irene Fast, and Mary E. Erickson, "Children's Disturbed Reactions to the Death of a Sibling," *American Journal of Orthopsychiatry* 34 (July 1964):741-51.

78. James R. Morrissey, "A Note on Interviews with Children Facing Imminent Death," *Social Casework* 44 (June 1963):343-45.

79. Cain, Fast, and Erickson, "Children's Disturbed Reactions."

80. Erikson, *Childhood*.

81. Davis, *Passage*.

82. Ibid., p. 148.

83. Teilhard de Chardin, *Phenomenon.*

Suggested Readings

Axline, Virginia M., *Play Therapy,* rev. ed. (Boston: Houghton Mifflin, 1969; available in paperback as a Ballantine Book).

Although directed at psychologists, psychiatrists, and social case workers, this book may be helpful to parents, teachers, and all who interact with children.

Easson, William M., *The Dying Child* (Springfield, Il.: Charles C Thomas, 1970).

This book is meant for anyone who deals with the dying child or adolescent, including parent, doctor, clergyman, and teacher.

Kübler-Ross, Elisabeth, *On Death and Dying* (New York: Macmillan, 1969).

Written by a pioneer in dealing with terminal patients, this book helps the reader gain insight into the dying patient's point of view.

Moustakas, Clark E., *Loneliness* (Englewood Cliffs, N.J.: Prentice-Hall, 1961).

Loneliness is an absorbing book for all who care to confront the meaning of loneliness and the solitude of suffering.

Quint, Jeanne C., *The Nurse and the Dying Patient* (New York: Macmillan Company, 1967).

Based on a sociological study of life in a large metropolitan hospital this book may be of help to all who interact with dying children and adults.

Rogers, Carl R., *On Becoming a Person* (Boston: Houghton Mifflin, 1961; also available in paperback as a Sentry edition).

Written by a leading psychotherapist this book is a classic in helping people develop closer interpersonal relations.

Teilhard de Chardin, Pierre, *The Phenomenon of Man* (New York: Harper and Row, 1959; available in paperback as a Harper Torchbook).

This book is a unique contribution to the development of a theory of man which unifies science and religion. A help to all who search for a deeper understanding of man's place in the universe.

Verwoerdt, Adriaan, *Communication With the Fatally Ill* (Springfield, Il.: Charles C Thomas, 1966).

Written for physicians from physiological, psychological, and sociological perspectives, this book introduces theoretical considerations only to clarify practical problems. Although slightly more technical than *The Dying Child,* it is one of only a few sources of its kind and may be of much use in understanding the dying child, his parents, and his siblings.

The contents presented in the following chapter are derived from the plenary sessions at a retreat held at Hotel Valley Ho, Scottsdale, Arizona, on May 17-19, 1973. Most of the specific comments and information exchanged there have since been incorporated into the individual chapters in the present volume. The remaining general observations are rearranged and edited into this chapter. For convenience, several headings and specific references have been added by the editor. Although discursive in nature, this format is expected to encourage the reader to become a part of the meeting. Please feel and think along with all the participants.

5

Death in the Life of Children: Discussion

edited by
Kaoru Yamamoto

—One of the difficulties in this area of inquiry (death) is that, although many secondary references are available, most of them seem to be based upon very flimsy, fragmentary, and fugitive (not readily accessible) sources.

—Right. For example, someone makes assumptions to argue his or her case. Then, everyone starts citing the source to treat these untested assumptions as if they were facts. After a while, all sorts of trappings of scholarship are built on this shaky basis. Little critical scrutiny, that is.[1]

—Descriptions of developmental trends in death-related attitudes are a tenuous enterprise when technical requirements in research are examined. Most studies do not give us any indication of representativeness of the results, due to their haphazard sampling procedures.

—Well, I don't know about that. I have some faith in these data because they seem to fit the developmental model of Piaget.

—Wait a minute. That's not much consolation, either. Isn't one of the reasons for the apparent fit between the data and the so-called model actually that we have built our model to fit our data, and then turned around to argue that the data fit the model. That's a circular argument which does not help much.[2]

—With all the secondary information on secondary information, I sometimes wonder what sort of cards we are playing.

—There is, however, a risk in our being hung up on the so-called technical rigor; to miss out on clinical wisdom. These observations may not fit the canons of empirical research, but they tend to be more meaningful to practitioners and professionals-in-preparation, you know.

—We can talk about death in terms of statistics without involving people at all. People's feelings about death, and feelings about facts concerning death.

—Yes, our task is to learn from all sources of knowledge without losing our critical stance and capacity for understanding, I guess.

—I think I can quarrel with that "critical" quality, though. Isn't myth-making what we have always done, at least for five thousand years? Words based upon someone else's words. If one goes after that someone, he simply points to still another party. And you come back to yourself in a full circle. But once we have built a myth, we don't have to worry about the validity of its datum base.

—Myth-making is not always a debilitating function. Without myths, we would be in a terrible mess. A myth serves as a glue to bind people together.

—Well, our scientific discourse is supposed to save us from that, isn't it?

—Scientific discourse itself is a myth, I believe, a special kind of myth, but still a myth.[3]

Things to Believe

—In any case, death remains a touchy area for exploration. Like someone I know who was going to run a study of adolescent girls with behavior problems. She was asked to insert a couple of questions on death, and she was very much concerned about when in her interview she was going to ask these. Worrying about upsetting people, you know.

—She had good reason to worry, because we are not supposed to break down someone's defense (successful ways of coping, so far as the person involved is concerned) unless we can help him to construct a better coping system. Usually we are helpless in building a better mechanism after tearing a person apart. I suppose this particular subject, death, poses a very difficult problem here.

—Not only because it is sensitive, but also because there is so much dogmatism about the subject, it is hard to deal with.

—And because youngsters actually have little contact with death. America is a death-deprived culture now.

—But does it have to be so avoided in conversation? You know, America is said to be death-deprived, but the largest amount of life insurance is sold in this country. So, some aspects of death are quite palpable.

—Life is placed at a premium. Not only insurance, which is, incidentally, not called "death insurance"(!), but medicine. You take certain pills, and you will live.

—Not only that, taking the right kind of medicine will make you younger! An invitation for reversal of life processes.

—That's where we need clear models of life, not false and shallow ones. I remember a statement Erikson made: "healthy children will not fear life if their elders have integrity enough not to fear death."[4]

—I do not think the physical processes themselves are controversial, but the value judgment involved is. It is because children ask questions like, "Where is he (the dead) now?" or "What happens to her now?" That leads us immediately into the realm of religion, and it is so easy for us to step on others' toes in so many different ways. It is therefore understandable for the teacher to be wary of this domain.

—You certainly get into value domains quickly.

—You know, it is in a sense surprising to see the same explanations repeated in the responses of many children, as well as adults, on what is going to happen to us after death. Studies, though most are based on shaky data, give the impression that maybe there has been an increase, say among adolescents, in the belief of reincarnation and the like.

—Just asking them about what they are afraid of most tends to bring out the fear of death. If you allow them to express their feelings freely, it comes out.

—Or, in their plays and dreams. I was a bit surprised to find out the possible significance of the familiar game of peek-a-boo in this matter of life and death. Disappearance and reappearance, and all that.[5]

—What about this death-deprivation you spoke of. Aren't our children bombarded daily with violence and death on TV? Kids are playing war games from early childhood.

—But it's all "out there." No direct involvement and no feelings.

—Particularly in relation to their own death which is, to begin with, an idea foreign to them.

—Conceiving of death, especially one's own, and being concerned about death in general are two different facets of the problem.

—Are there studies on children's concepts of death as a function of their exposure to mass media?

—No, precious few on that *specific* association.[6]

—Speaking of media, most descriptions of death are of the sudden, one-shot variety. Long suffering, prolonged cases of death are seldom depicted.

—That slow, suffering type is very common, though hidden, and it probably affects the life of many people for a sustained period of

time. This is a source of major stress and, if we seriously consider
preparation for death, this reality must be faced and adequately
handled.

—Rare exceptions to the general rule include a film called, *Cries and
Whispers,* depicting the final days of a dying person, and the reactions of her sisters, as well as her servant girl.

—Also a new movie, *Love.* A story of an old woman just fading out;
not suffering too much.

—And that piece, *Brian's Song.* Well it was perhaps much romanticized; remember that story of friendship between two football players, one of whom died?

—Let me raise a question about what represents a mature concept of
death. I am a bit embarrassed to acknowledge a lot of child-like
thinking here. Is the process linear and unidimensional? Aren't there
many different ways of thinking about death all in a mature fashion?

—There is always a danger in age-grading, because we are so inclined
to pigeonhole people. Actually, the range or variation among individuals allegedly at the same developmental stage is fantastically
large, and whenever we refer to a modal trend or modal concept of
death, this fact must be kept in mind. Otherwise, narrow
categorization can be very harmful.

—Or else, many so-called adults are dead! Their thinking does not look
anything like the mature model.

—The other side of the coin is that some children can speak of age-ism,
how they are discriminated against because of their chronological
age, how parents drive them crazy by treating them on age-graded
basis.

—That invites the question of whether what is should indeed be. What
adults do or wish to do should be the goals for children?

—Children's rights are related to that, I guess. And what's meant by
"mature" and "immature"? Some children may be very mature *for
their age,* but they are still immature from the standards applicable to
older children or adults. So, how does one define children's rights?

—A part of the difficulty in making the jump of faith from observations
to curriculum is related to this matter of what we judge to be mature
and healthy in our attitudes toward death at various levels of
development. We do make decisions about this, but we are mostly
unaware of the basis for our decisions and acts.

—Right, any knowledge of human development as such cannot tell us
what to do and what not to do. Ends do not contain in them
specifications for means.

—I think that's why we cannot separate descriptions from value judgments. There is no such thing as value-free, objective descriptions.

—Maybe we have been too preoccupied with *what* children think of death to look into the *how*, the processes of thinking engaged in by children. Levels of thinking in children. Rather than just memorizing and repeating certain responses, being able to offer some justification for one's position. That's probably what we should be asking of children.

—In other words, to have a coherent way to take a look at death, instead of internalizing someone else's interpretations and clinging to them without any thoughtful basis? Why do you believe . . . someone asks, and we should be able to offer some logical basis for our beliefs. Is that what you are saying?

—Aren't you advocating intellectualization here? An allegiance to rationality at the risk of overlooking emotions?

—No, unless I am mistaken, what is being sought here is that, over and beyond merely releasing emotions, we must clarify them and finally accept them. Otherwise, blind emotions will still be running our life. *We* must become the master by rationally examining our feelings. I think that's important.

—Aiming at logical ways of thinking seems to be the best justification for the schools' work on the subject. Also, to counter some upset parents. To help children to develop a more rational way of looking at death.

—I am not sure. I feel it is asking too much of the teacher to defend her efforts on that specific a basis. I think it is justification enough that death *is*, and we cannot ignore it. That broad rationale is more fundamental, isn't it?

Head and Heart

—I believe that basically we have to deal with the matter in total honesty. That is, we have to present all sorts of postulations without defending or criticizing any. Your opinion is as good as mine. And you have to clarify and legitimatize all positions—I guess?

—Yes, after all, teachers don't have a magical key to resolve the mysteries of life.

—But, basically, the responsibility for such resolution rests with the family, I submit.

—I don't think that all explanations are equally good enough. When we inject ourselves in someone else's life, as in teaching, we violate this other person's domain or territory (or whatever the expression may be); we influence each other just by being there, by being alive—so, that part does not bother me. But I cannot go along with the position that one belief is as good as another. What children believe can hurt them. They can still choose and make their decisions out of the available options, but I am not going along with the position of anything goes, hands off.

—Like, up until a certain level of development, children tend to believe that every action of theirs is directly related to the events which (happen to) follow. So, if a child is angry and slams a door, and that night her ailing mother dies, she is likely to deduce a causal explanation for these two and carry around the guilt feelings of "I killed my mother." That can hurt her.

—Wait a minute, I don't think that's what I was trying to say to begin with. Clusters of interpretations associated with religious groups and other philosophical positions are not idiosyncratic (i.e., peculiar to individuals; particularistic) or totally eclectic. They in fact have some legitimacy. The alternative is that you are indeed imposing an interpretation which you yourself find difficult to defend and which has less justification than that which you are attempting to replace.

—I think what he was saying was not a challenge to your position, but something like this. Since you are violating this person's domain, he or she has the right to know where *you* stand, what *you* believe in. You cannot hide behind the stance of neutrality and cannot fake. That's where people get into trouble by telling children what they themselves do not believe in, right?

—That's right, that's where I was. And it seems we were actually agreeing with each other!

—Many children believe that the dead person is merely asleep. The concept of irreversibility does not arrive early. Now, does that hurt them?

—But for some of us, say, those raised in fundamentalist Christian denominations, "reversibility" is a cardinal principle of faith.

—Whether reversible or irreversible, the important thing is to help children come to terms with the reality of death, isn't it? To accept it—that cuts across religions.

—The question I am raising is of the nature of that so-called reality itself. To some, reversibility *is* reality.

—Maybe we are hung up too much on what the teachers say, rather than on what they do in organizing children's experiences and allowing them to express and exchange their own feelings. Instead of saying this is what I as a teacher see as an expert and an authority figure, I should probably be tapping what children see and encourage in its sharing with each other. . . .

—We can give children assurance, the needed sense of security, by being there without, at the same time, pretending to have all the answers ourselves.

—In actuality, how many possible interpretations are there of death? Basically, many common features are found in varied interpretations. Maybe there are not that many toes we can step on after all.

—Probably the teacher's contribution is not in clarifying these interpretations as such, but in clarifying feelings in children.

—That's a good point. That's probably the most "professional" approach. Beyond that, especially in the substantive realm, you can step on others' toes. We are not equipped to resolve all the difficulties which thus arise, and probably no one is.

—On the other hand, it also takes faith to work on feelings. If you believe that clarification of feelings always leads to better situations you go ahead and do so. If you are not so sure about this, chances are you refrain from opening up the Pandora's box.

—Most of us in helping professions have been *taught* that clarification and acceptance of feelings help, and merely believed it without much examination.

—Yes, if you believe in the basic goodness of human beings and in their life-enhancing, self-directing motive, clarification works. If you believe that human beings are essentially evil, dumb, and need external directions, I don't know what clarification as such accomplishes.[7]

—You don't have to go that far, either. From my personal experience, when my wife's father died, my attempts at clarification of her emotional tangles didn't seem to help. As a matter of fact, that almost wrecked our marriage. Wounds opened up, which she had tried to repress. She became unglued after having somehow managed to glue herself together. I was of no help.

—Don't you think, though, that, with ungluing and all, clarification of her feelings would have helped in the long run?

—Perhaps, but "would have" is a tenuous basis to operate from.

—Why did you have to do anything? Ungluing was an integral part of her grieving and reconstructing, I suspect.

—Yes, I am sure of that, but he had to live with her, you see. With strangers, he could have done a beautiful job.

—Maybe my intensive loving relationship interfered. I could have done it with my students, my associates, etc. Maybe I was too close to her.

—That's quite plausible. In general, however, the more teachers know about children in their particular context of life, the better the teacher can understand them and be of assistance to them. Their family, religion, and many other dimensions which make up their life space.

—At the same time, school should be one place where children can separate themselves from all these sources of influence and examine themselves as individuals, shouldn't it?

—Who is *the teacher* when we speak of her or him working with children?

—The teacher may be seen as a person who cares for and comforts pupils, but the teacher can also be seen as someone with a major intent to cause children to learn.

—I don't follow you.

—Let me take a concrete example. In *Man: A Course of Study*,[8] one of the first things a teacher does is to show children a life rope, a piece of string, and ask them to put down on a sheet of paper significant events in their life. So, they ask, "You mean what we have done?," "What we are going to do?," and so forth. It's very ambiguous. Now, one of the things many children do is to omit death, the end of this string. But that is crucial, because the very next activity is to study life cycles and compare them among different animals and human beings. Salmons have generations, but theirs are different than ours.

—What age group are you talking about?

—Fifth graders, well, fourth through sixth. Many student teachers also want to omit that death end of the string. Actually, the intent of the teacher ought to be to teach pupils that death is a part of life. The substantive side of the teacher's activities should not be overlooked in our emphasis upon caring and comforting.

—Some states do not allow teachers to use that program of study. Besides, there are people who object to certain segments of the curriculum.

—Like Emerson's journal, in which he describes his life with Eskimos? An episode there tells of these people's leaving a grandma on ice to die.

—To understand other cultures, one must study their handling of birth, other critical experiences, death, and contingent rites of passage. That helps tremendously in understanding our own culture, don't you think? Substantively, as well as emotionally.

—Another episode involves hunting of animals. Many adults who first see the film react like children do. They don't like the bloody scenes, blood spewing out of caribous they killed, or walruses on ice.

—There is an educational folklore which says that the teacher's job is to hold children's hands, to be a nice person, to love. That's true, that's overriding. But there is this other aspect too. The teacher must induce learning in the pupils, learning not only about themselves, but also learning about things outside of themselves.

—It must be mentioned, however, that many teachers, not to speak of parents, object to curricular materials which encourage such approaches, and stick to good old textbooks.

—Many of them would gladly restrict their activities to conveying the so-called facts, nothing beyond that.

—Yes, some balance should be struck, granted. My point is that death is not merely a personal question but also an instructional question. When Mary's father died, wonder how Mary felt?—that's an instructional question.

—To encourage children to clarify and examine feelings in such a context is an instructional challenge. We must be concerned not only with what comes into the classroom, but also with what teachers do in it. Or, when ancient Greeks are studied, say in the second grade, how did they live, we ask, and one of the revealing facets of their culture, any culture, is their burial practice.

—In teaching, we should be careful about drumming up the experience of death into something sinister and monstrous by paying too much attention to the traumatic aspects when our overall purpose is to treat death as a natural part of life.

—You remember, in Mark Twain's story, Tom's coming back to watch his own funeral? In all the classes I have come across in which this anecdote is discussed, the focus seems always on the comic side of the experience. Never Twain's attitude about religion, never feelings of the people in mourning, never the boy's own conflicting emotions . . . teachers, it seems, never handle the total implications of this death. These, however, allow us to study death as a natural part of life.

—Incidentally, in Protestant and Catholic churches primarily, there has been a strong movement toward viewing death as a natural event, rather than an unnatural event. Death education has been receiving much emphasis in institutional religion.[9]

—The kind of education we are interested in providing is not ideas only but things at the feeling level. To introduce more humaneness into education in general. To influence our orientation to life itself.

For the Living

—Speaking of death education, there are two facets to the story. We can give our teachers, nurses, ministers, etc., all the nice curricular materials and stuff with which to work with their clients. But when, specifically, are we to work with these professionals-to-be to clarify their own feelings? Young adults and adolescents need to work through their own feelings before working with clients.

—The sooner in the preparation program for professionals, the better. Not necessarily to have the right answer at the right time, but to be prepared, to be able to think about it before being pushed precipitously to face the experience.

—Thinking per se may not be that great, though. I have in mind this tendency for denial. Many have some ideas about death, but live all their life and eventually die without ever facing up to death. For teachers to be of help to children, therefore, it may be necessary to involve them in some actual death experiences. What I am talking about is the difference between intellectual comprehension and total understanding with emotions and everything.

—But the thing of it is that death is a low base rate (frequency of occurrence) experience in a typical teacher's life. Or a dentist's or a social worker's. Some professionals will live all their professional life without coming face to face with their client's death. Therefore, it may not make much sense to build a whole curriculum to clarify our feelings about death itself. It will be better if this is couched in a larger scheme of clarification of feelings about ourselves in all their complex aspects. Another hopeful means may be simulation exercises, in which we simulate our acts in encounters with death.

—In my student teaching experience, one of the older children in the adjacent room threw a dead bird into my room to stir up quite a commotion. Many pupils were disturbed, others gave all sorts of explanations, and one of the girls had been so secluded as to be horrified, not to know what to do, started crying, and all that. My concern was not to allow a panic to set in and not to confuse them further by injecting my own interpretations.

—That is a crisis situation which demands quick thinking and action.

—What, by the way, did you do with that bird?

—We buried it.

—Did you have a funeral ceremony?

—Yes, someone suggested saying a few words over the grave. Another said to put up a cross. Anything kids suggested was O.K. by me.

—What did you say?

—Well, some neutral, nice thing or two! But I heard from a couple of disturbed mothers next day anyway.

—Perhaps the important thing here is that children had the ceremony whatever it was. Funeral was for the children, not for the bird.

—I have very ambivalent feelings, primarily negative, about anthropomorphism seen in, say, a pet's grave and the like. Animals are not humans, and birds don't bury birds. As a sensitive teacher, if children want to bury a bird, I may feel that helps them, but, on the other hand, that may simply obscure the critical distinction between human beings and other animals.

—The important thing is that the burial and funeral were for the children, not for the bird, isn't it? It served as a release. It's a sort of role playing, and even using toys would help.

—I understand that, but this role playing is different. You see, little girls play mom by dressing up in her clothes and shoes, but they have seen mother dress up. In this case, however, they have never seen a funeral.

—But how do you explain that to five year olds? We bury humans in the ground, but throw cats and birds in a garbage can?

—I had an experience when I was babysitting for a family that was out of town. Their dog died. According to the health department, there was an ordinance to the effect that the body had to be put in a box and placed on a certain spot on the curb to be picked up by city personnel. Now, the children, aged three, seven, and nine, were very distressed to learn they could not bury the dog. So, I put the body in a box as specified, but took off the dog's collar and buried it. The children were satisfied with that. They showed a definite need to do something.

—One time I buried my own pet. I had been feeling very sad, but it felt so good to put the spade in the ground that, by the time I put dirt on top of the body, I came to terms with myself. I thought then that it must be much easier for us to handle our feelings if families could, like in olden days, go out, dig holes, and bury the dead by themselves.

—To feel spent, the physical exhaustion itself, may have that therapeutic effect, you know.

—It gives me a strange feeling to see the memorial ground for pets down the street spruced up with a tiny ambulance and all that, or to hear of those Hollywood personalities sending their dogs and cats to psychiatrists. But, when you have a pet in the home, it becomes like a member of the family.

—Just burying it, and burying it with ritual, gives a child a sense of completion, I guess. Now the child can see the pet resting at peace, instead of lying around out there.

—I have been thinking. There is a difference between burying a pet and burying a person, a friend, a relative, or anyone else. In the case of a pet, you feel sort of guilty, you had better do something, and a burial gives you a sense of satisfaction—now you have done it! In the case of people, burial is expected and handled by specialists. So, burying may not offer the same kind of satisfaction.

—Remember that 75 percent of all funerals nowadays are held in mortuaries, nowhere else. Hardly ever at home, even though many (American) Indians prefer funerals at home.

—In our fairly new congregation, a committee drew up a rule book governing the use of the chapel for this or that purpose—marriage, recreation, community sing, or what have you. Interestingly, they forgot to mention anything at all about funerals!

—We seldom have a child younger than ten being brought to a funeral at the mortuary. Participation in a funeral in all its aspects is rarer than we think among children.

—What about a child's funeral? Do the child's friends come?

—It depends upon the child's parents. Some teachers have brought their class, but most won't. Some let the classmates write a letter, and most write to the dead child, rather than to the parents. Most teachers seem to remove the child's desk in the room very quickly.

—So far as teachers are concerned, they try not to show any reactions, any emotions, to all these experiences. The school behaves as if there were no death.

—I have never thought of the fact that you mentioned: birds don't bury birds. Burial, certainly funeral itself, seems to be a very peculiarly human experience, doesn't it?

—Making a will, making arrangements for one's funeral and burial, and all those things—these are not inconsequential in understanding death in America. A cultural historian's perspective, so to speak. Where one wants to die, in Texas, Indiana, or Paris, is of much significance in his or her life.

—There are many cases in which people specified before their death the format and contents of their own funeral as a joyful celebration. In plain language, to boot.

—What about hippies?

—Many of them have brought up new ways to say goodbye. Like, one group sent flowers in the shape of a motorcycle. That was their way of saying, "Well, George, you left us, but we loved you."

—Children tend to be fascinated by a cemetery, though perhaps a bit scared. That's a part of the child's conception of death. It used to be there were many tombstones, nowadays there are just small plaques. Wonder whether children's reactions are becoming different.

—That's a meaningful tradition, you know. Perhaps of less significance nowadays, but our language still carries many expressions with flavors from the yore.

—I understand eulogies have changed over years. Epitaphs on the gravestones. There are some fascinating accounts of these, and their possible implications.[10]

—Say, those children of yours saw the dead bird in its actual appearance, unlike our prettied-up corpses, didn't they? I have been a volunteer aide in an emergency room, and exposure there to actual dead bodies was a shocking thing to anyone who had seen only the corpses in a casket. I am not sure, though, whether young children should be exposed to corpses.

—Some authorities are emphatic about not showing children corpses. Others disagree.

—I have heard that there are cases in which schizophrenia resulted from children's seeing corpses.

—No, wait a minute, that's a careless way to look at the relationship. That one thing followed another does not mean the first was the cause of the second. Like, in schizophrenics, the memory functions are known to be slanted, and they may recall the experience with the corpse particularly vividly. The causal connection, if any at all, may run opposite to the easy association, you know. Chances are that seeing a corpse did not make the person schizophrenic. The experience may have accentuated or brought to surface an already existing tendency to schizophrenic responses.

—Nowadays even some hospitals don't encourage next of kin to come confirm the fact of death in the patient's room. The body directly goes to a mortuary, and family members do not have, or won't opt for, an opportunity to establish the reality.

—Of course, letting family members see the body, often grossly mutilated, may not help them at all. Pointless, often.

—But that sense of closure or completion is important. Use of cosmetics on the corpse is not critical. What is important is to confirm that the person is dead by seeing the body. When such confirmation is not possible, like a son who was mutilated in Vietnam or missing in action, emotional difficulties easily arise.

—What bothers me is to know what body of knowledge we refer people to, when we make these pronouncements and recommendations. I don't think there is any consistent body of knowledge.

—Yes, I see your point. Under certain circumstances, why not this? But, then, why this?

—The same comments apply to children's attendance at a funeral.

—It is obvious that we should refrain from saying dogmatically what all children should do or should not do. What works best for one child may not work at all for another. Family contexts, religion, ethnic background, and other combinations rule out the possibility of an overall, rigid rule.

—I believe it is important for us to deal with our personal feelings through rituals and other means. However, experiencing is not enough—we must understand these feelings. There are many experiences in school that are not productive in this sense. In other words, how to make a meaning out of such words as funeral, burial, or what have you. Burying a pet may serve to handle the feelings of grief immediately, but for teachers to persist at that level would be unproductive for educational purposes.

—You are concerned with putting an instructional dimension on top of, shall we say, the emotional dimension?

—Right, I would like to have more to our understanding of grief situation than burying the body and forgetting it. The intellectual side, if you will. What would a teacher do once it has been buried?

—Creating a ritual itself serves some of that intellectual function, I suspect.

—And having some project to occupy oneself, having something to do, is important in sustaining us in crisis, as witnessed by people who went through and survived concentration camps, prison camps, and similar experiences. Maybe rituals are helpful in this sense also.

—When the time comes for me to bury my parents, I hope I have the strength to serve as one of the pall bearers. To do something in that situation will help me integrate my thought, feelings, and action, I believe.

—Yes, that's true too for dying patients just lying there, passively waiting their final moment. If they can be helped to take a stand or to do something, that final life task itself would make an enormous difference in giving meaning to their life.

—Meaningfulness of what we are doing, and meaningfulness of life, this we cannot impose upon anyone else. This is a decision each person has to make for himself, no one can make it for him. Another thing is that, even in a most restricted context such as concentration camp or terminal illness, a person can still make a decision and face the consequences. That's what freedom is about.

To Lose a Loved One

Editor's note: *At this point, the retreat participants listened to Julie's (pseudonym) taped account, described in the Prologue. The ensuing* *discussion is subsumed in this section. Before reading on, you may wish to refresh your memory by referring back to pages 3-8.*

—Actually, much of Julie's pain stemmed from the conflicts in the family, not from the demise of her sister, right?

—My first association with a similar case was a mother who was hospitalized for severe depression after the death of her child. She made a few attempts at killing herself, and so forth. Previous to that, she spent an excessive amount of time in the hospital. She really took care of the child. Now what was behind all this was a serious marital conflict. Marriage was on the rocks, and finally when the child was diagnosed as suffering from leukemia, she expended these extreme efforts. On the surface, she was a grieving mother, but in actuality this was a somewhat unrealistic effort on her part to resolve the difficulty. The tension was certainly aggravated by her child's illness, but it was not brought on by that.

—What are you saying? These situations create additional stress on an already existing conflict?[11]

—Yes, that, and also that an excessive devotion on the part of a parent or anyone else may signal something else.

—Death may be used as a dumping ground for marital troubles, right?

—To change the subject a little, Anna Freud was heard describing a change in her interpretation of death as a crisis in a child's life. Since the whole family context must be taken into consideration, she now seems to feel that perhaps death of a parent in childhood is less damaging, psychiatrically speaking, than in adolescence when youngsters are striving to gain independence, trying to break away from parents. Now, if a young child loses a parent, he or she may have other chances, so to speak, to mend the loss, but an adolescent will not have that opportunity again and may suffer from a sense of guilt for a long time.

—Yes, she may be right. I have an artist friend who ran away from home at adolescence to be independent, and then her father died soon afterward. This has left a bitter taste in her, and she has never quit talking about that.

—That also relates to Julie. At the time she was thirteen, when her peer relations were pushing her toward independence, she had a mother who was overprotecting her.

—Was Julie embarrassed to tell about all the family squabbles, and so forth?

—No, I don't think so. She was home over the weekend and was under no pressure. She told us in small group (class) situations some of the same.

—Is she living at home?

—She is in a residence hall; in a teacher education curriculum.

—Maybe, the marriage was not on such a shaky ground. Death was certainly a traumatic experience, but they managed to stay together.

—There is no marriage on such a solid ground to begin with. It has to adjust to whatever comes along and remain flexible.

—What about the picture? Of June in her casket, I mean.

—I think the picture should not have been taken.

—Why? So long as the picture was there, Julie had a choice to look at it or not to look at it.

—That was not the motivation for picture-taking, though.

—I wonder why she did not wish to see it.

—Of course, leukemia is not a particularly pleasant condition to look at.

—Could have been another thing too. If Julie was placing herself in the role of a mother figure, looking at the picture might be too punishing.

—I think her explanation was understandable—not to remember her sister in an ugly light, but as a healthy, beautiful child.

—I doubt if anything could have been more horrifying to her than taking a look at the last picture of her sister.

—Have any functions been served in her not participating in the funeral?

—When we were talking about the importance of rituals. . . . I lost my father at the same age as she did, you know, but rituals did not help me, and it took a long time before I actually faced the reality. Maybe rituals help. . . .

—Not someone else's, though. To be of assistance, rituals must have personal significance. Not the *ritualistic* rituals, if you know what I mean. You must *actively* take part in it, even create it, to answer *your* needs. Not the usual, spectator kind.

—Seeing that movie was a good catharsis. She could cry and release her emotions because it touched her, after all these years, with its secret significance. Different experiences, pictures, books, or what have you, serve this purpose of catharsis.

—The movie she went to see, *Gone with the Wind,* seemed particularly significant. Nine years or eight years later, you know.

—Death remains a shadow over one's life in any case.

—One of my friends fell apart seeing that same movie and kept on saying that it's too sad, too sad, with all those deaths and everything. I wonder what that kind of person does in actual situations? Well, at least, the exposure is good.

—Movies or books allow you some distance, a margin of safety; they allow you to respond a bit more freely than in actual experiences, I suppose.

—Do you suppose Julie was partially resentful of the amount of grief her parents were showing when she was the one who should be rightfully grieving, more than the parents I mean, due to her very close relation with June in a maternal role?

—It doesn't mean she actually took over the mother role, does it? The point is what she felt. Not the fact whether she was taking over the mother role, but if she had felt close, then some resentment may have been there.

—She could still grieve for her sister as a sibling, but resent the parental inattention.

—I thought it interesting to note that she said something like, "We must do something," "We are still here," etc. Almost saying, "Hey, we are here! Don't forget us!"

—When a child is dying from a protracted illness, and this is understandable, parents tend to become preoccupied with that particular child and to neglect others.

—In our work, we inquire about the home situation in these cases to make sure that such negligence is not happening.

—The fact that this was a nuclear family without grandparents living with them may have added to the difficulty.

—And after the child's death, it does not help to have parents blaming themselves and fighting with each other. That shatters the tenuous sense of security for the remaining children.

—Well, to change the stream of thought a little, we have in our church a former Vietnam prisoner of war. When we talk about something, anything, in his company, we realize that, for seven years, he doesn't have any recollections of what we are talking about. We wish to include him in our interaction, but we feel ill at ease because of this awareness. In a sense it's similar to a person whose loved one died. We want to say something, but we don't know what or how.

—You don't know where to step because you don't want to hurt the person further, I guess.

—Each person has to work his grief out by himself.

—But we don't have to keep on re-inventing the wheel!

—I agree that there is this thing in education and culture that people are supposed to resolve their own problem by themselves. But, if you fellows build instructional materials with all sorts of support systems, so as to, well, structure grieving for others, what would that do to the bereaved pupils and teachers, those people most directly involved?

—The "support systems" in that context may be too formal to be of much use in actual encounters with death. The same thing as the ritualistic rituals mentioned earlier.

—There was a discussion at a conference about returning Vietnam veterans who essentially indicated that they welcome psychiatric and other help, but they will seek it on their own terms when they need it. Not when we *impose* our goodwill upon them.

—Then there is the matter of helpers. Kübler-Ross told us at one of her conferences that the most effective helpers she has found in working with the dying have been people from, say, black communities, who experienced death either as a child or in adolescence, or who, in any case, had had familiarities with loss. She says their ways of dealing with death are different. Wonder what their different tactics are.

—That's interesting. There has been a program we are now looking into; the widow-to-widow program, because it appears much easier for a widow to talk with another widow than anyone else. Maybe because of the common experience, they can share feelings more easily.[12]

—Let me bring up a point here. In our discourse this evening, we again used the word, "loss." We are almost afraid to use the direct expression, "death," which may stand for low grief situations. The death of her sister was a "loss" to this girl, Julie. The image of "high grief" death and that of "low grief" death may be significantly different—our language reflects this difference. I don't think we show the same reaction to thousands of, say, French soldiers who lost their lives in the war. A boy down the street who died in the Battle of the Bulge causes this sense of "loss," but not those thousands.

—Words we use help differentiate some of the intense feelings we have. Some of the variance in situations, levels of intensity of grief, for instance, may be partially explained by such discrimination.

—We use many expressions: left, gone away, passed away, passed on, went away, gone beyond. If we aren't calling a spade a spade, haven't morticians encouraged this trend?

—Well, maybe, but the use of such euphemisms may serve to avoid another round of crying and fighting, as seen in Julie's experience. That helps children under such circumstances.

—There is another thing which seems to have received little attention so far. That is the case, for example, of Julie's parents being led around by the nose by a quack. This is a serious issue especially in cases of terminal illnesses. Many families squander their resources in these hopeless pursuits, resources which can be used for more constructive purposes.

—That may serve for assuaging some of their guilt feelings, though, by allowing them to say that they have tried everything which could have been done.

—I remember a patient with a brain tumor. My assignment was to see that the family resources were preserved by letting them accept the terminality of his condition.

—In any event, let's remember that there is this time dimension to death. It's not a "done with and that's it" kind of thing. It continues to be interpreted and experienced by the bereaved.[13]

—That's an important point to make. Death is not something for us to accept just like that. It has to be assimilated in relation to something or someone.

—That may be critical in children. They do not have much experience to relate their reaction to. We must be there to facilitate this process.

—This idea of assimilation is important, I think. Death has to be assimilated by each person so that he may then live his life, write his own story, so to speak, and die his own death.

To Care and Grieve

—What about a person who falls apart? Parents who lost a child, for instance? What are we to do when they fall apart?

—Let the parents fall apart. Let them express their grief. I often send children out and let parents show their feelings without much restraint.

—People don't like to see expressions of sorrow in public. We would rather give them sedatives and quiet them down.

—But why remove their other children from them? Why not let them share the sorrow?

—Because adults often need to be alone to express their grief. Frequently, a man cries in front of me, a nurse. He won't cry in front of his child or his wife.

—I tend to feel that that's one of the reasons why the child grows up to be an adult who won't and cannot express his emotions more openly and freely.

—That may be so, that may be our cultural pattern—men don't cry, and all that.

—I had an experience with my daughter and her pets. A dog and a cat joined our family at about the same time, and one (the cat) died at Thanksgiving time one year and the other died at about the same time the next year. Both were at the veterinarian's, and she did not want a funeral for them. The grief she expressed at the death of the cat, her pet of eight years, was the most difficult experience for her to handle up to that time, and also the most significant learning experience at the same time. She had been the only child, and the anger she felt for that cat for leaving her, and the guilt she felt for not having visited the cat at the hospital, neglecting her, or not feeding her properly were very intense. But she did not want a funeral. Nor did she want to replace the cat immediately. She did, oh, about six months later. It took her that long to come to terms with the fact of death and her emotions about it, I guess.

—Under the same circumstances, I think I would not have gone to the vet's either to claim the body to bury it. The cat was there and done with. That's that. I would have hated to reinitiate my involvement with the cat. If it had died at home, my reaction might have been different.

—The feelings in these situations can be very intense, indeed. I once had a counseling relationship with a lady whose husband had been a pharmacist. When she lost her canary, which was the only living thing in the house then, her grief was such that she had to remove herself from the house to work through her emotion. She took a two-week vacation for that purpose.

—Was that a case of delayed grief for her husband?

—Well, perhaps so.

—It may not take another living being to elicit that sort of reaction. I knew of a boy whose father was killed in Vietnam. He did not believe the fact of his father's death and had much difficulty in resolving his feelings. What worked for him, surprisingly, was that story, "A Red Balloon." In one section of the book, a group of bad boys throw stones at the balloon and the story says, "Then, Pascal's balloon was lying on the ground dead, and he felt very sad," or something like that. This helped the boy to relate to the death of his father.

—We, teachers, must be careful here in not going overboard in passive listening and so forth. In this highly mobile society with small nuclear families, it may be important for us to be equally concerned with helping children to construct some alternative means for dealing with their grief. These may be rituals, replacements, or what have you. I once read a story called, I guess, "Growing Time," in which a pet dog dies and the parents bring home a puppy for the child. The idea conveyed was that life goes on, carried by this puppy from the one which died. Would this kind of thing be considered by teachers?

—In the case of my daughter, she and I spent a lot of time discussing the death of that cat. The important thing appears to be to give children a sufficient amount of time to complete their grief work before moving onto reconstruction.

—One of my neighbors lost her husband in an accident, and we wanted to convey our sense of sorrow to the family. But the five year old girl did not seem to grasp the situation and smiled at me as usual, and all that. What am I to do? To remind her of the reality, or to play along as if nothing had happened?

—We tend to get hung up on *what* we are going to say. The important thing is not what but how, I believe. Attitudes, or what you bring to that situation as a person—that's critical. The fact of your being there when needed matters. You cannot really rehearse what to say or do. It has to come from the whole being of you in the particular context.

—What about organ banking and transplanting? I know of a mother whose child, upon death, gave her kidney to another lady. The mother sends a card to the lady every year on the child's birthday. This may be a little pathological, but that's one way to continue believing in the everlasting life of her child.

—It's rather unusual for a hospital to release the name of the recipient of an organ, though.

—Did you read about the mother who asked doctors to pull that machine off to let her child die rather than being kept "alive" on the strength of the machine? That involves a high drama with emotions and everything.

—Well, that happens everyday in hospitals. Wonder why that particular incident got so much attention.

—The moral question of giving someone, say, ten more days of life when the quality of that life is minimal is a difficult one to resolve.

—Then there is also the matter of selection of patients for a limited number of machines for intensive care.

—Some teaching hospitals seem to regard patients as a tool for teaching, rather than as human beings.

—Hold it, we may be too harsh on the medical profession here. They are dealing with this matter of life and death every day, and they must make more decisions, command decisions at that. And you and I know that the more command decisions you must make, the more mistakes you are prone to commit. Many of them are struggling mighty hard, and credit should be given them.

—The same sort of thing should be said about morticians. Many funeral directors work hard to be of assistance to the mourning family, but they also receive much criticism.

—It is easy for us to drop in the trap of paying attention to some unusual, specific instances and forget about the overall trend.[14]

—That's a good point. On that score, what's the new trend in the so-called "funeral industry"? (An unfortunate, though revealing, expression, I must say.)

—We have started thinking that the funeral should not be the end of our service to families. On the contrary, we think of the funeral as the starting point, to be followed up in our helping attempts afterwards in their mourning and reconstruction periods. As you know, that's actually when they need support, probably more than during the period immediately following a crisis. Say, about a month later and on.

—Ministers are in a strategic position in such efforts, are they not?

—But at least a half of the funerals we conduct are for families not affiliated with churches. No support comes from them, not from community, not from doctors; then where does the support come from? We are not trying to intrude into some other professionals' work area, but just to complement their service where it is lacking.

—But funeral directors may not be the best person to do it. Like, when my father died when I was thirteen, the funeral director came over to put his hand on my shoulder to say, "I am so terribly sorry." I thought to myself, "For crying out loud, what do you know about me? You didn't know my dad, you did not know the family, you did not know anything!" I resented it as a superficial gesture, trying to express something which he probably didn't feel.

—But that could have been his way. What can a person say under such circumstances?

—Yes, that's a point. What can anyone say in that sort of situation?

—What does the class say to the parent? What does a teacher say?

—Funeral directors are in the same position as doctors here. You are giving service for which you charge a fee. In a sense, making money out of someone's misery—that may be the thing which people resent.

—I think that's one of the reasons why we must be careful in expressing our sentiments to someone whose life we don't know too well.

—That's where the importance of being "tuned in" to other people's feelings comes in; of getting the "vibes" (vibrations), so as not to end up in some cross-communications. It takes a sensitive teacher to stay tuned in, rather than merely idea-oriented.[15]

—Well, the focus here should be on the "vibes" rather than on the "words," right? Not any superficial conversation, but some genuine expression of emotions.

—What we are really talking about is nonverbal communication which comes through loud and clear in you and your acts. Don't contradict it with your words to cause mixed messages to confuse children.

—Children must have someone who can feel *with* them. Talking with someone helps, if the person is tuned in. If children repress all their feelings without expressing them in some fashion, it is indeed dangerous.

—In various ways, it seems to me, we are saying that you don't treat death problems unless in the total context of the particular child's life, that is to say, unless on a broader relationship basis. Otherwise, teachers and others may be simply interfering with someone's life in such a shallow way as to harm the person, rather than help the person.

—Well, let's get back to this matter of grieving—grieving is good and necessary, and so on. Most of us do not grieve for those children dying in Vietnam, Africa, or Pakistan, or for the numerous daily deaths on our highways. These are apparently low grief situations. But how do we deal with them in a responsible fashion?

—I don't know how to handle that.

—I don't, either. I know we should grieve for the lives lost, but we don't.

—Several years ago, for example, the whole nation came to a standstill to watch and experience the deaths of two past presidents (Truman and Johnson). Families must have talked about death and life, and children must have experienced something.

—In one of our classrooms, pupils carried another pupil around to simulate a funeral—the teacher didn't do anything to take advantage of this, though.

—I would say that, in the age in which we live with all the carnage on the highway, homicides, wars, etc., we cannot possibly respond in a high grief manner, in the same fashion as to the loss of significant others. Intellectually, I ask myself, "What kind of human being are you?," but I cannot be torn up by every death I read about and encounter. The question is how to deal with this dilemma humanely and sanely.

—In school we don't study about high grief deaths. In these more common, low grief situations, on the other hand, we may not feel deeply enough to move us to some constructive action. We should get upset and angry, but nonpersonal deaths do not arouse us.

—I have to make efforts to think about individuals involved before I can be moved in these cases. The fact that I must force myself in itself tells something. I commute on freeways and see several accidents everyday. The first one I come across I say to myself, "Oh, how awful!" By the time the fifth or sixth one comes into my view, I am just driving by, saying things like, "Well, there is another one." I am counting off numbers, instead of being personally affected. By then, I am saturated.

—In the thirties, there was a famous picture of a crying Chinese baby left on railroad tracks in Canton, or wherever that was. That picture always tears me up. It evokes all sorts of things in me, and I am moved by it far more than most anything I have seen or heard. Grief?—I am not sure; anger?—yes.

—And a certain amount of guilt for not doing anything or being unable to do anything?

—Aren't we getting into the matter of mere semantics, here?

—Well, I tell you, semantics here makes a real difference. To sweep all this under the rug, without differentiating among these feelings, is to lose the richness and dimensions which make meaning for life.

—These deaths range far and wide, covering all kinds. With some, I can become reconciled, like the death of my father. But with others, like napalm bombing, especially when children are involved, I cannot. I have never discussed things like the latter with my class, because I don't know how to handle them.

—When I contrast my life with my father's, and my father's life with that of my grandfather's, a question comes to my mind. Though mortality rates were much higher in those early days, how much death did they really have to confront in their life time? Theirs were very personal dealings with deaths in their immediate families. Until some of them went overseas in World War I, not many of them faced a large-scale death situation with which we are familiar. In our life time, in contrast, we hear of six million Jews exterminated in concentration camps, plus all the casualties in the Second World War, Korean War, Vietnam, highway accidents, and so on, and so forth. We are surrounded by people, and by death. All of a sudden, I feel overwhelmed, we are not deprived of death at all. Therefore, I have to put it off and limit my awareness to the ones close to me. I say, "Sorry, but I cannot take this all." It sounds superficial and hypocritical, but I cannot do otherwise.

—You are honest. It is a protective response.

—When we say "sorry," we are also saying sorry for ourselves.

—Or that we understand. We know the shoes you are in.

—In a similar vein, many clinicians have developed a style of handling patients, a set of bedside manners, which is often called callous. Actually, it is their defense to protect themselves. In order to survive in that kind of setting and cope with the immense stress, doctors and nurses need that type of response. Not that the specific modes of response so developed have necessarily salutary consequences.[16]

Being Helpful

—Institutions are primarily self-serving. In a sense, hospitals are there for communion of doctors, nurses, and other medical personnel. In mental hospitals, for instance, if you had good patients, cooperative, helpful, and not too crazy, you let them do all the work; bad patients, on the other hand, run you out of business. So you train good patients for your own sake, and keep them there. The same thing goes for prisons, schools, or what have you.[17] Now, this we have to counteract and counteract systematically. We have to remind ourselves constantly that, left alone, institutions tend to serve themselves by exploiting their clients. This is a real danger.

—In my work, I have been handling something like thirty-five deaths a year, either dying in the emergency room or dead on arrival. To give help to the family and, at the same time, not to be broken up myself, I try to imagine myself to be one of the hundred and thousands of people the deceased might have known and who might have loved him or her. I must go out there to work with the family and, in this manner, I can feel a bit of the sense of loss they are feeling and can probably be of better assistance.

—Attitude of indifference is far more harmful, so far as a helping person is concerned, than a blundering attempt. Doing something which may bring out some pains and disturbance is far better than not caring at all.

—Remember that doing nothing is itself a decision—it is a form of action.

—Anything a person does, or does not do, counts in that sense.

—A teacher can provide materials on death, academic sort of, which is justified in the curriculum. Should she also provide emotional support on a personal basis? Can she really go both ways?

—In the life of a teacher, it has to be both ways. For example, dealing with children whose classmate has died—it must be both ways—that's the reality.

—But, if a child doesn't die *in* the classroom, aren't we teachers taking on another responsibility here to prepare the rest of the group, a responsibility which they should not perhaps assume? *In* the classroom, we have to respond, yes. Are we to take on the added responsibility of setting up a curriculum of death education for all cases?

—The important thing about being a teacher is being ready, able, and willing to handle all fields where one can be of help, involving children, parents, etc. I don't think everyone can do that to the same degree, though.

—And I don't believe that setting up a formal curriculum that is narrowly focussed on death as such is the answer. By institutionalizing the procedure, we are likely to miss out on the most important part of such an *education*. Teaching, here more than anywhere else, must be done in context and spirit, through personal caring and modeling. This is not something to be handed out in small, convenient packages or units from 9 a.m. to 10 a.m., and then be dropped for the rest of the day. It cannot be adequately handled by adults who are tired of living, but afraid of dying, on a part-time basis! This involves the teacher as a whole being.

—How school acts here is probably a function of what kind of support the society gives. Teachers may be open for exploration of this subject, but without a strong support, they cannot do it alone. The total milieu or atmosphere counts.

—Like them or not, there are some minicourses on death available.[18] Some systems have adopted them for junior high, but others have had trouble with the board.

—There are some new nursery programs intending to prepare young children for death with specially prepared books, and other materials.[19]

—Of course, we may come to depend too heavily upon the formal institutions of school. Just like riding academies, dancing schools, so on, and so forth, ad infinitum. That's a danger we have to watch out for.

—There have also been some serious general discussion on death education as preparation for life.[20]

—That's a good concept—to prepare for life by examining death.

—Well, this book is an example of that, I think. In a sense, the whole thing presents an exercise in anticipatory grief.

—It is also a reminder, I hope, that life is not merely life after death. Life is also for here and now.

—What about the issue of self-destruction, particularly suicide? Some recent sources say that more than 25,000 people take their lives each year in the United States, and that 0.5 to 3 percent of these are less than twenty years old.[21] The figures do not include those classified as accidental death.

—The threat seems to be growing in the younger population, at least attempts at suicide, under the influence perhaps of drugs.

—Suicide as another anger reaction may be a defensible way to approach this. A means to get back at parents?

—When, for instance, a boy kills himself, would the family's reaction to the experience be different than that to other kinds of death?

—Perhaps more guilt feelings?

—I don't agree with interpreting all suicides as an anger reaction, nor do I believe that anyone who commits suicide is by definition unstable, mentally ill, or what. Some suicides are perfectly rational, I think.

—But, in children, couldn't we say that some sort of emotional disturbance is there as a precedent?

—Not necessarily. Uniform cause-effect correspondence may not be presumed.

—I had a teacher, a former student of mine, who was teaching in high school. On one Friday afternoon, a child handed over a note to her saying that he had had it, he was going to kill himself over the weekend. The teacher couldn't find any help from the principal, other teachers, and counselor; so she came back all the way to my office.

—In our school also, a child left that type of note in a place clearly visible to his teacher, and that caused much anguish in teachers.

—What can you do in those situations?

—As mentioned before, ignoring the cry for help may be far worse than trying to be of assistance in no matter how unskillful ways.

—It is so easy to overlook that sort of cry, though. Maybe insensitivity is cultural?[22]

—Distress signals should not be ignored, even though there may be many false ones. Families should be informed of such potentially self-destructive children. That is basically a family problem in my judgment.

—From the teacher's viewpoint, however, there is a logistics problem. She is there to work with all the children, twenty-five, thirty-five, or fifty of them, and she must balance that fundamental responsibility with preoccupation with a single child.

—And it may be akin to being concerned *after* the horse has left the barn. Teachers' unique contribution is in the preventive area, not in the crisis-intervention or remedial area.

—Another thing for teachers to consider is the legal aspects of their action in such cases. Many of the existing laws may be obsolete or peculiar but they are still there. With the best of intentions, teachers may be opening themselves up for liabilities.

—The danger of being caught between the devil and the deep sea is fortunately much smaller for teachers in the institutional context of school than for clinicians. Besides, emergencies require some quick actions, and if concern about legal aspects inhibits teachers' caring, that would be very unfortunate.

—A young nurse who worked with me killed herself while on leave. She had had some psychiatric problems, but she was a nice, competent person. Because we loved her very much, we had a lot of guilt feelings later. We got together and talked things over so as not to remain crippled by guilt.

—For a child merely to attempt to take his or her own life is too sad for me even to contemplate. What do we do to make them so unhappy to begin with?

—Without much forethought, some children may kill themselves with the abundance of firearms, drugs, and other potentially dangerous agents in their life. Many suicides are accidental, you know.

—Some thirty years ago, there was a report of chain suicides, somewhere in Missouri or Kansas, of up to fifty. I am aware of no systematic reports or studies on that.

—In institutional settings, for example, in state hospitals, that is not too uncommon, even though not publicized.

—Let me make a sort of closing point on suicide. If a person is really determined to kill himself, no one else can prevent that person from committing suicide, be it in the setting of school, home, hospital, prison, or elsewhere.

—Right, the decision is finally a matter of choice, of one's attitude toward life. In that sense, the person's decision may have to be respected.

—Our obligations cannot go beyond a certain point. We do whatever we can do in response to pleas for help, but it is ultimately the individual's life and his choice.

The Social Matrix

—Does death, as a particularly significant experience in human life, warrant a closer examination over and beyond the general processes of coping?

—From my viewpoint, the answer is "no." Death is just another change; what counts is change.

—In terms of divorce rates and other indications, however, there are differences in kind, not merely in the quantitative variation in stress.

—I tend to feel that death is the biggest crisis in life.

—Not necessarily. In a family, for instance, the presence of a severely retarded child may pose a bigger crisis, due partially to its interminable nature or continuous stress.

—That's an interesting possibility to look into. A series of studies at the University of Washington Medical School indicated that death of spouse tends to be rated as the single, most impactful personal experience by people in many different cultures.[23] Because they have concentrated on the relationship between changes in life and incidence of illness, that sort of sustained stress was not included in exploration.

—Cues coming from those family members who are not talking and behaving as if no death took place, suggest to friends that the family wishes to stay closed to maintain balance.

—An open family may have to regress back to a closed stance for reconstruction purposes.

—Remember that these categories are not fixed. That is to say, a closed family can become open, and an open family may change to be closed.

—I see a closed family system as serving some useful purposes at times. In the same manner, perhaps, as neuroses and psychoses fulfill certain purposes. The choice of strategies may be unfortunate, but these defense mechanisms perform definite functions.

—If a family is closed, there is nothing much a teacher can *do*—that's the impression I get. But *understanding* may be a different story. The teacher can certainly listen closely and act with deeper understanding.

—I don't know too many family therapists around in school systems. If the suggestion is that a child needs to see a family therapist whenever death, especially that of a parent, comes to his or her life, I would say such help is not readily available. In extreme cases, the family can surely seek out a qualified person, but ordinarily it's not there.

—Yes, I believe that we have to separate this crisis intervention part from the understanding part mentioned earlier. The latter is more preventive in orientation, affects more people, and is probably more basic.

—More often than not, school psychologists and counselors have not been particularly helpful in such attempts. Historically, psychological services in school have not been known for their success.

—A part, an important part, of that failure comes from our traditional emphasis upon individuals as the basic unit. Our psychologists and counselors have always worked on an individual basis, after the classic medical or psychoanalytic model. Family therapy approach tries to take a look at the same experience from a slightly different perspective.

—The important thing here is to shift our focus from individuals to dyads, triads, and so forth, I suppose. To understand children in their social relations.

—Are there any alternatives to referral to practicing clinicians? Is there anything else a teacher can *do?*

—I suspect that the best route teachers can take is to deepen their understanding, as you said, and to improve their educative functions.

—Yes, something other than purely therapeutic roles. Teachers must handle children from all sorts of family systems and still convey the necessary comprehension and compassion. What they do in their educative capacity may help open up a closed family, you see. It is a very ticklish process, though.

—Well, if the classroom is open, that sort of thing may be more readily handled.

—There is another aspect to this matter of family. In school, we study family, and death in the family can be intellectually examined without anyone having personally experienced death. The same as, say, unemployment, civil unrest, or what have you. We can study death in the family from stances different than that of therapy. Should the teacher propose to take the class to a funeral to introduce the concept of death and the feelings of family members?

—That's a delicate question. In any case, family's feelings about race, sex, death, religion, or any socially sensitive issues must be carefully taken into consideration. Each family has its right to choose and build its own life style, you know.

—Now what if the teacher dies? The classroom in this situation is rather similar to the family, and someone may have to come in to intervene to open it up or to sustain its openness.

—I think it is important for teachers to mobilize all social support systems for such a purpose, without trying to go at it alone. Families, other agencies, individuals, and so forth.

—The purpose of opening up a family is to help individual members in it. If, in my bias, families are perfectly successful, they will eliminate themselves.

—I don't buy that at all. To open the family to give members a chance to grow—that I wholeheartedly agree with. But families won't eliminate themselves in that process.

—I, too, agree with the intended goals, but I believe that your description is overly optimistic. I do not see all families and all relationships becoming open. They may become more open, yes, but the situation is one of degree, not an open-closed dichotomy.

—Bruno Bettelheim makes a very interesting observation about the

Diary of Anne Frank, a point I have not seen raised by others.[24] He feels that the Franks' downfall was largely due to their efforts to keep the family intact. They wanted to stay together as a family under the extraordinary circumstances and, as a result, were wiped out. Many other Dutch Jew families disbanded themselves to scatter among gentile friends; for example, this child joining family *A* to become one of its members, so far as outsiders were concerned, that child joining family *B,* etc. Most of these families survived because they were willing to adjust the institution of family to cope with the particular stress, while the Franks perished in their attempt to maintain the family intact. A very noble and adaptive thing to do, perhaps, in other situations, but their efforts to save the institution resulted in the destruction of all its members.

—That's a very good point. In fact, the Franks had a visa to come to the United States but, after receiving it, Mr. Frank changed his mind for whatever reasons. Exactly the same situation was seen in many other countries under Nazi occupation.

—What about the various ethnic groups, say, Greeks, Italians, and so forth, in the United States? They give much support to each other within their own community, but the community itself remains very closed to outsiders. A very tight network to provide much social support, and it is social support which has been stressed in crisis intervention.

—When I was at a general hospital as a chaplain a patient called me to come to help him die. He was from northern Italy. All the family was present, and he moved positively toward death. A very open family situation within that closely knit network, I guess.

—In the Jewish tradition, there is this custom of sitting *shiva* where ten men join the family to mourn for seven days after the funeral of a close relative. There must be ten men available to support the family, and they go at any time of the day or night when the call comes.

—The custom of wake or watching is a long-standing one, in which a religious vigil over the dead is combined with celebration of life for the living. It lifts up the group, adults and children alike, even though the young have been increasingly kept out of such an experience.

—Speaking of these religious or, for that matter, any other cultural practices, however, there is always the danger of pigeonholing people. The fact that someone happens to be of Jewish, or Catholic, or other faith does not mean that his or her actions conform to a certain stereotyped set. In funeral practices, for example, that person may radically deviate from the popular ideas about the given tradition.

—Right, and many elements in the so-called theological interpretations are actually human elements, nothing to do with the alleged association with the particular religion. They are there, and many people fall back upon these common threads.

—Religion has to take on individual meaning over and beyond institutional meaning. That's one of the difficulties with institutionalized religion.

—It is true that cultures or subcultures may differ markedly in handling death situations. In long suffering death, for instance, Navahos give a large amount of group support. Once the person has died, they forget about him—they burn his house. But during his suffering, a tremendous community support is provided.

—What about his family? Do they go to another house?

—Yes, to another hogan, because the ghost may be there in the old one to haunt people.

—These ethnic variations are fascinating. Like the famed Negro funerals in the South, say in New Orleans, with a big band and all. To examine other cultures is to know ourselves better.[25]

—Also to take a closer look, through literature, arts, music, and the like, at what our own expressed thoughts and emotions are.[26]

—Let me raise a point here. The idea of balance, homeostasis, or equilibrium is very common in our thinking, for example, in discussing personality, family, or classroom. The concept must, however, be interpreted to mean nothing static. Instead of responding merely to external disturbances to reset the original balance and then rest again, individuals and small groups actually create an imbalance themselves so that they may re-integrate at a higher level. If this active process is not there, the person or system is essentially dead in its present state of frozen balance.

—Right, once I reach a certain level of maturity, there is no place for me to go, if a narrow, static interpretation is followed. I must, immediately or simultaneously, seek another, higher level of maturity. An open system is a system in motion, not one content with its present balance.[27]

—Yes, it's something like riding a bicycle. At every moment, the rider may be described to be in balance, but the reason he or she can maintain that balance is that the whole system, both the bicycle and the rider, is moving. To stay open, the system must discard the attained balance to move on to the next, and the next.

—Don't get "maintaining balance" confused with "maintaining the status quo," that's the message.

—In the family system, pains are caused when individuals in the family wish to grow and seek integration at the next higher level.

—People seek change, and yet fear change. It is this which is operating here. If the family wants to maintain its present balance as such, it cannot allow members to change. Then, having a balance defeats its very purpose.

—It seems that what happens in the family is that, "O.K., I am willing to change but it is enough for me to cope with my own changes. I cannot handle your changes at the same time, so don't you change." The so-called relationship rules are then trying to maintain homeostasis at the cost of other people's nonchange.

—I see a peculiar paradox here. On the one hand, we say we are striving for change. On the other hand, we have this concept of homeostasis which suggests to me some sort of stability, either structural or functional. So, we have a system in which change may be valued but, at the same time, may introduce dysfunctions. So far as a group of people—young, healthy, career-oriented, mobile, etc.—are concerned, change may be something desired, but those are not at all characteristic of the life situation of many, many, many people. What most families might strive for is stability, not change, isn't it?

—Stability is not possible, I suspect.

—Well, that sounds very noble philosophically, but any "change" presupposes "stability," doesn't it?

—And there are things which do not change. Men have not yet given birth to a baby and, more seriously, death remains irreversible.

—Also, changes have directions. They are not automatically for the better, by any means. Growth is for the better, yes; mere change, no.

—I wonder whether all this is not the reason why we have so many closed families. It is much easier to close up than to face everything out there. If you try to stay open, chances are that you come under a strong pressure to change.

—Change, when it happens, tends to breed more change.

—We may need some buffers to change. Rituals may serve that protective function also.

—Let's not kid ourselves, any change is very threatening, very threatening. Eric Hoffer tells a story that, after picking beans for two weeks, it was a major and threatening shift to pick cauliflowers! It didn't come easy.

—The concept of stable versus changeable society also applies in this context. A good example of a stable society is the medieval society—everything has been spelled out and accepted by most members. This is a highly predictable situation. Now, however, that does not exist. Change is predictable, anything else is not. Readiness for change is the thing we ought to be aiming at in education.

—Teachers must make all sorts of decisions to act here and now. But these short-range actions take on meaning only in their long-range perspectives. Their immediate skills and knowledge count, to be sure, but their basic philosophy and style of life will have a more permeating influence upon their pupils. It makes a difference if they believe in education for growth, rather than in education for stability per se.

—I believe that, fundamentally, teaching is an act of faith. Teachers must believe noble beliefs and dream lofty dreams today, because these will mold the world of tomorrow, the world of our children.

Notes

1. There are, however, treatises purporting to offer such examination. For example: Richard G. Dumont and Dennis C. Foss, *The American View of Death: Acceptance or Denial?* (Cambridge, Ma.: Schenkman, 1972); John Hinton, *Dying* (Baltimore: Penguin Books, 1967); Robert Kastenbaum and Ruth Aisenberg, *The Psychology of Death* (New York: Springer Publishing Co., 1972, Concise Edition, 1976); and Glenn M. Vernon, *Sociology of Death* (New York: Ronald Press, 1970).

2. This is a danger rather familiar to workers in social sciences. Thus, for instance, H. J. Butcher has this to say in *Human Intelligence* (New York: Harper and Row, 1973), p. 189:

As with Freud, it is difficult to say to what extent Piaget has devised a highly abstract, *a priori* framework, and has then suited his techniques of observation to this very personal observation.

3. For more formal discussions of related matters, consult such sources as: William R. Coulson and Carl R. Rogers, eds., *Man and the Science of Man* (Columbus, Oh.: Charles E. Merrill Publishing Co., 1968); Abraham H. Maslow, *The Psychology of Science* (New York: Harper and Row, 1966); Michael Polanyi, *Personal Knowledge* (Chicago: University of Chicago Press, 1958); and Pitrim Sorokin, *Fads and Foibles in Modern Sociology and Related Sciences* (Chicago: Henry Regnery, 1956).

4. Erik H. Erikson, *Childhood and Society*, 2nd ed. (New York: W. W. Norton, 1963), p. 269.

5. Ibid., pp. 209-46 (Chapter 6, "Toys and Reasons"); Adah Maurer, "The Child's Knowledge of Non-Existence," *Journal of Existential Psychology* 2 (Fall 1961):193-212; and Adah Maurer, "Maturation of Concepts of Death," *British Journal of Medical Psychology* 39 (March 1966):35-41.

6. For reviews of studies on the possible influence of TV viewing on children in general, consult the following: Gerald S. Lesser, *Children and Television: Lessons from Sesame Street* (New York: Random House, 1974); Eleanor E. Maccoby, "Effects of the Mass Media," in *Review of Child Development Research,* Vol. I, ed. Martin L. Hoffman and Lois W. Hoffman (New York: Russell Sage Foundation, 1964), pp. 323-48; John P. Murray, "Television and Violence: Implications of the Surgeon General's Research Program," *American Psychologist* 28 (June 1973):472-78; Aletha H. Stein, "Mass Media and Young Children's Development," in *Early Childhood Education,* 71st Yearbook of the

National Society for the Study of Education, Part II, ed. Ira J. Gordon (Chicago: University of Chicago Press, 1972), pp. 181-202; and Aletha H. Stein and Lynette K. Friedrich, "Impact of Television on Children and Youth," in *Review of Child Development Research*, Vol. V, ed. E. Mavis Hetherington (Chicago: University of Chicago Press, 1975), pp. 183-256.

7. Interested readers may study references such as: Charlotte Bühler and Melanie Allen, *Introduction to Humanistic Psychology* (Belmont, Ca.: Brooks/Cole, 1972); Floyd W. Matson, *The Broken Image* (Garden City, N.J.: Doubleday, 1966); and C. H. Patterson, *Humanistic Education* (Englewood Cliffs, N.J.: Prentice-Hall, 1973).

8. The following sources present a detailed description (the first) and an extensive critique (the second): Jerome S. Bruner, *Toward a Theory of Instruction* (New York: W. W. Norton, 1968), pp. 73-101, Chapter 4; and Richard M. Jones, *Fantasy and Feeling in Education* (New York: Harper and Row, 1970).

9. See, for example: Carl G. Carlozzi, *Death and Contemporary Man* (Grand Rapids, Mi.: William B. Ferdmans Publishing Co., 1968); Marie Fargues, *The Child and the Mystery of Death* (Glen Rock, N.J.: Paulist Press, 1966); Earl A. Grollman, ed., *Explaining Death to Children* (Boston: Beacon Press, 1967), see, in particular: Edgar N. Jackson, "The Theological, Psychological, and Philosophical Dimensions of Death in Protestantism," pp. 171-95; Thomas J. Riley, "Catholic Teachings, the Child, and a Philosophy for Life and Death," pp. 199-220; and Earl A. Grollman, "The Ritualistic and Theological Approach of the Jew," pp. 223-45; Edgar N. Jackson, *Telling a Child about Death* (New York: Channel Press, 1965); Hoover Rupert, *Where Is Thy Sting?: Death in Christian Perspective* (Nashville, Tn.: Graded Press, 1969). An example of religious education curriculum on death may be found in the "Parish Education" materials, particularly the *Teacher's Manuals* for various age levels, from the Anglican Church of Canada, Church House, Toronto 285, Ontario, Canada.

10. The relevant documentation includes the following: William H. Beable, *Epitaphs: Graveyard Humor and Eulogy* (Chicago: Gale Research Co., 1971); Raymond L. Brown, *Book of Epitaphs* (New York: Taplinger Publishing Co., 1969); John R. Kippax, *Churchyard Literature* (New York: Gordon Press, 1969); and Thomas J. Pettigrew, *Chronicles of the Tombs* (New York: AMS Press, 1968).

11. A recent study of relevance here is the following: Eric Bermann, *Scapegoat: The Impact of Death-Fear on an American Family* (Ann Arbor, Mi.: University of Michigan Press, 1973).

12. Organizations working on this principle include the "Parents without Partners," "N.A.I.M. Conference," and "Society of the Compassionate Friends." Many communities have active local chapters. In England, there is the "Cruse, National Organization for Widows and their Children." Good sources for the bereaved are: Clarissa Start, *When You're a Widow* (St. Louis: Concordia Publishing House, 1968); Simon Stephens, *Death Comes Home* (New York: Morehouse-Barlow, 1973); and Margaret Torrie, *Begin Again* (London: J. M. Dent and Sons, 1970).

13. Ira O. Glick, Robert S. Weiss, and Collin M. Parkes, *The First Year of Bereavement* (New York: Wiley-Interscience, 1974); and Collin M. Parkes, *Bereavement: Studies of Grief in Adult Life* (New York: International Universities Press, 1972).

14. An interesting observation on the relationship of medical ethics with the image of man is given in the following source: Talcott Parsons, Renée C. Fox, and Victor M. Lidz, "The 'Gift of Life' and Its Reciprocation," in *Death in American Experience*, ed. Arien Mack (New York: Schocken Books, 1973), pp. 1-49.

15. Clark Moustakas, *The Authentic Teacher* (Cambridge, Ma.: Howard A. Doyle Publishing Co., 1966); and Theodor Reik, *Listening with the Third Ear* (New York: Pyramid Publications, 1948).

16. Some relevant materials may be gleaned from sources such as the following: Barney G. Glaser and Anselm L. Strauss, *Awareness of Dying* (Chicago: Aldine Publishing Co., 1965); Barney G. Glaser and Anselm L. Strauss, *Time for Dying* (Chicago: Aldine Publishing Co., 1968); David Sudnow, *Passing On* (Englewood Cliffs, N.J.: Prentice-Hall, 1967); and Avery D. Weisman, *On Dying and Denying* (New York: Behavioral Publications, 1972).

17. Erving Goffman, *Asylums* (Garden City, N.Y.: Doubleday, 1961); Anthony M. Platt, *Child Savers* (Chicago: University of Chicago Press, 1969); and Thomas S. Szasz, *Ideology and Insanity* (Garden City, N.Y.: Doubleday, 1970).

18. The titles below are merely examples: David W. Berg and George G. Daugherty, eds., *The Individual, Society, and Death: An Anthology of Readings*, with *Student Activity Books, Teacher's Resource Book*, and *Audio-Visual Components* (filmstrips and cassette tapes), DeKalb, Il.: Perspectives on Death (P. O. Box 213), 1972-73; Elisabeth Kübler-Ross, A Cassette Tape Library on "Coping with Death and Dying," Flossmoor, Il.: Ross Medical Associates (1925 Sylvan Street), 1974; and University of Minnesota, Center for Death Education and Research, A Cassette Tape Library on "Death, Grief, and Bereavement," Minneapolis: Author (1167 Social Science Bldg.), 1971-73.

19. Examples of materials good to use with children are: Anne Frank, *Diary of Anne Frank* (Garden City, N.Y.: Doubleday, 1952); Fred Gibson, *Old Yeller* (New York: Harper & Row, 1958); Earl A. Grollman, *Talking about Death* (Boston: Beacon Press, 1970); Miska Miles, *Annie and the Old One* (Boston: Little, Brown, 1971); National Instructional Television Center, "In My Memory," A film available from the Center, Box A, Bloomington, Indiana 47401; Doris B. Smith, *A Taste of Blackberries* (New York: Thomas Y. Crowell, 1973); and E. B. White, *Charlotte's Web* (New York: Harper & Row, 1952).

20. For instance, see the following: "Death and Education," *Pastoral Psychology*, November 1971; Betty R. Green and Donald P. Irish, eds., *Death Education: Preparation for Living* (Cambridge, Ma.: Schenkman Publishing Co., 1971); and Earl A. Grollman, *Concerning Death: A Practical Guide for the Living* (Boston: Beacon Press, 1974).

21. Earl A. Grollman, *Suicide* (Boston: Beacon Press, 1971); Albert Schrut, "Suicidal Adolescents and Children," *Journal of American Medical Association* 188 (June 1964):1103-1107. Literature on suicide is by now voluminous. Only a sample of available sources is given below for reader's convenience. Jacques Choron, *Suicide* (New York: Charles Scribner's Sons, 1972); Norman L. Farberow and Edwin S. Shneidman, eds., *The Cry for Help* (New York: McGraw-Hill, 1961); Stuart M. Finch and Elva O. Poznanski, *Adolescent Suicide* (Springfield, Il.: Charles C Thomas, 1971); Jack P. Gibbs, *Suicide* (New York: Harper and Row, 1968); David Lester, *Why People Kill*

Themselves (Springfield, Il.: Charles C Thomas, 1972); Karl A. Menninger, *Man Against Himself* (New York: Harcourt, Brace, 1938); Seymour Perlin, ed., *A Handbook for the Study of Suicide* (New York: Oxford University Press, 1975); Harvey L. Resnik, *Suicidal Behaviors: Diagnosis and Management* (Boston: Little, Brown, 1968); Edwin S. Shneidman, ed., *Suicidology: Contemporary Developments* (New York: Grune & Stratton, 1976); Erwin Stengel, *Suicide and Attempted Suicide* (Baltimore: Penguin Books, 1964); and Samuel Wallace, *After Suicide* (New York: John Wiley and Sons, 1973).

22. A fascinating, little study in this connection is reported in: Leland Moss, "Help Wanted: A Limited Study of Response to One Person's Cry for Help," in *Death and the College Student*, ed. Edwin S. Shneidman (New York: Behavioral Publications, 1972), pp. 49-67.

23. Thomas H. Holmes and Minoru Masuda, "Life Change and Illness Susceptibility," in *Stressful Life Events*, ed. Barbara S. and Bruce P. Dohrenwend (New York: John Wiley and Sons, 1974), pp. 45-72; and Alvin Toffler, *Future Shock* (New York: Bantam Books, 1971), pp. 327-33.

24. Bruno Bettelheim, *The Informed Heart* (New York: Avon Books, 1971), pp. 247-55.

25. Sources here include: E. James Anthony and Cyrille Koupernik, eds., *The Child in His Family*, Vol. II, *The Impact of Disease and Death* (New York: John Wiley and Sons, 1973); Johannes Fabian, "How Others Die—Reflections on the Anthropology of Death," in *Death in American Experience*, ed. Arien Mack (New York: Schocken Books, 1973), pp. 177-201; Geoffrey Gorer, *Death, Grief, and Mourning* (Garden City, N.Y.: Doubleday, 1965); Robert W. Habenstein and William M. Lamers, *Funeral Customs the World Over* (Milwaukee: National Funeral Directors Association, 1960); Maurice Lamm, *The Jewish Way in Death and Mourning* (New York: Jonathan David Co., 1969); Oscar Lewis, *A Death in the Sanchez Family* (New York: Random House, 1970); Robert J. Lifton, "On Death and Death Symbolism: The Hiroshima Disaster," in *The Phenomenon of Death*, ed. Edith Wyschograd (New York: Harper and Row, 1973), pp. 69-109; and David G. Mandelbaum, "Social Uses of Funeral Rites," in *The Meaning of Death*, ed. Herman Feifel (New York: McGraw-Hill, 1959), pp. 189-217; see also: Mircea Eliade, *Death, Afterlife, and Eschatology* (New York: Harper & Row, 1974); and Richard A. Kalish and David K. Reynolds, *Death and Ethnicity* (Los Angeles: University of Southern California Press, 1976).

26. Harold Bloom, "Death and the Native Strain in American Poetry," in *Death in American Experience*, ed. Arien Mack (New York: Schocken Books, 1973), pp. 83-96; Carla Gottlieb, "Modern Art and Death," in *The Meaning of Death*, ed. Herman Feifel (New York: McGraw-Hill, 1959), pp. 157-88; Frederick J. Hoffman, "Mortality and Modern Literature," in *The Meaning of Death*, ed. Herman Feifel (New York: McGraw-Hill, 1959); and Benjamin Nelson, "The Games of Life and the Dances of Death," in *The Phenomenon of Death*, ed. Edith Wyschograd (New York: Harper and Row, 1973), pp. 113-31.

27. For some related discussions, see the following: Gordon Allport, *Pattern and Growth in Personality* (New York: Holt, Rinehart and Winston, 1961); Ludwig von Bertalanffy, *General System Theory* (New York: George Braziller, 1968); and Abraham H. Maslow, *Toward a Psychology of Being*, 2nd ed. (Princeton, N.J.: D. Van Nostrand, 1968).

This chapter, prepared by a perceptive teacher, not only presents a humane examination of death in the school program, but also summarizes the major themes and sentiments of the whole book. There is certainly much to be done, but there is also much that can be done at the hand of thoughtful people like the author herself.

6

Teachers, School Children, and Death

Beverly Hardcastle Lewis*

Every teacher must in some way meet the variety of emotions that children bring with them to school. How the teacher does this depends on the type of person he is and what he believes. But when we work with children who need help, it is hard to ignore the need before us in favor of something less meaningful and less real.[1]

Of all the emotions that children bring with them to school those associated with death are perhaps the strongest. How teachers meet these emotions, how teachers respond to a child in grief, depends greatly upon how they view their role as a teacher and how they regard the teacher-student relationship. If they are sensitive to the affective dimension of the relationship, then they will wish to respond in some instrumental way. At such a point they may wish for guidance so as to support and help their pupils in the most effective manner possible. Some teachers, however, feel that the affective domain lies outside of their realm of responsibility. To these teachers, emotions and feelings get in the way of the work at hand which is, allegedly, to "educate" the child. For these teachers grief emotions, all emotions, are irrelevant to education in their classrooms. At the base of this belief is a denial of the wholeness of the child. To the music teacher the child is a set of vocal chords; to the art teacher the child is a pair of hands; to the physical education teacher the child is a set of muscles; to the classroom teacher the child is an intellect; to the school psychologist the child is a complex of emotions; and to each the child is nothing more, according to this belief. Though schools do specialize instruction along these lines, they do so in order to serve the child better, not to categorize him or her. The child remains whole throughout the process. Specialized teachers may focus on specific aspects of a child, but they create a harmful distortion of reality if in the focusing process they blur out the existence of all the other aspects of the child.

153

To regard emotions as hindering irrelevancies in the classroom is also to miss quite simply and sadly their value. Joseph Church writes:

> Feelings are the substrate and the raw material of cognition as opposed to reflexive action, and our human capacities for thought are no greater than our human capacities for feeling. . . . Certainly it is possible to be retentive without great feeling, but learning without the understanding that emotion gives is barren and perhaps even dangerous.[2]

A number of educators—Sylvia Ashton-Warner, Sybil Marshall, John Holt, Lillian Weber, Clark Moustakas, Carl Rogers, and others[3]—share this belief and advocate centering the educational experience on children's feelings. The child-centered curriculum, the open classroom, the integrated day, the hidden curriculum innovations all spring from a common valuing of the affective dimension, the feeling dimension of the teaching-learning situation. Donald Barr, a strong critic of the new technological devices, taps this dimension when he values teachers on the ground that the "devices lack wonderment, respect, and love."[4]

While it becomes difficult to deny this dimension—few teachers regard their classrooms as sterile learning factories—it is challenging to embrace it. Forceful answers and clear guidelines are not offered here. To recognize, receive, and respond to emotions is urged instead, especially when they are the intense emotions associated with grief. To ignore these, to suppress or dismiss these is to reject the child.

Again, the question of how arises. How does the teacher respond to the grieving child? An answer begins within the teacher and is continually shaped by her uniqueness. She needs to confront the concept of death to determine her own personal view. She needs to base her reaction to grief on her own grieving experiences. Considering her own thoughts on life and death, reviewing her own experiences with death seems an appropriate starting point for the teacher if she wishes to prepare for an honest, supportive response to the grief of a child. Before the teacher responds to someone else's feelings, she needs to explore her own.

Teacher Beliefs and Societal Influences

As teachers explore their own feelings about death, they may benefit by becoming aware of some of the ways society influences and shapes their thinking. These influences are discussed fully in earlier chapters. Two ways, however, stand out as being particularly relevant to teachers and will be considered again here.

The first is a habit of mind, a way that we have become duped by our own energetic health and safety campaigns. Unconsciously we have come to view death as a mistake, a sign of weakness, an accident, but not as a natural phenomenon. As teachers we promote these misconceptions when we overemphasize good health habits and safety precautions. Year after year we repeat the same messages, reinforcing public service announcements on television, radio, in newspapers and magazines. Buttons, displays, and posters further echo the life saving messages. Since the same approach is used to convince us to purchase one brand of toothpaste over another, we find our acceptance of the health and safety messages operating on the same semi-conscious level. With the acceptance of the rules, we expect some sort of guarantee. So, if we fasten our seatbelts, then we won't die in an automobile accident. If we stop smoking, then we won't die of cancer or heart disease. If we remove all safety hazards from our homes, then we won't die in a home accident. Unverbalized but sensed in this attitude is the next step: if we follow the rules, we won't die. Robert Fulton refers to this phenomenon as the dying of death and compares it with past views of death in this way:

> An increasing number of Americans no longer view death as the result of Divine displeasure or as the price of mortal trespass; rather, in our modern, secular society death is coming to be seen as the result of personal negligence or of an unforeseen accident. Death is now a temporal matter that man treats much as he would an avoidable illness or physical stigma.[5]

As teachers search for their own feelings in regard to death they should consider this careless habit of the mind and deliberately seek a more natural view of life and death. An awareness of this influence could lead to the restoration of a more open, less cloaked view of death.

The second striking societal influence on teachers is more awesome in its effects, for it reflects a trend of actions and conditions rather than isolated attitudes or ideas and as such it cannot be managed and dealt with easily; indeed it cannot be manipulated as ideas can. This societal influence, or the societal demand, is the development of the nuclear family. These small family units which have moved away from the larger, rooted family are more fragile and more dependent upon the community than the larger family units were.

Though there are clearly advantages and values gained in the nuclear family setting, a natural and open acceptance of death is not one of them. "The family as such, begins with the marriage and ends with or is broken by the death of one of the parents. This threat hangs so heavily over all the members of the small family unit that they face it only with difficulty."[6] The child's natural fears of abandonment become intensified in such a setting. Should a death or divorce threaten, the child's once rhetorical question, "But who will take care of me?" becomes a very practical one, "Who will, indeed?" As teachers examine their thoughts, they may wish to consider their response to the nuclear family in a time of crisis.

An awareness of societal influences and the self-awareness, which comes from a consideration of one's own thoughts and experiences, should result in what Joseph Church defines for us as thematizations. These are guiding statements of personal philosophy which shape a person's conception of himself and, as such, play a significant part in directing his behavior. To thematize about death and about one's relationship to a grieving child thus becomes imperative, if the teacher wishes to respond meaningfully to classroom experiences involving death. Further, the teacher should revise her thematizations from time to time so that they reflect the influences of new experiences or insights. When the search of self has brought about initial thematizations about death and grief, then, perhaps, the teacher may benefit by looking to other teachers and their experiences with death and school children.

What Other Teachers Experience and Practice

To gain some insight into how other teachers viewed these issues, an informal survey was conducted in February 1973 by the writer. Through the form of a questionnaire, information was sought in three broad areas: the frequency of the problem of a grieving child; the manner in which teachers dealt with grief; and the extent of direct teaching on death. The questionnaire is shown in Table 1. Teachers were invited to comment further on the back of the questionnaire and a number of them did so. Where possible, personal interviews were conducted with those teachers who had experienced the death of a pupil. The survey was made in order to gain information from teachers who were willing to share their experiences; it was not an attempt to analyze the status of death education in the schools.

An Exploratory Survey in Five Schools

The elementary schools participating in the informal survey were somewhat scattered geographically: two schools in northwestern New York; one school in Iowa City, Iowa; one school in Kirkwood, Missouri, a suburb of St. Louis; and one school in Falls Church, Virginia, a suburb of Washington, D.C. The school populations would not fall into any extreme groups—none were extremely poor (slum) schools; none were catering specifically to the extremely wealthy; none were religiously directed schools; and none were private schools. None of the schools were truly rural; none were inner city schools. Of the total 136 teachers, 107, or 78.7 percent, gave usable responses. The response rates varied from 100 percent in Kirkwood to 68.2 percent in Geneseo, New York.

In general the teachers indicated an honest concern with the problem. Some volunteered guidance; others shared personal experiences. Most

Table 1

Death Questionnaire
Have any of your pupils died this year?
Have you ever had a pupil die?
Have any of your pupils lost close relatives or friends this year?
Have you ever needed to comfort one of your pupils in grief?
If so, do you explain to the class why the child is grieving?
If so, do you feel free to share your religious views at such a time?
If so, do you keep the reason for the child's upset a private matter?
Have any of your pupils ever expressed a real concern about his own death?
Have you ever taught directly about death? (In social studies, science, etc.)

indicated a special regard for the individual case, for the individual child. Whether they were inclined to share a child's grief with the class was dependent upon the child. Whether they shared their religious views with the child was again dependent upon the individual case and then these were supplied only as far as the child's needs required. That the individual case should be considered over any blanket program was perhaps the clearest message obtained by the questionnaire.

A more detailed tabulation of the responses teachers made to the questionnaire is presented in Table 2. For an indication of the frequency of death occurrences, we note that, of the 107 respondents, 44 percent had pupils who lost close relatives or friends during the year. Forty-six percent of responding teachers stated that they had had to comfort a child in grief at some point in their teaching careers. Twenty of the 107 teachers had lost a pupil at some point during their teaching years. In these cases, grief was on a class-wide basis, and also a personal grief for the teacher.

Table 2
Teacher Responses on Death Questionnaire

School Location	Number of Teachers				
	Total	Responding	Those Who Lost Pupils at Some Time	Those with Pupils Who Lost Relatives or Close Friends This Year	Those Who Ever Needed to Comfort a Pupil in Grief
Geneseo, N.Y.	44	30	9	16	19
Iowa City, Iowa	13	10	2	3	5
Falls Church, Va.	25	19	2	5	9
Kirkwood, Mo.	22	22	3	10	6
Avon, N.Y.	32	26	4	13	10
Total	136	107	20	47	49

When asked if they would share their religious views with a child at a time of death, twenty-five teachers replied that they would, forty-seven replied that they would not, and thirty-one preferred not to comment or if they did comment they qualified their selection extensively with written remarks. Here, as in the general case, emphasis was placed on the needs of the individual child and his or her individual experience.

The response to the question regarding the publicness of the grief was quite mixed. There were adamant comments on both sides. Forty-six teachers said that they would explain the cause of a child's grief to the class, nineteen said that they would not, and thirty-six qualified their remarks indicating that they would or they would not depending upon the individual case. Some teachers noted that the reaction of the other children to the grieving child could act as a guide in this matter. A third grade teacher in Falls Church wrote:

> I would normally keep a child's grief over a personal loss private, but if his grief was outwardly shown in the classroom, I feel that it would bring about a natural discussion due to his peers' curiosity. As of yet the situation has not arisen.

The significance of the death to the child would also act as a guideline, wrote other teachers. A fifth grade teacher in Avon commented:

> There have been times when cousins or aunts or uncles died, but one time the child's mother died and that time the children and I did discuss it.

Only 14 of the 107 teachers have had pupils express a real concern over death to them. The written comments on this question indicated that a general concern over death had increased.

Challenges for the Teacher

Earlier chapters of this book refer to parents' reluctance to discuss death with their children. We have noted that in the nuclear family the subject of death is often a taboo. While, in the past, parents could talk about death but not sex with their children, "Now parents talk openly with their children about sex . . . but are strangely confounded when they try to speak of death, dying, or the emotions relating to these evidences of the end of the life cycle."[7] This need for frank discussion apparently has been felt more and more in the schools and classrooms. A guidance counselor offered:

> I frequently am asked by teachers how they should respond—my recommendation is to be alert and talk about it if the child feels the need (especially *listen* to him). In group work, I have shown a TV film to the fifth and sixth graders. The response was interest, sharing of experiences freely and willingly. A few parents objected as they felt this matter should be handled strictly in the home. However, there was no reluctance on the part of the children to work with it.

"A few parents objected," but what of the majority? Have they remained silent because they have created the need and thus enjoy seeing the schools accept the responsibility? In their silence may lie their support. What matters most, however, is that the children's needs be met, and the situation seems more hopeful now that teachers have begun to respond to the need.

When a Child Grieves

Before we help a child read a book, learn a division algorithm, design a science experiment, write a story, or mould a relief map, we need to know where he is on the continuum of development for the particular skill or concept area being used. We need to know what his previous learning experiences have been, and we need to know roughly where he is in the progression of cognitive stages of growth as outlined by, for instance, Piaget.[8] We then accept the child where he is and adapt our curricular goals to him. While we as teachers recognize that each child is different, we also recognize with Piaget that the basic sequence of cognitive stages appears constant, with each child moving at his own rate. It thus may be beneficial to review the sequence of stages in the comprehension of death.

Levels of Comprehension

Descriptive studies have been made on these developmental stages and are discussed fully in Chapter 2.[9] Here let us review some of the characteristics as they pertain to the classroom. The idea that death is reversible, which exists until at least the age of four, lies behind thoughts or remarks that may strike the preschool or kindergarten teacher as being humorous or incongruous. One child to another: "Is your granddaddy still dead?" Or another to her teacher: "Miss Joan, Miss Joan! I saw your picture in the newspaper! What happened, did you die or something!" (This a comment on our concept of news as well.)

The magic and joy found in the concept of reversibility are appealing. Fifth and sixth graders, formally beyond this stage, were caught off guard by a story in a social studies booklet which related a Buddhist child's explanations of an earlier life. The story was passed around the room and shared with friends like a forbidden fruit, the concept of reincarnation delighting them. In our culture, however, the idea that death is reversible is mostly limited to those in the three to five year old age group, an age group that watches for hours television cartoons which support reversibility. Cartoon characters suffer stylized death blows time and time again but always pop up and continue where they left off.

The age of six seems to mark a change in children's attitudes toward death, for their interest in death increases and their play becomes more violent in nature. Gesell also notes for us:

> At the same time the six-year-old worries about illnesses, death of the mother, and begins to connect old age with death. He may become interested in rituals and be disturbed by pictures and stories of dying or dead animals, but he does not yet believe that he himself will die.[10]

It was at this age that I personally recall having a bird cemetery, scouring the neighborhood with a friend in search of small, limp carcasses. Then we would bury them and conduct rather solemn and elaborate ceremonies for them. The ritual, perhaps, held the attraction. More than half of a class of fifth and sixth grade children recalled creating similar burial activities. It would be interesting to relate a study of cemetery play activities with mourning experiences and age levels.

Between the ages of five and nine, "there is a strong tendency to interpret death in anthropomorphic terms: death is a person."[11] This gives the child a way to get out of death, by not getting caught. Games of hide and seek and jokes about the "boogey man" which are popular with this age group are perhaps forms of acting out the fears of death and also a playing with the concept of death as a personal possibility.

At the age of seven, eight, and nine the child begins to have "a reasonably clear idea of the causes of death, is interested in what may happen after death and is able to accept that death is the common lot of humanity, animals, and plants, and that one day he himself might die."[12] The acceptance of one's own death is gradual and complex. At this stage, children tend to be unable to deny death or accept it. They seem to be trying on the idea of death in order to accommodate it. Children who were discussing the death of one of their friends with their teacher asked such specific questions about the death that one would think that they were placing themselves in their friend's position to discover what death really was.

> What happened in the ambulance? Where is he now? What happens at a funeral? What does he look like? How is he dressed? What happens after the funeral?

By the age of ten, children tend to grasp the concept of death much as adults do. They are equipped "with most of the intellectual tools necessary to understand both life and death in a logical manner."[13]

In a number of studies, findings have indicated that children's reactions to death are similar to those of adults but differ in degree. In one study included in the book *Children and the Death of a President*, Roberta Sigel compared the reactions of school children and adults to President Kennedy's death. She noted:

> The children's behavior was also strikingly similar to adults'. . . . It may also be an illustration of adults' tendency to minimize the extent to which children are capable of experiencing rather adult reactions.[14]

The study was based on the responses of over one thousand fourth, sixth, eighth, tenth, and twelfth grade students. Sigel also notes that children do not display their grief as openly as adults nor for as long a period of time.

Children in the writer's classroom, aged eleven and twelve, display an attitude toward death which reflects the attitude of adult society. It may be casual and lightly ironic at times. When a class president was being elected the two candidates found themselves being guarded by self-appointed secret service agents. When later one child returned to the classroom and asked about who had won the election, another child dead-panned: "Julie did, but she's been assassinated already."

These children could also deal with serious questions regarding death. In one reading group, two factions argued over the two views of death in Pearl Buck's *The Big Wave*. One group felt that it was better to live securely within the walls of the old Gentleman's fort rather than to risk death from the volcano or wave on the mountain or beach. The larger faction believed that it would be better to live actively in the open, risking death, than it would be to hide from life and live dully to an old age.

Children in this age group, the ten's to twelve's, could openly and reasonably talk about capital punishment. Some felt no one had a right to take another person's life even if that person had done so himself. Others believed that not only should the one who had committed the crime be punished with death, but that the criminal should receive the death in the same form that he or she gave it. The arguments were not unlike those offered by adults.

The contrast between this age group and the five's is great—from reversibility to reason. Knowing something of the sequence of the stages which fall between the extremes helps the teacher understand the child and his or her growth.

Significance of the Death

When a child grieves the teacher should consider the significance of the death to the child. As has been noted in earlier chapters, our society tends to segregate the elderly and the dying from the more active, younger population. The likelihood that a child would develop a significant relationship with an elderly relative is diminished by this trend. The death of a grandparent living in a distant retirement center or nursing home is not as likely to upset a child as would the death of a grandparent who had been living in the child's home. There are, of course, many exceptions, and many close and meaningful relationships have been maintained and enriched despite geographical distances. While family relationship is less solid as an indicator of the significance of a death to the child, the teacher may fairly easily determine how upset the child is through gentle questioning.

The most significant deaths for a child to deal with are those of his mother, father, or a sibling. The effects of such losses can be devastating. Emotional and mental problems may occur immediately, later in their life, or perhaps not at all. The resulting difficulties are unpredictable, the potential for problems is great. Considering the death fear of nuclear families and considering the role parents play in the development of the school child's personality, it is not surprising that the death of a parent during childhood could have foreboding consequences.

Psychiatrists and psychologists seem particularly pessimistic about the possibility of mental or emotional disturbances as a consequence of death loss during childhood of parents or a sibling. Rosenblatt writes:

> . . . I am inclined to feel that if we wish to prevent children from developing emotional illnesses as a consequence of losing loved ones in death, we shall have to do away with death itself.[15]

Similarly, Moriarty states:

> It is the thesis of this book [*The Loss of Loved Ones*] that the loss of loved ones, especially through death is one of the most important causes of major mental illness. These illnesses may start immediately after the death of a loved one or they may appear much later in life. Children who lose loved ones, mothers, fathers or siblings in their early childhood are profoundly affected by this.[16]

The consequences to the child of a death are not certain, but the fact that there is a potential for difficulties is clear. The teacher must respond to this possibility. She cannot ignore a significant death experience of one of her school children. She must consider the matter as serious even if the child does not evidence apparent difficulty or upset.

Kliman has organized a checklist of symptoms or signs which may occur after a loss and which the teacher should be alert for. If enough of these signs appear, help for the child should be sought. For the classroom teacher two criteria which Kliman considers valid bases for preventive intervention should be noted. These are: (1) when "suicide is the cause of a parent's death" and (2) "when a girl under eight loses her mother."[17] In such cases the teacher should turn to the psychologist (clinical, counseling, school); counselor (pastoral, family, school); psychiatrist; psychiatric social worker or nurse; or other professional who is qualified to deal intensively with emotional problems. This does not mean that the teacher avoids the problem or transfers the responsibility; rather, it is that, in so availing herself of outside assistance, the teacher will be in a better position to maximize her unique contribution to the child's welfare through her close relationship with him, and to help him through his grieving experiences.

Pity and Sympathy

The teacher's initial reaction to a child who encounters a significant loss may be that of pity. It is sad to see a young dependent child experience a loss of any kind. While pity is not an unreasonable response, it should be avoided because of its crippling nature. Implied within pity is a sense of condescension or contempt. Dreikurs writes: "Pity is a negative emotion—it belittles the individual, weakens his self-reliance and destroys his faith in life."[18] If the teacher feels pity for the child, she should seek to overcome it so that self-pity and low self-expectations will not be promoted and will not have an opportunity to develop.

Instead of pity, adults are reminded to respond with:

. . . sympathy and understanding by supporting the child in his grief as well as his courageous search for a way forward. This in no way means that we abandon the child to his trouble. On the contrary—we rally to support him just as we do to an adult in trouble.[19]

A Constellation of Feelings

To supply the support and encouragement needed in a time of grieving, the teacher must also become aware of the constellation of feelings with which the child may be struggling. The child may speak of these. More likely, the child may not be able to define them, but they are sensed by him and shape his actions. The feelings are powerful ones, sometimes contradictory ones; they occur as the child struggles to accept or deny the death in his experience. Moriarty enumerates them as "the intensification of dependence, loneliness, uncertainty, fears of loving and hating, guilt, shame, feelings of not belonging and being different."[20]

These feelings are accessible, especially in the initial stages of grief. If the teacher becomes attuned to them she may respond to opportunities to draw out the child, listen to him, or protect him, as each opportunity dictates. She may regard the child as "a walking wound," an expression President Kennedy's widow used to describe her feelings in the months after her husband's death. As a walking wound, the child is sensitive, vulnerable, and needs to be protected from careless remarks.

Guilt

Let us look closely at some of these feelings. The feeling of guilt after a parent dies is a common reaction. All of us think, feel, and act in unkind ways toward those whom we love. We express our anger toward them at some points during our lives. These angry actions and thoughts are recalled and sometimes amplified after the loved one dies. We feel guilt over them; children may carry the sense of guilt to that of blame and self-accusation. They may believe that in some way their anger caused the death.

The guilt may grow, especially as we unconsciously superhumanize the one who has died. We select from our memories the good things the person has done; we block out the mistakes or unkindnesses. We idealize the dead also simply because they have passed through the experience of dying. Freud points to this: "Toward the person who has died we adopt a special attitude something like admiration for someone who has accomplished a very difficult task."[21] Our angry thoughts or actions, focussed on the now near sainted dead, seem blacker and the guilt deepens.

We may even feel guilt in our own sense of joy in being alive, savoring life, carrying on. Need a child wear the mask of mourning when he or she feels some joy? The following account was shared in response to the informal survey:

Mrs. N.'s husband died several years ago leaving her with four small children. He had been ill for a long time. Her children never seemed to have had a feeling of insecurity either during their father's illness or after his death and were unaware of financial circumstances, insurance, etc. After her husband's death, the children snapped back immediately to the business of living and didn't seem to grieve excessively. Her husband's death occurred a few days before the Christmas holidays. Her little boy was to be in the Christmas pageant. . . .

There was no classroom discussion of the death as far as Mrs. N. knows but her son did overhear the cafeteria woman say, "Isn't that the boy who just lost his father, what's he doing here?" Mrs. N. feels that this statement could have upset her child and was uncalled for.

Sometimes the teacher is in a position to ward off painful comments or to soften them should they occur. If the teacher's actions stem from an understanding of the child's feelings he or she will find ways to support and help in the child's management of guilt feelings.

Dependency

Intensified dependency is a second feeling which may result from a loss. The child may require more guidance at school; may lean on the teacher more; may confide in her more. If the teacher uses this opportunity to offer support and accepts this role with full awareness of the desirability of guiding the child through this stage, she can be instrumental in the child's adjustment to the death and to his or her altered life.

Teachers may miss the opportunity to fill the dependency need. One mother recalled such a case. Her daughter, in fifth grade, returned to school from an absence due to her grandmother's death and funeral. The mother felt badly because the death was such a shock and the family was so unprepared for the funeral and estate arrangements that little time was spent consoling their daughter with her own grief. Relatives from out of town needed to be cared for and legal matters had to be managed. As the child was not demanding in her nature, she did not get the attention she needed. When the girl returned to school after the funeral she seemed to request support there for she volunteered an explanation for her absence. The teacher's reply was: "Really? We didn't even notice that you were absent." Perhaps this was fumbled support. More likely it was an off-hand remark, unthinking. Regardless of the teacher's reasons, she missed an opportunity to be supportive to the child. Further, the child was hurt by the comment, for she mentioned it to her mother. Certainly if the child had reported that her mother or father had died, the teacher would have been more responsive.

Dependency intensification is especially significant with the death of a parent in a nuclear family. For practical as well as emotional purposes the child and remaining parent are more dependent upon people in their immediate environment outside their family. The teacher, because she guides the child in school, may become more important to the child. She should be aware of her increased influence and act with it delicately and instrumentally.

Exclusion

The sense of being different or of not belonging also accompanies a loss. This is one area in which the teacher may contribute markedly to the child's adjustment to a new life. An open acceptance of the child and his grief, rather than a hush and denial can promote the child's feelings of belonging despite the immediate difficulties. The sense of being different, of being separate and removed is so easily promoted.

In one case reported, the cause of the death in the family was surrounded with some degree of shame. Out of kindness, little was said about the death, and when the child returned to school after the funeral no one spoke to her of it. Her peers seemed to be on guard and her teachers seemed polite but distant. The girl's posture and expression then, and for many weeks afterward, indicated a sense of little self-value. She did become an isolate for a period. She was avoided by others; they were awkward and ill at ease when with her. In addition, the girl herself seemed to seek solitude.

A deliberate and warm acceptance of the child when she returned to school could have perhaps countered the shame she evidenced and the isolation she experienced. A group recognition of the loss as a loss which was difficult and sad for the girl could have opened up her relations with the class who in turn could have shared their own experiences with death and grief. The silence surrounding the death had the corollary effect of increasing children's own anxiety about the possibility of their experiencing a similar loss, silence, and exclusion. The denial and the silence served as negative examples for each child's view of mourning, each child's concept of grief.

"Where can one turn in tragedy if no one understands or will admit that there is tragedy? But if tragedy can be admitted, we shall find our comfort in what we can mean to each other."[22] A high regard for this perspective and a concern over the attitude of death as unnatural and pornographic lay behind actions and responses to the grief of a child in the writer's schoolroom. Since the experience occurred while this chapter was being written, I could not have been more mentally prepared. I had come to the conclusion that, should a death occur in the lives of any of my students, I would seek to share the grief with the child and with the class openly and naturally, unless, of course, there was some indication that this would be harmful to the child. I did not want to promote the development of the feeling that the child was different and removed from the class. I did not want to see grief covered up and camouflaged like some ugly sore. Instead, I wanted the child to feel my support and that of his classmates at a time of crisis.

These were my beliefs, yet to act on them was not so simple as it was to value them. One of my students came to school with swollen eyes and clearly had been crying. She was a mature sixth grade student, so I believed her to have good reasons but perhaps personal ones for her upset. During morning announcements she wrote a note and handed it to me: "I'm sorry that I didn't do my homework last night, but my grandmother died and I had to go out of town." After my initial freeze of shock, I knew what to do, but did not know how to do it. Quietly I asked her if she would mind if I told the class why she was upset. She agreed to this so quickly that I asked her again to be certain that she understood. Again she nodded, so I made a fumbling but earnest explanation to the class. Their response was quick and natural, open, yet gentle. They spoke of their own experiences with death—"I know how she feels because my grandfather died last year"—and offered support and sympathy to their classmate in simple gestures of concern. Several girls rushed in to mend fences with their friend, apparently over a recent squabble. Others gently "fought" to have her on their team in recess games.

Two aspects of that day strike me in retrospect. First, the children seemed more expressive physically than on other days—walking hand in hand or with arms around each other's shoulders. The sense of a football huddle suits the impression. Secondly, the affective dimension of the informal conversations seemed stronger than usual; the conversations were about feelings and concerns which were important to the speakers.

At the conclusion of the day I felt convinced that, if a grieving child grants the teacher permission and if circumstances are such that further harm would not come to the child, then a very sad experience can be met somewhat instrumentally by sharing the grief and the reason for it with the class, and all the children involved will themselves gain from the experience. The class benefits as a unit of mutual support; individuals observe a grieving experience and thus become perhaps better able to grieve with less confusion or fear should they encounter a similar experience; and finally the child who is grieving is not having the experience compounded by school and social problems of exclusion, but rather is finding that people care for her and support her at a difficult time.

The children in this case reacted with ease, supporting the child in a natural manner. Whether they would have responded as openly or as well to the death of a classmate's parent or sibling is not clear. Such a death would hold their own fears of abandonment and loss. The freely expressed sympathy and the open caring might not have been possible.

Grief and the Work of Mourning

In addition to a consideration of the child's level of comprehension, the significance of the death to the child, and an awareness of the constellation of feelings the child is struggling with, the teacher needs to know what is entailed in grief and the work of mourning. This subject is dealt with thoroughly and beautifully in Chapter 3; however, because the teacher needs to alert herself for the difficulties which may arise from the mourning experience, let us review some of the concepts here and apply them to the classroom situation. "Now that teachers are concerned with the education of the whole child and have access to personal and family records in case of difficulty it may be the school that finally brings the problem [of bereavement] to light and helps to solve it."[23]

"The wise management of grief in children as well as adults revolves around two major factors: one, the encouragement and facilitation of the normal mourning process, and two, the prevention of delayed and/or distorted grief responses."[24] What then is the normal mourning process? If teachers are to be of help at this crucial point they must know what to look for and where they may be instrumental. Kliman outlines the mourning process for us in this way:

> The work of mourning can be divided conveniently into three areas . . . (1) testing and accepting the reality of the loss; (2) remembering—working over and decathecting the memories concerning the lost object; (3) cultivating substitute object relationships. A good deal of mourning work in all three areas can be expected of a healthy child. A marked lack of or extremely intense work may be poor prognostic signs.[25]

These clear distinctions can guide us and help us understand the child's behavior. They explain for us, perhaps, things which we sense as right but did not know why they were right. On several occasions I have been startled by the bluntness with which children have spoken of deaths of their parents or friends. When a fifth grade child was killed, children throughout the school were upset, and they spoke of it over and over again. "Did you know about . . . ?," "Have you heard about . . . ?", and similar queries could be heard through the halls and in the classrooms. Even when the listener had heard and did know, the story was retold. In one case a child told me the story two times during the day. At the end of the second time he realized what he had done and he caught his breath, and then smiled at himself and me. He had told the story not for my sake, he realized, but for his own. It seemed and felt right at the time. The boy was, it may be suggested, testing and attempting to accept the reality of the loss. On another occasion, a child was called from my room and taken home. His brother had been killed in an automobile accident a few hours earlier. When the class and I talked about what had happened one child spoke forcefully and even proudly about the death of his own father in an automobile accident. Here, too, the proud, blunt statement seemed right. It may be the case that the child had tested and accepted the reality of his loss reasonably well, and his pride would reside in that very accomplishment.

A school psychologist tells us that the first two stages of the three-step mourning process are clearly ones in which the alert and sensitive teacher may aid the child in his mourning work.[26] The teacher is encouraged to help the child at this point by providing opportunities for the expression of his grief either verbally, in writing, or even in art. In addition to listening actively and readily, the teacher may gently elicit the child's feelings. Moller describes the child's sense of upset and the value of discussing the feelings which he may not be verbalizing:

> Quite suddenly their unsuspecting trust in the security of family life is broken. Overcome by shock and apathy they lapse into a long period of apprehensiveness. It is imperative to give bereaved children an opportunity to talk about their bafflement. . . . In school, psychologists, social workers, guidance counselors, or teachers should try to stimulate discussions on the subject to help the child work through his grief.[27]

Similar advice is given to us by Mitchell for the purpose of revealing and relieving feelings of guilt which the child may be experiencing:

> It might be advisable for parents and teachers to bring guilt feelings out into the open, casually, with children who do not express their

feelings. They can make sure that the child realizes that the death of a friend or relative, and particularly one who was disliked, occurred naturally and was in no way connected with the child's behavior.[28]

As the classroom teacher seeks ways to help a child she should avoid the two extreme responses. On the one hand, she should not silently ignore the problem, for such a response could promote suppression on the child's part and would then work counter to the healthy though painful work of confronting reality. On the other hand, she should not rush to the child with reassurances, leaving the child no room for his own responses. Rather she should openly but gently observe and support the child in his mourning and at times she may wish to intervene to stimulate the process actively.

The immediate or delayed consequences of suppressed grief may be great. These include school phobia, under-achievement, learning disabilities, speech difficulties, discipline problems, and deeper psychological disturbances.[29] While these reactions to death may be considered the concerns of the school counselor or psychologist, it is in most cases the classroom teacher who must recognize the need and move to solve it. Further, the teacher is uniquely qualified to help through his or her natural, already-established relationship with the child. Thus, though counsel is sought, the charge remains the teacher's.

Reactions to a loss may continue several years after the loss itself. According to one study "teachers found it hard to accept the fact that, even two or three years after the original deprivation, a child could still be uninterested in classroom subjects, fail to pay attention, and not work up to his capacity."[30] When a teacher becomes aware of a problem and wants to understand it, she should look beyond the recent past for possible causes.

A Common Loss

When a child in the classroom dies, the teacher must consider the effects of the loss on individual children in the room, on the group as a whole, and on herself as well. The responses of four interviewed teachers concerning deaths in their classrooms were especially helpful as they were shared with me.[31]

Two of the teachers said that they had cried in front of their classes. In both cases the children expressed surprise at first but were then supportive and understanding. All four teachers discussed the death with their classes. Two mentioned the awkwardness and sadness of having to remove the dead child's desk and things from the room. The subject of the child's death was discussed by these teachers whenever it was brought in the classroom. All mentioned that the subject was brought up from time to time many months after the loss.

In all four cases the teachers and children did something in response to the death, some form of memorial. For a middle school child who was killed, his former teacher collected money from children and donated books to the school library in his name. This was especially nice because, after the initial strong emotional response to the death, a period of time elapsed while the books were being ordered. During this delay the response to the child's death deepened and calmed. When the books arrived they were placed on display by the librarian, and children and teachers were thus silently reminded of the loss. In another case, the children wrote letters to the child's mother telling her what they liked about the child. (These were never delivered because the teacher was told by other teachers that the letters would be too painful for the mother to read. In retrospect, the teacher wished that she had delivered them after all.) In still another case, the dead child's class was given a memorial book by another class which had been working with them. The teachers felt that these formal expressions were good for the children and appropriate for the grieving families.

The teacher who collected money for the book memorial mentioned above seemed comfortable in her dealings with death. She was personally saddened by her former pupil's death, yet she was willing to share her feelings with her school children and to respond to theirs. She felt it was valuable to help the class to try to understand the family's feeling of loss. Further she advises the teacher to call on the family and express her honest feelings. Her presence and words can mean a lot to the family.

One class responded to the death of a child in another class with curiosity and questions which the teacher thought might have been based on fear of concrete aspects of death. The teacher finally arranged to have her husband, a funeral director, answer the children's questions. The children went to the funeral parlor for this. The teacher felt that the experience was valuable for the children because familiarity usually reduces fear.

Though our hearts are with the teacher who responded to the first question of the informal survey ("Have any of your pupils died this year?") with a "No, thank God!," we may still benefit from these teachers' experiences with a common loss.

Death as a Subject

Because society in the seventies treats death as a taboo topic to be disguised by euphemisms, and because more and more of the elderly and the dying are isolated in nursing homes and hospital wards, segregated from the rest of society, the time has perhaps come for positive and direct death education in the schools. Indeed this is being done in some elementary schools, high schools, and colleges.[32] Direct education in death also occurs when the need arises as we have noted in earlier sections of this chapter. The specific counseling and guidance given to individual children in their mourning work may also be looked upon as direct education in death. What, however, should we as classroom teachers do when specific incidents do not define or highlight the need for us?

A Natural Integration into the Curricula

I personally do not feel that the need for instruction is great enough to merit a direct death-education course. I feel equally negative about the complete avoidance of the subject of death in our classrooms. We should neither force-feed our children with death instruction nor starve them with the absence of it. A natural, comfortable integration of death as a concept, as a shaping influence, may enter into much of the already existing curricula. Let us briefly consider how this might be done.

Social studies. Perhaps one of the most inclusive and useful definitions of this area of study is the following:

> The social studies [are] rooted in history and the social sciences to provide for inquiry into social, economic, and political activities [with a focus on the aspects of]: variety and change of human behavior in groups; interaction of people with their human and physical environment; relationships among people, between people and institutions, between people and the earth, and between people and value systems.[33]

We may say that man lies at the center of all of these, and, though the concern is with his life, it is at the same time also with his death. The regard for the first is shaped by the second.

As an example of such an orientation, we may mention an elementary school level social studies program, simply entitled *Man: A Course of Study,* developed by the Education Development Center,

Inc., under grants from the National Science Foundation. Its primary concern is with answers to the question, "What makes man human?" As answers are sought, concepts emerge, for instance—life cycles, survival, myth making, and death. Guiding questions from the introductory manual indicate how naturally death fits into the study:

> What things happen during one person's lifetime that happen to all people, to all living things? How does life go on even though individuals die? Some questions have no final answers; yet they may lead to a greater understanding of one's own past and place in the world today.[34]

To answer these questions children study selected forms of life—the salmon, the chimpanzee, baboon, and eventually man, the Netsilik Eskimo.

A second social studies program, also suitable to the natural integration of death as a subject, has been prepared by the Social Science Staff of the Educational Research Council of America. This program is entitled *The Human Adventure*. It is designed to be studied by children in the upper elementary grades. The outlook and tone of this program is similar to that of *Man: A Course of Study*, but it is more concerned with civilized man and the influence of ideas and values. From the program's introduction we note:

> The social science program must, therefore, pay constant attention to the values that direct men's choices and behavior. . . . Above all, the student should learn to inquire into the possible existence of universal values, that is, values shared by rational men everywhere. This concept of Natural Law is an important counterbalance to the cultural relativism (and consequent cynicism) that often results from analysis of successive religions and cultures.[35]

Some concepts and experiences children enter into in this program are directly concerned with death. In the study of Confucianism, children learn of the high regard that is placed on the whole family, whether the members are living or dead. It is reported that, when a Chinese child is asked who his relatives are, he automatically includes the dead as well as the living. Rituals and festivals such as the Ch'ing Ming Festival ("Cleaning the Ancestors' Graves Day") are also studied. In the study of Buddhists and Hindus in India this program exposes children to the concept of reincarnation and shows ways that such an idea can control and shape behavior. Death is included naturally in the program, providing interest and insight into the culture being studied.

The materials for all social studies programs may be adapted to include the concept of death in some way. If the lives of famous Americans are to be the material for the program, the deaths as well as the lives should be considered. What did Lincoln's death mean to those left to govern the country? Why was the country so guilt-ridden when John Kennedy was killed? What meaning can we find in the death as well as the life of Martin Luther King? In those courses of study that call for overviewing the geography and customs of different countries, such matters as the burial, mourning activities, and regard for the dead should not be neglected, or worse yet deliberately deleted. In all of these approaches, death is included naturally, being neither forced nor repressed.

Science. In the early years of elementary school, children learn to distinguish the characteristics of living things. In such studies they may touch on death characteristics for comparative purposes. In the middle school years the human body, its make-up and functioning, is studied somewhat in depth. Children seem particularly interested in the study of the heart and the respiratory system which are, needless to say, critical sources for the continuance of life. As children learn more, they may foresee the possibilities of the elimination of death or the prolonging of life. They may ask us unanswerable questions. Mitchell suggests a positive direction for our responses. In one of her classes a discussion of living and nonliving things led to a discussion of dead bodies which in turn led to a discussion of atoms and then to a discussion of electrons. A child in her class finally burst out with:

"They [electrons] *could* go on forever. Bits of me can go on forever and ever and ever." I realized then that probably this is the way to help children overcome their fears of death—by telling as much of the truth as we know. Similarly, when the curious child asks what happens to *me* after death or to grandma one need not say "You or she will disappear for ever" but rather "People are still trying to find out, just as they are trying to find out what is in space."[36]

Mitchell's response supports both the causes of science and the efforts to regard death openly.

The creative arts. These may be considered as expressions of feelings. They may act as vessels for the simple release of emotions. The angry painting, the joyous dance, the sad story reflect the inner child and catch and shape the spilling feeling. Death may be played with safely in this realm as children draw monsters, write murder mysteries, dramatize a death or drone a funeral dirge. It may be play, this peeking at death, but it is purposeful play.

The arts may also act as serious working ground for coming to terms with a feeling. Children may not be able to define the feeling, it may be too strong, too frightening, or pervasive, but they may be able to express the feeling in their drawings, music, creative drama, poetry, or other art form. They then may deal with the feeling or communicate it more easily and perhaps more gradually and securely. We have such an example in Chapter 4 where a child comes to terms with his fear of death through his drawings.

Finally the arts may act as windows to self-understanding. As children learn to interpret moods and emotions in a work of art, they become aware of the shades of their own moods and feelings. For this reason teachers may wish to begin art appreciation programs. A number of these are available commercially in kit form containing filmstrips, records of commentary, and a short teacher's guide book. A particularly enjoyable kit, entitled *Understanding Art: Abstraction and Representation*, involves the children in the creation of art as well as the viewing of it. A sample activity:

> Have your students make a "realistic" picture of any subject that they desire—but—in which they must get a feeling of mood, and expression. Something violent or something calm. Something sad or joyful. Compare the results with the work of the major artist whose works appear in the filmstrip.[37]

The arts are to be encouraged for they give children opportunities to express themselves, their inner selves. Sylvia Ashton-Warner, the guardian of this child right, tells us:

> Touch the true voice of feeling and it will create its own style and vocabulary. The words which caption the native imagery I call the Key Vocabulary, for they unlock the mind.[38]

Literature. Just as death occurs in life, so it occurs in literature; and here, perhaps, is the most fruitful area in which to work. Death seems to be placed in the appropriate perspective in good literature, that is to say, it neither dominates nor is denied. Literature also provides readers with the vicarious experiences of death of oneself and of others. Grief, mourning, and other feelings are engaged more deeply in literature than they can be, say, on television. Finally, literature may provide the opportunity for a release of emotions over a real loss.

As a vicarious experience with death, literature may evoke feelings of anger, sorrow, frustration, and helplessness. The place and purpose, justice and meaning of death may become matters of immediate concern to the active reader. Real tears may be shed, real anger may burn but, if the reader so chooses, he can stand back and assure himself that no one really died, that what he feels is a response to something fictional, unreal. The experience, however, has raised questions which would have been raised with a real personal experience. The fictional, reading experience may also be regarded as a practice or rehearsal for the reader's confrontation with his own grief or his own death.

Literature may also act as a release for suppressed grief which resulted from previous losses in the reader's experiences. One high school student reported that it was not until she had read about the deaths of her favorite characters in *The Three Musketeers* that she cried over her father's death.[39]

If the teacher uses literature as a means of teaching about death, she needs to be selective. Many books contain death, some contain grief, yet their values vary widely. Some are written sentimentally, eliciting a feeling of pity from the reader; others are written artistically with sensitivity and dignity. If a book meets the standards of fine literature, it should manage the subject of death well, if not significantly. There are several guides for the teacher as she evaluates the quality of writing in a children's book. She may use her own literary sense; she may consider the awards[40] given to the book; she may seek the librarian's guidance. The nonfiction books should not be neglected. In recent years a number of books have been written for children with the goal of informing them about the subject of death. History books, war stories, and biographies also offer perspectives on death.

Of all the books that I have personally reviewed, the single book which encountered death most directly and beautifully was *The Big Wave* by Pearl Buck. The story is really a parable about how to live with the idea of death. She introduces her book to her young readers in this way:

> It was during the war and I saw that many children were afraid, even American children. They were not used to the idea of death. They thought that death comes only to old people. But during the war they learned that death comes also to the young, if we allow it. . . . I thought then that I would like to write a story . . . that could help other children not to be afraid of death, because life is stronger than death. Life goes on and on, whatever happens. So I wrote this book, *The Big Wave*.[41]

Whatever Happens

Pearl Buck's help is direct, simple, and artistic. In school, we as teachers seek the same. When children grieve, they need our support and that of other children. Polite silences will not serve them. In classrooms, we as teachers act as guides, frail ones perhaps, to lead the grieving children, and so we must confront our own thoughts before meeting those of others. Finally, we, as teachers, must respond to the sadness as well as the joy of human life.

Notes

* The author gratefully acknowledges the assistance given by Mrs. Barbara Nolan, school psychologist, Holcomb Campus School, State University of New York; Dr. William Pinar, College of Education, The University of Rochester, New York; and other friends, in their thoughtful examinations of an earlier version of the manuscript.

1. Clark Moustakas, *The Authentic Teacher* (Cambridge, Ma.: Howard A. Doyle Publishing Co., 1967), p. 21.

2. Joseph Church, *Language and the Discovery of Reality* (New York: Random House, 1961), p. 202.

3. For fuller explanations of this approach to education the following sources are strongly recommended: Sylvia Ashton-Warner, *Teacher* (New York: Simon and Schuster, 1966); Joseph D. Hassett and Arline Weisberg, *Open Education: Alternatives within Our Tradition* (Englewood Cliffs, N.J.: Prentice-Hall, 1972); Alvin Hertzberg, and Edward F. Stone, *Schools Are For Children* (New York: Schocken Books, 1971); John Holt, *How Children Fail* (New York: Pitman, 1964); Sybil Marshall, *An Experiment in Education* (New York: Cambridge University Press, 1966); Moustakas, *Authentic Teacher;* and Kaoru Yamamoto, ed., *The Child and His Image* (Boston: Houghton Mifflin, 1972).

4. Donald Barr, *Who Pushed Humpty Dumpty?* (New York: Atheneum, 1971), p. 142.

5. Robert Fulton, "On the Dying of Death," in *Explaining Death to Children,* ed. Earl A. Grollman (Boston: Beacon Press, 1967), pp. 31-47, quoted from p. 31.

6. Edgar N. Jackson, "The Theological, Psychological, and Philosophical Dimensions of Death in Protestantism," in *Explaining Death to Children,* ed. Earl A. Grollman (Boston: Beacon Press, 1967), pp. 171-95, quoted from p. 177.

7. Ibid., p. 172.

8. See: John L. Phillips, Jr., *The Origins of Intellect: Piaget's Theory* (San Francisco: W. H. Freeman and Company, 1969); also see, Hans G. Furth, *Piaget for Teachers* (Englewood Cliffs, N.J.: Prentice Hall, 1970).

9. For additional reading see: Robert Kastenbaum, "The Child's Understanding of Death: How Does It Develop?," in *Explaining Death to Children,* ed. Earl A. Grollman (Boston: Beacon Press, 1967), pp. 89-108; also see, Marjorie Editha Mitchell, *The Child's Attitude to Death* (New York: Schocken Books, 1967), pp. 55-64; and Maria H. Nagy, "The Child's View of Death," *Journal of Genetic Psychology* 73 (September 1948): 3-27.

10. Mitchell, *Child's Attitude*, p. 62.

11. Kastenbaum, "Child's Understanding," p. 102.

12. Mitchell, *Child's Attitude*, p. 62.

13. Kastenbaum, "Child's Understanding," p. 104.

14. Roberta S. Sigel, "An Exploration into Some Aspects of Political Socialization: School Children's Reactions to the Death of a President," in *Children and The Death of a President*, ed. Martha Wolfenstein and Gilbert Kliman (Gloucester, Ma.: Peter Smith, 1969), p. 49.

15. Bernard Rosenblatt, "Reactions of Children to the Death of Loved Ones—Some Notes Based on Psychoanalytic Theory," in *The Loss of Loved Ones*, ed. David M. Moriarty (Springfield, Il.: Charles C Thomas, 1967), pp. 135-45, quoted from p. 145.

16. David M. Moriarty, ed., *The Loss of Loved Ones* (Springfield, Il.: Charles C Thomas, 1967), p. 13.

17. Gilbert Kliman, *Psychological Emergencies of Childhood* (New York: Grune & Stratton, 1971), p. 89.

18. Rudolf Dreikurs and Vicki Soltz, *Children: The Challenge* (New York: Duell, Sloan and Pearce, 1964), p. 245.

19. Ibid., p. 246.

20. Moriarty, *The Loss*, p. 115.

21. Max Schur, *Freud: Living and Dying* (New York: International Universities Press, 1972), p. 529.

22. Hella Moller, "Death: Handling the Subject and Affected Students in the Schools," in *Explaining Death To Children*, ed. Earl A. Grollman (Boston: Beacon Press, 1967), pp. 145-67, quoted from pp. 147-48.

23. Mitchell, *Child's Attitude*, p. 106.

24. Fulton, "On the Dying," pp. 46-47.

25. Kliman, *Psychological Emergencies*, p. 89.

26. The source is Mrs. Barbara Nolan, the school psychologist of Holcomb Campus School, State University of New York at Geneseo.

27. Moller, "Death," p. 163.

28. Mitchell, *Child's Attitude*, p. 107.

29. Kliman, *Psychological Emergencies*, pp. 89-90, presents a list of indicators for preventive intervention. Let me briefly summarize it here.

Single indicators (presence of any one of these suggests intervention):
Suicide of parent
Very poor relationship between child and parent, dead or surviving
Mentally ill parent, either dead or surviving
Maternal bereavement of a girl younger than eight

Joint indicators (any two of these suggest intervention):
Child less than four at bereavement
Child with a history of neurotic/psychotic illness
Child over four does not discuss dead parent or fact of death
Child over five refuses to take part in family funeral, services, etc.
Child over eight shedding no tears in first weeks after death
Child having unusually cheerful mood after parental death
If a boy, paternal death during adolescence

If a girl, maternal death from childbirth and tumors of sex organs
Abrupt and unexpected death
Death forcing geographical or economic displacement
Unavailability of suitable parent surrogate of the same sex
Pathologic mourning of remaining parent
Increasing physical intimacy between remaining parent and child
Long (six months plus), or disfiguring/degenerating terminal illness
Familial neglect, concealment, or delay in explaining death to child

30. Moller, "Death," p. 165.

31. Six teachers in the Geneseo school had lost, through death, a pupil in their classroom at some time during their teaching experience and were willing to discuss their experiences with me in interviews. The first four teachers described specific classroom death and grieving incidents, and it is on these that I base my comments in this section. The last two offered insights into the management of group mourning as they experienced deaths in ministerial roles. I am grateful to all six for sharing their thoughts and experiences: Ruth Hoppe, Mary Isgro, Betty Marks, Margaret Shipman, Dr. Malcolm Agostini, and Robert Holley. Also see: Fern H. Jacobi: "Death Touched Our School," *Childhood Education* 43 (October 1966): 85-86.

32. Specific educational instruction in the subject of death may be noted in the comments of the guidance counselor in St. Louis, which are quoted earlier in this chapter. For a useful descriptive account of the justification and the execution of a death mini-course at the junior high school level see: David W. Berg and George G. Daugherty, "Teaching About Death," *Today's Education* 62 (March 1973): 46-47. For evidences of course work in death at the college level see "Thanatology 1," *Time*, January 8, 1973, p. 36.

33. John U. Michaelis, *Social Studies for Children in a Democracy*, 4th ed. (Englewood Cliffs, N.J.: Prentice-Hall, 1968), p. 3.

34. The "Introductory Lessons" to *Man: A Course of Study* (Cambridge, Ma.: Education Development Center, Inc., 1969), p. 5.

35. Educational Research Council of America, *The Human Adventure*, Book 2, *Four World Views* (Boston: Allyn and Bacon, 1971), pp. 2-3, teacher's guide.

36. Mitchell, *Child's Attitude*, p. 76.

37. *Understanding Art: Abstraction and Representation* (Great Neck, N.Y.: Educational Dimensions Corporation), p. 5, teacher's guide.

38. Sylvia Ashton-Warner, *Spearpoint* (New York: Alfred A. Knopf, 1972), p. 91.

39. Martha Wolfenstein, "Death of a Parent and Death of a President: Children's Reactions to Two Kinds of Loss," in *Children and The Death of A President*, ed. Martha Wolfenstein and Gilbert Kliman (Gloucester, Ma.: Peter Smith, 1969), pp. 70-90, quoted from p. 81.

40. The Caldecott Medal Award is given annually for the most distinguished picture book for children. The Newbery Medal Award is given annually to the author of the most distinguished contribution to children's literature. For a complete list of other children's literature awards, see: Charlotte Huck and Doris Kuhn, *Children's Literature in the Elementary School* (New York: Holt, Rinehart and Winston, 1961), pp. 701-23.

41. Pearl Buck, *The Big Wave* (New York: J. Day, 1948).

Suggested Readings

The following authors express a special concern for the affective dimension of classrooms and education. While they may not discuss death and grief specifically, their concern for the recognition, acceptance, and response to children's feelings is so clearly defined and described that their thoughts and theories can easily be applied to a grief situation:

Ashton-Warner, Sylvia, *Spearpoint* (New York: Alfred A. Knopf, 1972).
Ashton-Warner, Sylvia, *Teacher* (New York: Simon and Schuster, 1966).
Hassett, Joseph D. and Weisberg, Arline, *Open Education: Alternatives Within Our Tradition* (Englewood Cliffs, N.J.: Prentice-Hall, 1972).
Hertzberg, Alvin and Stone, Edward F. *Schools Are For Children* (New York: Schocken Books, 1971).
Holt, John, *How Children Fail* (New York: Pitman, 1964).
Marshall, Sybil, *An Experiment in Education* (New York: Cambridge University Press, 1966).
Montagu, Ashley, *On Being Human* (New York: Hawthorn Books, Inc., 1966).
Moustakas, Clark, *The Authentic Teacher* (Cambridge, Ma.: Howard A. Doyle Publishing Co., 1967).
Yamamoto, Kaoru, ed., *The Child and His Image* (Boston: Houghton Mifflin 1972).

Two books that discuss death and grief with children in a direct and helpful manner are:

Grollman, Earl A., ed., *Explaining Death to Children* (Boston: Beacon Press, 1967), a fine collection of different perspectives on the subject. For the classroom teacher Hella Moller's chapter, "Death: Handling the Subject and Affected Students in Schools," is especially valuable.

Mitchell, Marjorie Editha, *The Child's Attitude to Death* (New York: Schocken Books, 1967). Though Mrs. Mitchell writes about children and education in England, the similarities are great enough for this to be a most useful book for American teachers and parents.

For practical curricular guides and ideas for teachers who wish to tap the affective dimensions of their classrooms, the following are recommended:

Cullum, Albert, *Push Back the Desks* (New York: Citation Press, 1967).
Koch, Kenneth, *Wishes, Lies, and Dreams—Teaching Children to Write Poetry* (New York: Chelsea House Publishers, 1970).
Petty, Walter T. and Bowen, Mary E., *Slithery Snakes and Other Aids to Children's Writing* (New York: Appleton-Century-Crofts, Division of Meredith Publishing Company, 1967).
Raths, Louis E.; Harmin, Merrill; and Simon, Sidney B., *Values and Teaching* (Columbus, Oh.: Charles E. Merrill Publishing Company, 1966).
Reasoner, Charles F., *Releasing Children to Literature* (New York: Dell Publishing Co., 1968).
Reasoner, Charles F., *Where the Readers Are* (New York: Dell Publishing Co., 1972).

Epilogue: Looking Beyond

Kaoru Yamamoto

"Man is an enigma. He is but a transient in the universe; yet he is aware of eternity. He is a feeble being; yet his faith moves a mountain."[1] These words, which I wrote for an introductory chapter of another, earlier cooperative endeavor, haunt me in addressing the present subject of death in the life of children.

Man is as much an enigma in death as in life. He lives to reveal glory and gloom, aspiration and apathy, dignity and degeneration, compassion and cruelty, in the ever-present shadow of death which reduces all organic matter to ashes. In every moment of his existence, death challenges man with the nagging question of ultimate futility and complete despair. After spending all his life in the quest for identity, man's last day is to be characterized by negation of his very self, by the impossibility of coexistence of being with nonbeing. Where death is, the person cannot be.

Man Alone

In dying, nevertheless, man reveals for the last time who he really is. "They died as they lived. . . . They each hung on to their habitual defenses—regressing, denying, withdrawing, projecting, as before."[2] Yes, man dies as he lives. Unless he has come to understand and accept himself in life, he will not face death graciously, and he will not suffer the process of dying valiantly. And, unless he is attuned to his own life and death, he cannot possibly touch others in any vital way at those moments of their greatest needs.

Although not many Westerners would regard death as an actual physical presence that continuously serves as an impartial judge and a wise counsel through their life,[3] there is no denying that man's attitudes to life and to death are closely intertwined. Just as there are enormous variations in his life styles, so there are many differences in

183

his orientation to death and dying.[4] Questions may be the same, but answers are, and have to be, uniquely his own.

Death, as organic "termination," is universal to all living matter, but man, and only man, anguishes over his "cessation," or the end of his conscious experience.[5] He, and he alone, dies a thousand deaths while alive, and repeatedly contemplates upon his total annihilation.

Meaning

Lepp, a French priest and psychotherapist, tersely summarized the significance of death in relation to life:

> Instead of thinking of death as the end . . . of life, I propose that we see it as the last act, the fulfillment of temporal existence. It would then follow that if we succeed in giving meaning to our lives, death would be by the same token meaningful.[6]

How, then, does one give life a meaning?

Bitter human experiences during the past several decades have made this query particularly trenchant. In the midst of man's large-scale destruction of human beings everywhere, be it through bullets, bombs, automobiles, fires, drugs, or anything else, the sense or non-sense of life itself becomes an urgent issue for consideration. Without pretending to be able to answer such a profound question myself, let me briefly recapitulate some points made by astute observers among us.

The meaning of life is not something to be found once and for all. The familiar expression, "search for meaning," would be misleading if it suggested an uncovering of already existing meaning buried somewhere out there. Rather, meaning has to be continuously defined and redefined in response to life's ever-changing context. As each man is singular, so also his meaning. As each experience of his life is unique, so also its meaning.

In his poignant discussion of life in Nazi concentration camps, Frankl points out that we should stop asking life of its meaning, but instead begin answering life its questions.[7] Life owes us nothing, but we owe life everything. This is so, because life provides us with a continuous opportunity, as well as challenge, to take a stand on whatever happens to confront us, to be conscious and responsible, and to be free and human. The task, or the privilege, is fundamentally individual in nature, and no one can substitute for anyone else. Life expects something of each person at every moment to the last of his days, and he retains the ultimate freedom in orienting himself to *his* destiny and coming up with *his* own way to bear *his* unique burden. Thus, "human life, under any circumstances, never ceases to have a meaning, and . . . this infinite meaning of life includes suffering and dying, privation and death."[8]

Bettelheim, another survivor of the horrendous, yet unmistakably human, institution of concentration and extermination camps, recounts a story of a woman prisoner who was marched naked to the gas chamber with the others. Somehow learning that she had been a dancer, the commanding SS officer ordered her to dance for him. Under these unbelievable circumstances, the lady danced, and while dancing, approached the officer to seize his gun to shoot to kill him. She herself was immediately shot to death. Senseless? Perhaps. "But isn't it probable," Bettelheim asks, "that despite the grotesque setting in which she danced, dancing made her once again a person?" A person who died in dignity to achieve her immortality by choosing the way in which she would face her inescapable fate?

> Exercising the last freedom that not even the concentration camp could take away—to decide how one wishes to think and feel about the conditions of one's life—this dancer threw off her real prison. This she could do because she was willing to risk her life to achieve autonomy once more. If we do that, then if we cannot live, at least we die as man.[9]

Community

Man dies alone. However, his death transcends the isolated phenomenon to affect all. John Donne was right in saying that the bell tolls for humanity. Every death diminishes you and me. Each, in his awkward way, responds to this reality.

Marks depicts a Miss Steineck, a fifth-grade teacher, who took on herself the task of breaking the news of the death of one of her pupils to the rest of the class. She fumbles about and tries to tell the group of her own childhood experience with the death of a pet crow. After having cried out her eyes for weeks, she recounts, she dreamed of Timmie, the crow, flying to her and asking her to remember him that way, a handsome bird with glistening feathers. The pet was dead, but she was not sad anymore. Alas, the class does not register any reaction at all. No emotions expressed, nothing. Miss Steineck feels betrayed and resumes the school routine of the day. The art (free drawing) period goes by eventlessly and, at the end of the session, children noisily scramble for the first place in line. Nonchalant, indifferent, cold-blooded little brats, fumes Miss Steineck; they don't really care.

She then notices the topmost picture of the pile on her desk. It depicts the deceased child doing something she enjoyed or was good at. The next does the same, the next, and the next. In their own ways, children were expressing strong emotions to the loss of one of their kind. Their lives have been unmistakably touched by the death of the classmate.

She laid the papers on the table. And then, to her own amazement, she found herself with her head on her desk, crying as she had not cried since Timmie died.[10]

Notwithstanding Donne's famed claim that no man is an island, we are actually separate islands in a common sea.[11] Each man is essentially and ultimately alone, and this quality of solitude has to be at the core of our orientation to, and comprehension of, life. To be capable of being alone, still, and at ease with ourselves seems to be a sign of human maturity.

It must, nevertheless, be remembered that a common sea surrounds us all, and that our fate is closely interrelated with each other's. "The fundamental fact of human existence is man with man. What is peculiarly characteristic of the human world is above all that something takes place between one being and another the like of which can be found nowhere in nature."[12]

In a typical paradox of life, individuation cannot be fulfilled by seeking further and further divergence. After striving hard to affirm his individuality, man must move back towards his brethren, must lose himself to rediscover it in others, and must grow to be a compassionate being.[13] Without this convergence, this uniting with humanity, he will suffer from crippling preoccupation with his own, minute being and eventual nothingness in the immense universe. He ends up with a feeling of utter frustration and despair. No, "personal destiny cannot be separated from the destiny of the human community," and "it is the duty of each one of us, particularly the duty of educators, to bring about the integration of the subjective, individual meaning of life with the communitarian significance of human existence."[14]

This sense of community is the backdrop of an awareness of meaningful life and death. If, in other words, human life is worth living for, it is also worth dying for. If a child touched the lives of those around him, the community has been enriched and deepened by his life and seemingly premature death. "The melody that the loved one played upon the piano of life will never be played quite that way again, but we must not close the keyboard and allow the instrument to gather dust."[15] The challenge is for the living, not for the dead who ran his race for us.

Rituals

Human communities have developed and practiced many rituals to reaffirm their solidarity in the face of critical events in life. Social *rites de passage* and religious sacraments represent, among other things, our attempts at corroboration of group cohesion. The race may be over for the deceased, but we are still alive and we are still answerable to life. By crying together, grieving together, and mourning together, we release our tension and give emotional support to the bereaved and to each other. We thus prepare for our tomorrow.

Eulogies may not convey much on the symbolic level, but their presymbolic or affective message is what actually counts.[16] It may appear disrespectful for people to eat together, drink together, and sing together in the presence (*sic*) of the dead, but these activities have always posed prominently in human rituals as means of asserting the solidarity of the brotherhood of man. The sacrament of Eucharist or Holy Communion is a classic example.

An important point to bear in mind is that these experiences ought to be shared by people to serve their purposes. Communality is the key for functional rituals; otherwise, they become empty forms without spirit. That is the danger in refined, systematic ceremonies, over against homemade varieties. The latter may be a little disorganized, but tend to be more flexible and spontaneous. They retain vivid significance to the participants. While institutionalized rituals, established customs, and traditions have their place and functions, those based upon intimately shared experiences, those small rituals which are meaningful only to family members and close friends, often serve better to strengthen mutual bonds in the face of both human joys and miseries. When a tightly knit group cares, shares, and dares together, the whole is larger than the sum of the parts. Individual members are uplifted and supported in their endeavors, be they in the moments of sorrow or in those of happiness. Obviously, under the guidance of exceptional teachers, some classrooms take on this viable characteristic.

Because of the sustaining and healing nature of the shared facing of common crises and victories, it is especially important for adults not to ignore the young at the most critical time of bereavement and mourning. Rabbi Liebman presents the point beautifully as follows.

The child can stand tears but not treachery, sorrow but not deceit. The little boy or girl should be dealt with in a straightforward, honest fashion; he should be allowed to share and participate in the family's woes as well as triumphs. The little organism is much tougher than we sometimes think. It will not dissolve in a little salt water shed by the childish eye. It will not break under honestly presented grief. It may break under the burden of exclusion and exile from the family circle, under the heavy load of adult evasion, half-truths, frozen emotions, hypocritical pretenses.[17]

Because, "The sabbath was made for man, not man for the sabbath" (Mark 2:28), it is essential to let rituals serve their intended purposes. If, for instance, expression of genuine sorrow is regarded unbecoming in a funeral, the whole intent of this ritual is defeated. If, likewise, opportunities for partaking of the painful yet salving feelings of loss and loneliness are denied, the process of reconstruction is unnecessarily obstructed or delayed. Unless adequate grief and renewal work has first been done, the bereaved can hardly help making a shrine out of his guilt and sorrow, and seeking "the living among the dead" (Luke 24:6). Only after the required spadework, he is in a position to build a new pattern of life to replace partially, and expand, that which included the dead. Only then, in other words, he is ready to let the interrupted melody continue with finer and finer arrangements.

Time and Hope

Especially in the face of children's deaths, we are reminded of the fact that duration is not the true test of richness or depth of life. Many thinkers have concluded that the finiteness of our presence in flesh is precisely the dimension which gives significance to our being. Frankl makes this point succinctly: ". . . to perpetuate something in itself meaningless is meaningless. If the thing is meaningless, it does not acquire meaning by being immortalized. Even when a torch goes out, its light has had meaning."[18]

Now

Young children live in the present, and the relational concept of the future and the past arrives much later as a correlate of general cognitive development.[19] Although our culture attaches a high premium to the future orientation, and places much pressure upon the young to align themselves in this valuation,[20] the price we pay for this may be amazingly high. In the typical interpretation, today is nothing but a preliminary for tomorrow (even though, technically, today is yesterday's tomorrow, and the past is now which was!), and it does not in itself hold much value. One toils for tomorrow all his life only to find that what he has been so assiduously working toward is none other than death itself. After preparing himself so long and hard for the future, he suddenly realizes that he is totally unprepared for the final change.

To live fully in the present is a difficult lesson for many to learn, and to appreciate and cherish life here and now is a hard task for most who have been raised in the tradition of privation and work ethics. On the other hand, a complete negation of this orientation fosters irresponsibility and exploitation. A sensible synthesis of containment and liberation, holding-on and letting-go, commitment and tentativeness, is what is desired here. "Might teachers and counselors, as well as parents, present a model which provides this balance, a model in whom there is enjoyment of today without tomorrow's being ignored?"[21]

No doubt under the heavy influence of Hebraic world view, we perceive time as rectilinear and sequential, a straight road running from oblivion to oblivion. The Greek and/or Indian view of cyclical time has not been incorporated in the mainstream of our thought, and eternity is nothing but an endless continuation of the present.[22] A dreary thought!

No matter how construed, time does *not*, and should not, define life, even though many of us are slaves of (physical) time. In its magnitude and complexity, life is somewhat like an ocean. Its tide may be closely followed, described, and even predicted, but an understanding of the astoundingly rich variety of organisms and phenomena it contains can never be attained by applying a single-dimensional scale of time.

Man is a transcendental being who lives in many different worlds on many different times.[23] What transpires in the *Umwelt*, the world of objects and of people treated as if they were things, may be conveniently located on the clock time or passing time (note, incidentally, the basically spatial character of this concept of time). If man is a particle driven inexorably by some built-in instincts, or controlled uniformly by external patterns of stimuli, in other words, if he is merely a *reactive* being, his world can be neatly encompassed by such quantitative time.

Man, however, is active, emergent, and interrelational. In his *Mitwelt*, the world of inner meanings in the brotherhood of man, physical time loses much of its relevance. Thus, for example, the depth and character of love or trust can never be assessed by the length of life, or by the number of years of acquaintance. The significance of an experience does not lie in its place on the horizontal, one-way time line, or in its duration, or in its continuity.

Finally, the *Eigenwelt*, one's fundamental relationship with his self, has little to do with the passing time. Our awareness in this realm is immediate and unique, and the so-called objective and normative approaches of analysis are especially maladroit in handling it. The *Eigenwelt*, nevertheless, is the center from which everything else flows, and many of man's most profound experiences are found here, be they "in green pastures" (creative or re-creative endeavors) or "through the valley of the shadow of death" (suffering). As so movingly written by Mrs. Lindbergh:

> The here, the now, and the individual, have always been the special concern of the saint, the artist, the poet, and—from time immemorial—the woman. In the small circle of the home she has never quite forgotten the particular uniqueness of each member of the family; the spontaneity of now; the vividness of here. This is the basic substance of life. . . . When we start at the center of ourselves, we discover something worthwhile extending toward the periphery of the circle. We find again some of the joy in the now, some of the peace in the here, some of the love in me and thee which go to make up the kingdom of heaven on earth.[24]

Tomorrow

Let us, by all means, look ahead, but let us live in the here and now, we said. But, look ahead to what kind of future? To what vision of tomorrow? Man's hope and fear reside in the future which, remember, *he* creates. *His* images of tomorrow powerfully influence his present, and his dreams guide his action today.

Suppose we identify, after Polak, two basic stances of optimism and pessimism towards each of the two basic dimensions of what is (*Sein*, or essence) and what should or can be (*Willen*, or influence).[25] Thus, the following scheme:

| | | Influence (*Willen*) | |
		Optimism	Pessimism
Essence (*Sein*)	Optimism	A	B
	Pessimism	C	D

Essence-optimism refers to a belief that the universe is in harmony under some systematic planning and benevolent guidance, while essence-pessimism assumes a chaotic or malevolent cosmos. Influence-optimism believes in the possibility of human intervention to change the course of events, but influence-pessimism allows man little role in such manipulation. In combination, then, these dichotomies give four different views of the future.

In cell B, essence-optimism and influence-pessimism, is found an image of man as a mere passenger in a universe lawfully and automatically moving toward its predestined goal. Although the future may be bright, this process scarcely needs human beings and the whole tone tends to be deterministic, be it expressed in a linear notion of evolution or in a cyclical idea of recurrence or reincarnation. More fatalistic still is the combination of essence-pessimism and influence-pessimism, shown in cell D. Here, man is utterly powerless in a tumultuous universe, the only course left to him being total resignation to the sinister destiny.

In cells A and C, on the other hand, man intervenes more or less directly to mold his future. If the combination is one between essence-pessimism and influence-optimism (cell C), he may resort to supplication for reconciliation with the willful and unpredictable supernatural,[26] or to reliance upon human rationality for control and conquest of fate. When the latter course is followed, man's hope is epitomized in utopianism. There have been many utopian systems proposed in history, and the current ones reflect the technological preoccupation of the contemporary age (see, e.g., Aldous Huxley's Brave New World, George Orwell's 1984, and B. F. Skinner's Walden II).

In cell A, essence-optimism and influence-optimism, the passive influencing takes the form of prayers for a savior's grace, while the active option is represented in the tradition of redemption through work (within the context of final dependence upon divine benevolence). Eschatological belief in the coming of the Kingdom of God seems to belong in A, and to a certain extent in B also.

Living or dying, it makes a difference which of these possible images of the future one holds. Unfortunately, clear visions of tomorrow have become rarer and rarer in our culture, and what is available in the name of the future is nothing but a simple extrapolation of the present, or a bigger, faster, richer, and cheaper today. Whether this-worldly (utopian) or other-worldly (eschatological) in orientation, a future which is *qualitatively* different than the present is essential in expanding our consciousness and challenging our potential. New dreams we have to dream, and new myths we must create, to sustain hope that is not contained in our earthly space, not restricted to our physical time, and, most certainly, not bound to the familiar species of *Homo sapiens*.[27] Although we are accustomed to thinking ourselves, as known to us, to be the culmination of the long progression in the genus of man, superior to every other being, that would be too limited a view of life, too superficial a picture of the whole scheme of things in the universe, and too confining an interpretation of (for myself, anyway) God's creation.

The Current Scene

To speak of death is to speak of life. Ironically, for various reasons, it has been difficult to give birth to this book itself. Even while the manuscript was in gestation, social scenes continued to change and affect the general thought and practice on death and dying.

By now, for example, the name of Karen Ann Quinlan is a familiar one to both the health professionals and the concerned public.[28] In April 1975, at the age of twenty-five, this young woman became comatose overnight and remained unconscious for an extended period of time. She was kept alive essentially by a technical life support system. Upon concluding that there was no likelihood of recovery, Karen Ann's parents requested two physicians to turn off the respirator and allow her to die. This the doctors refused to do, and the case was taken by the parents to the court for adjudication. After prolonged legal proceedings, the New Jersey Superior Court decided in November 1975 against the Quinlans' request.

However, their appeal to the New Jersey Supreme Court received a favorable ruling. The respirator could be turned off if, in physicians' unanimous opinion, Karen Ann had no reasonable chance of regaining conscious existence. No challenge was forthcoming from the New Jersey attorney general's office to ask the U. S. Supreme Court to hear the case. Nevertheless, the Quinlans did not immediately exercise the granted option to release their daughter to death.[29] While further discussion was being held among the parents, lawyers, physicians, and the court for clarification of the ruling details, Karen Ann's condition changed somewhat. She was finally removed from the respirator fourteen months after lapsing into coma, but her destination was a nursing home under the skilled care of medical and nursing personnel.

Even though clinicians have known other similar instances, the

Quinlan case served to focus people's attention on several moral, legal, and medical issues surrounding life and death. The question of euthanasia has been discussed anew from many perspectives,[30] and the ramifications of life-prolonging technological achievements have been pursued.[31] The question of sanctity versus quality of life is being examined in conjunction with the matter of the right to die, or death with dignity.[32] Medical practices and ethics have likewise been scrutinized as regards the criteria of death, as well as such interventions as abortion, genetic engineering, organ transplantation, hemodialysis, and dying.[33] Various suggestions, statements, bills, and acts have been proposed, enacted, or practiced on subjects like the patient's bill of rights, living will, and natural death.[34] A living will gives instructions on artificial prolongation or cessation of life in the face of conditions preventing a person's considered decision making. Such a statement does not carry any legal status except in California, where a new law went into effect on January 1, 1977. Legislation similar to California's "Natural Death Act" has nevertheless been introduced in at least twenty-five states, including Florida, Pennsylvania, New York, and Massachusetts.

An increasing amount of attention has also been paid to the processes of bereavement, grief, and mourning,[35] and sensitive accounts of personal loss and reconstruction are occasionally added to the literature.[36] Several guides for health professionals are now available to encourage better care for the dying and their families.[37] Slowly, numerous shortcomings are being recognized of the current institutional settings of hospital as a place to die in, and the idea of "hospice" has come to be taken as a serious alternative.[38] This arrangement developed in England, which has now twenty-five hospices including St. Christopher's in London and St. Barnabas's near Brighton, to give the terminally ill a familial context in which to spend their last days. Thus, in addition to offering medical and nursing services, such *hospi*table pla*ces* have capabilities to accommodate families, look after younger children, allow able patients to continue to work, and provide emotional support and spiritual guidance to all, so as to insure a good home-care environment. In the United States and Canada, there are presently only a handful of operational hospices in places like Branford, Connecticut; Santa Barbara, California; Tucson, Arizona; New York, New York (St. Luke's Hospital Center); and Montreal, Canada (Royal Victorian Hospital).

Materials potentially useful for the improvement of one's quality of life and preparation for death have continued to be written for the general public.[39] In school, the once taboo topic of death has entered the realm of curricular reality,[40] while the development of lifelong education directed at the elderly has received an impetus from the awareness that meaningful death seldom follows meaningless life.[41] At least two extensive bibliographies on death and dying are now available to workers in this general field.[42] Finally, a few treatises have appeared on "life after life" to invite further thoughts on the mystery of human life and destiny.[43]

All told, there is no denying that more discussion on the subject of death and dying is being held among more people now than in the recent past. More things are in the public view, and more activities are in evidence. The overall trend is an encouraging one, but two observations should nevertheless be made here. First, the focus of inquiry and discussion has remained on adults, and the young ones are still relatively neglected. This is partially reflected in the far smaller number of specialized works on death in the life of children.[44] Second, whether or not the heightened interest in death and dying is indeed anything but another cultural mask of defense remains to be seen.[45] It may be that the old stereotypes and practices are merely replaced with new fads and biases. Paradoxically, the more one talks, the less one may have to think about what is (and is not) being said. The more continuously one talks, the longer one may be able to postpone facing the lurking guilt, fear, and anxiety. To be alone and at ease with oneself is still a severe test to most of us, both in life and in death.

Freedom, Life, and Death

Man's understanding of himself remains meager and lopsided, particularly under the *Zeitgeist* which values the tangible over intangibles, information over understanding, doing over being, and rationality over totality. Unsettling questions of human existence are avoided, and answers evaded. The voice of the supreme concern has been lost in the din of daily routines.[46] Man, however, is still man, and *his* meaning for *his* life and death cannot be given by anyone or anything else, not even by the powerful technological tools of his creation!

Liebman reminds us of an important distinction between the two senses of the word, "end." One is *finis*, the matter of form, the end of a sequence, a story, or a drama. The other is *telos*, the matter of substance, the completion, perfection, or consummation. In his incisive words:

Death has often written *finis* to a life that has had no "end," no "purpose." The worst tragedy that can befall a human being is to come to the end (*finis*) without ever having possessed any end (*telos*)—without ever having sought for any great aim in the midst of his life career.[47]

The challenge, therefore, is starkly personal in the first instance. If man's life is an aimless drifting, his death is equally meaningless; if his death is purposeless, his life itself has been wasted. Man's ultimate freedom is in his choice of what he makes of his life and death.

Notes

1. Kaoru Yamamoto, "The Concept of Self: Introduction," in *The Child and His Image: Self Concept in the Early Years*, ed. Kaoru Yamamoto (Boston: Houghton Mifflin, 1972), pp. 1-25, quoted from p. 1.

2. Daniel Cappon, "The Psychology of Dying," in *Death: Interpretations*, ed. Hendrik M. Ruitenbeek (New York: Dell Publishing Co., 1969), pp. 61-72, quoted from p. 61 and p. 62. This does not rule out the possibility of a person's growth during the last phase of his life. After all, man is an active and open being unto the last.

3. Carlos Castaneda, *Journey to Ixtlan* (New York: Simon and Schuster, 1972). For a survey of various views of death in the West, see: Philippe Ariès, *Western Attitudes toward Death* (Baltimore: Johns Hopkins University Press, 1974); and Jacques Choron, *Death and the Western Thought* (New York: Collier Books, 1963).

4. Different deaths in different personal and social contexts are told in such sources as: James Agee, *A Death in the Family* (New York: Avon Books, 1963); Steward Alsop, *Stay of Execution* (New York: Charles E. Tuttle, 1974); Robert Anderson, *After* (New York: Random House, 1973); John Gunther, *Death Be Not Proud* (New York: Harper & Row, 1949); Oscar Lewis, *A Death in the Sanchez Family* (New York: Random House, 1970); Doris Lund, *Eric* (Philadelphia: J. B. Lippincott, 1974); Alexander Solzhenitsyn, *Cancer Ward* (New York: Bantam Books, 1969); and Lael Tucker Wertenbaker, *Death of a Man* (Boston: Beacon Press, 1974). Also of interest is the following treatise by a scholar, written in his last days of terminal cancer: Ernest Becker, *The Denial of Death* (New York: The Free Press, 1973).

5. This distinction is discussed in: Edwin S. Shneidman, "Orientations toward Death," in *The Study of Lives*, ed. Robert W. White (New York: Atherton Press, 1963), pp. 200-27.

6. Ignace Lepp, *Death and Its Mysteries* (New York: Macmillan, 1969), p. 142.

7. Viktor E. Frankl, *Man's Search for Meaning* (New York: Washington Square Press, 1963); also see: Viktor E. Frankl, *The Will to Meaning* (New York: The New American Library, 1969).

8. Frankl, *Man's Search*, pp. 131-32.

9. Bruno Bettelheim, *The Informed Heart* (New York: Avon Books, 1971), p. 259.

10. Marjorie Marks, "Death in the Fifth Grade," in *Child Development through Literature*, ed. Elliott D. Landau, Sherrie L. Epstein, and Ann P. Stone

196   DEATH IN THE LIFE OF CHILDREN

(Englewood Cliffs, N.J.: Prentice-Hall, 1972), pp. 418-21, quoted from p. 421. For a concise description of the characteristics of children's reactions to death of loved ones, in contrast to those of adults', see: Martha Wolfenstein, "Death of a Parent and Death of a President: Children's Reactions to Two Kinds of Loss," in *Children and the Death of a President*, ed. Martha Wolfenstein and Gilbert Kliman (Garden City, N.Y.: Doubleday, 1966), pp. 70-90. Further information is to be found in the following source: Erna Furman, *A Child's Parent Dies* (New Haven, Ct.: Yale University Press, 1974).

11. Anne M. Lindbergh, *Gift from the Sea* (New York: Random House, 1955), pp. 37-59.

12. Martin Buber, *Between Man and Man* (New York: Macmillan, 1965), p. 203.

13. For related discussions, see, e.g.: Erik H. Erikson, *Insight and Responsibility* (New York: W. W. Norton, 1964), pp. 109-57; and Pierre Teilhard de Chardin, *The Phenomenon of Man* (New York: Harper & Row, 1961), pp. 237-99.

14. Lepp, *Death*, p. 145.

15. Joshua L. Liebman, *Peace of Mind* (New York: Simon and Schuster, 1946), p. 109.

16. For an examination of these matters, see: S. I. Hayakawa, *Language in Thought and Action*, 2nd ed. (New York: Harcourt, Brace & World, 1964), pp. 69-81. Related information of significance is found in: Jerome D. Frank, *Persuasion and Healing* (New York: Schocken Books, 1963).

17. Liebman, *Peace*, p. 123.

18. Viktor E. Frankl, *The Doctor and the Soul* (New York: Bantam Books, 1969), p. 55.

19. Leonard W. Doob, *Patterning of Time* (New Haven, Ct.: Yale University Press, 1971), pp. 247-52; and Jean Piaget, *The Child's Conception of Time* (New York: Ballantine Books, 1971).

20. See the following for diverse orientations to time found in different cultures: Edward T. Hall, *The Silent Language* (Garden City, N.Y.: Doubleday, 1959), pp. 23-41; and Florence R. Kluckhohn and Fred L. Strodtbeck, *Variations in Value Orientations* (New York: Harper & Row, 1961).

21. C. Gilbert Wrenn, *The World of the Contemporary Counselor* (Boston: Houghton Mifflin, 1973), p. 106.

22. J. B. Priestley, *Man and Time* (New York: Dell Publishing Co., 1968); and Henri M. Yaker, "Time in the Biblical and Greek Worlds," in *The Future of Time*, ed. Henri Yaker, Humphrey Osmond, and Frances Cheek (Garden City, N.Y.: Doubleday, 1972), pp. 15-35.

23. Rollo May, "Contributions of Existential Psychotherapy," in *Existence*, ed. Rollo May, Ernest Angel, and Henri F. Ellenberger (New York: Simon and Schuster, 1967), pp. 37-91.

24. Lindbergh, *Gift*, pp. 127-28.

25. Fred Polak, *The Image of the Future* (San Francisco: Jossey-Bass, 1973).

26. For a somewhat related discussion, see: William F. May, "The Sacral Power of Death in Contemporary Experience," in *Death in American Experience*, ed. Arien Mack (New York: Schocken Books, 1973), pp. 97-122.

27. Pierre Teilhard de Chardin, *The Future of Man* (New York: Harper & Row, 1964).

28. For the legal details of this case, consult the following: University Publications of America, *In the Matter of Karen Quinlan,* Vol. 1, *The Complete Legal Briefs, Court Proceedings, and Decision in the Superior Court of New Jersey,* and Vol. 2, *The Complete Briefs, Oral Arguments, and Opinion in the New Jersey Supreme Court* (Washington, D.C.: Author, 1976).

29. The family's own account of the agonizing experience appears in: Joseph Quinlan and Julia Quinlan, *Karen Ann: The Quinlans Tell Their Story* (Garden City, N.Y.: Doubleday, 1977).

30. John A. Behnke and Sissela Bok, eds., *The Dilemmas of Euthanasia* (Garden City, N.Y.: Doubleday, 1975); A. B. Downing, ed., *Euthanasia and the Right to Death* (London: Peter Owen, 1969); Jonathan Gould, and Lord Craigmyle, eds., *Your Death Warrant?* (New York: Arlington House, 1971); Marvin Kohl, ed., *Beneficent Euthanasia* (Buffalo, N.Y.: Prometheus Books, 1975); Daniel C. Maguire, *Death by Choice* (Garden City, N.Y.: Doubleday, 1974); Maurice Natanson, ed., "The Nature of Death," *Journal of Medicine and Philosophy* 3 (March 1978); Joseph V. Sullivan, *The Morality of Mercy Killing* (Westminster, Md.: Newman Press, 1950); Charles W. Triche, III, *The Euthanasia Controversy, 1812-1974* (Troy, N.Y.: Whitstone Publishing Co., 1975); and Richard Trubo, *An Act of Mercy* (Los Angeles: Nash Publishing Co., 1973).

31. Diana Crane, *The Sanctity of Social Life* (New York: Russell Sage Foundation, 1975); Donald Cutler, ed., *Updating Life and Death* (Boston: Beacon Press, 1969); Norman B. Levy, ed., *Living or Dying* (Springfield, Il.: Charles C Thomas, 1974); and Robert M. Veatch, *Death, Dying, and the Biological Revolution* (New Haven, Ct.: Yale University Press, 1976).

32. Group for the Advancement of Psychiatry, *The Right to Die* (New York: Jason Aronson, 1974); Marvin Kohl, *The Morality of Killing* (New York: Humanities Press, 1974); Marya Mannes, *Last Rights* (New York: William Morrow, 1974); O. Ruth Russell, *Freedom to Die,* rev. ed. (New York: Human Sciences Press, 1977); and Robert H. Williams, ed., *To Live and To Die* (New York: Springer-Verlag, 1973).

33. Dennis J. Horan and David Mall, eds., *Death, Dying, and Euthanasia* (Washington, D.C.: University Publications of America, 1977); Eike-Henner W. Kluge, *The Practice of Death* (New Haven, Ct.: Yale University Press, 1975); Lyn H. Lofland, ed., *Toward a Sociology of Death and Dying* (Beverly Hills, Ca.: Sage Publications, 1976); Nancy Ostheimer and John M. Ostheimer, eds., *Life or Death—Who Controls?* (New York: Springer Publishing Co., 1976); Robert M. Veatch, *Case Studies in Medical Ethics* (Cambridge, Ma.: Harvard University Press, 1977); and Arthur Winter, ed., *The Moment of Death* (Springfield, Il.: Charles C Thomas, 1969).

34. American Hospital Association, "Statement on a Patient's Bill of Rights," Chicago: Author (840 N. Lake Shore Drive, 60611), 1972; Euthanasia Educational Council, "A Living Will," rev. ed., New York: Author (250 West 57th Street, 10019), 1974; and Society for the Right to Die, "Death with Dignity: Legislative Manual," New York: Author (250 West 57th Street, 10019), 1975.

35. Ira O. Glick, Robert S. Weiss, and C. Murray Parkes, *The First Year of Bereavement* (New York: Wiley-Interscience, 1974); Vanderlyn R. Pine, Austin H. Kutscher, David Peretz, Robert C. Slater, and Robert DeBellis, *Acute Grief and the Funeral* (Springfield, Il.: Charles C Thomas, 1976); Bernard

Schoenberg et al., eds. *Anticipatory Grief* (New York: Columbia University Press, 1974); and Bernard Schoenberg et al., eds., *Bereavement* (New York: Columbia University Press, 1975).

36. Nina L. Herrmann, *Go Out in Joy* (Atlanta: John Knox Press, 1977); C. S. Lewis, *A Grief Observed* (New York: Bantam Books, 1976); Stephen S. Rosenfeld, *The Time of Their Dying* (New York: W. W. Norton, 1977); Ted Rosenthal, *How Could I Not Be among You?* (New York: Avon Books, 1975); and Lael T. Wertenbaker, *Death of a Man* (Boston: Beacon Press, 1974).

37. Ruth D. Abrams, *Not Alone with Cancer* (Springfield, Il.: Charles C Thomas, 1974); David Barton, *Dying and Death* (Baltimore: Williams and Wilkins, 1977); Ann M. Earle, Nina T. Argondizzo, and Austin H. Kutscher, eds., *The Nurse as Caregiver* (New York: Columbia University Press, 1976); Charlotte Epstein, *Nursing the Dying Patient* (Reston, Va.: Reston Publishing Co., 1975); Melvin J. Krant, *Dying and Dignity* (Springfield, Il.: Charles C Thomas, 1974); Elisabeth Kübler-Ross, *Questions and Answers on Death and Dying* (New York: Macmillan, 1974); Austin H. Kutscher and Michael R. Goldberg, eds., *Caring for the Dying Patient and His Family* (New York: Foundation of Thanatology, 1973); and Elizabeth R. Prichard et al., *The Family and Death* (New York: Columbia University Press, 1977).

38. Joan Craven and Florence S. Wald, "Hospice Care for Dying Patients," *American Journal of Nursing* 75 (October 1975):1816-1822; Robert E. Neale, "A Place to Live, a Place to Die," *Hastings Center Report* 2 (June 1972):12-14; Parker Rossman, *Hospice* (New York: Association Press, 1977); Ciceley Saunders, "The Moment of Truth: Care of the Dying Person," in *Death and Dignity*, ed. Leonard Pearson (Cleveland: Case-Western Reserve University Press, 1969), pp. 49-78; Ciceley Saunders, "St. Christopher's Hospice," in *Death: Current Perspectives*, ed. Edwin S. Shneidman (Palo Alto, Ca.: Mayfield Publishing Co., 1976); and Sandol Stoddard, *Hospice Movement* (New York: Stein and Day, 1977).

39. Lynn Caine, *Widow* (New York: William Morrow, 1974); David C. Gordon, *Overcoming the Fear of Death* (Baltimore: Penguin Books, 1972); Earl A. Grollman, ed., *Concerning Death* (Boston: Beacon Press, 1974); Earl A. Grollman, *Living—When a Loved One Has Died* (Boston: Beacon Press, 1977); Robert E. Kavanaugh, *Facing Death* (Baltimore: Penguin Books, 1974); Elisabeth Kübler-Ross, *Death: The Final Stage of Growth* (Englewood Cliffs, N.J.: Prentice-Hall, 1975); and Peter Marris, *Loss and Change* (Garden City, N.Y.: Doubleday, 1975).

40. Loren Bensley, *Death Education as a Learning Experience* (Washington, D.C.: ERIC Clearinghouse in Teacher Education, 1975); Robert J. Kastenbaum, *Death, Society, and Human Experience* (St. Louis: C. V. Mosby, 1977); Gretchen C. Mills, Ray Reisler, Alice E. Robinson, and Gretchen Vermilye, *Discussing Death: A Guide to Death Education* (Homewood, Il.: ETC Publications, 1976); Frances G. Scott and Ruth M. Brewer, eds., *Confrontations of Death* (Corvallis, Or.: Continuing Education Publications, 1971); and Hannelore Wass, ed., *Death Education* (Washington, D.C.: Hemisphere Publishing Corporation, 1025 Vermont Avenue, N.W., 20005). [This is a new quarterly journal with its volume 1, number 1, in Spring 1977.]

41. Ravrinda H. Dave, ed., *Foundations of Lifelong Education* (London:

Pergamon Press, 1976); and Malcolm S. Knowles, "Adult Education: New Dimensions," *Educational Leadership* 33 (November 1975):85-88.

42. Robert Fulton, ed., *Death, Grief and Bereavement: A Bibliography, 1845-1975* (New York: Arno Press, 1977); and G. Howard Poteet, ed., *Death and Dying: A Bibliography, 1950-1974* (Troy, N.Y: Whitston Publishing Co., 1976).

43. Raymond A. Moody, Jr., *Life after Life* (New York: Bantam Books, 1975); Raymond A. Moody, Jr., *Reflections on Life after Life* (Atlanta: Mockingbird Books, 1977); Karlis Osis and Erlendur Haraldsson, *At the Hour of Death* (New York: Avon Books, 1977); and Arnold Toynbee, Arthur Koestler et al., *Life after Death* (New York: McGraw-Hill, 1976).

44. Eric Bermann, *Scapegoat: The Impact of Death-Fear on an American Family* (Ann Arbor: University of Michigan Press, 1973); Joanne Bernstein, "Helping Young Children Cope with Death," in *Current Topics in Early Childhood Education*, Vol. 1, ed. Lilian G. Katz (Norwood, N.J.: ABLEX Publishing Corporation, 1977); Lindy Burton, ed., *Care of the Child Facing Death* (Boston: Routledge and Kegan Paul, 1974); Erna Furman, *A Child's Parent Dies* (New Haven, Ct.: Yale University Press, 1974); Harriet S. Schiff, *The Bereaved Parent* (New York: Crown Publishers, 1977); and Rose Zeligs, *Children's Experience with Death* (Springfield, Il.: Charles C Thomas, 1974).

45. Ernest Becker, *The Denial of Death* (New York: The Free Press, 1973).

46. For discussion of this point, see sources such as the following: Peter L. Berger, *A Rumor of Angels* (Garden City, N.Y.: Doubleday, 1970); Carl G. Jung, ed., *Man and His Symbols* (New York: Dell Publishing Co., 1968); Paul Tillich, *Dynamics of Faith* (New York: Harper & Row, 1957).

47. Liebman, *Peace*, pp. 134-35. For an examination of the paradox of *finis* vs. *telos*, see: A. Roy Eckardt, "Death in the Judaic and Christian Traditions," in *Death in American Experience*, ed. Arien Mack (New York: Schocken Books, 1973), pp. 123-48.